Mapping Manager Development

MANAGEMENT IN DIGITAL TIMES

Edited by Piotr Olaf Żylicz

VOLUME 2

Piotr Olaf Żylicz / Vartika Dutta / Rathish Bhat

Mapping Manager Development

Current and Upcoming Trends

PETER LANG

Lausanne · Berlin · Bruxelles · Chennai · New York · Oxford

Bibliographic Information published by the Deutsche Nationalbibliothek
The Deutsche Nationalbibliothek lists this publication in the Deutsche Nationalbibliografie; detailed bibliographic data isavailable in the internet at http://dnb.d-nb.de.

Library of Congress Cataloging-in-Publication Data
A CIP catalog record for this book has been applied for at the Library of Congress.

The book was published with financial support from WSB Merito University in Warsaw.

Cover illustration: Courtesy of Benjamin Ben Chaim

ISSN 2194-5918
ISBN 978-3-631-86419-7 (Print)
E-ISBN 978-3-631-90468-8 (E-PDF)
E-ISBN 978-3-631-90469-5 (E-PUB)
DOI 10.3726/b20980

Published by Peter Lang GmbH, Berlin, Deutschland

info@peterlang.com - www.peterlang.com

This publication has been peer reviewed.

Table of Contents

Piotr Olaf Żylicz, WSB University, Poland

Vartika Dutta, Indian Institute of Management Amritsar, India

Rathish Bhatt, Goa Institute of Management, India

Introduction: Macro Contexts of Managers Development

Abstract: COVID-19 and its consequences are the most shared experience in human history. They had an impact on societies, national economies, international cooperation, and the functioning of organizations. It also influenced how people, including managers, develop. We discuss two macro contexts of the development: trends of change in Learning & Development and implicit patterns and relevant impact of national cultures.

Keywords: Managers, Learning & Development, Implicit cultural models

'It's critical to support people for who they are.'

Karol Cyrulik, WSB Merito University

The book is about the concepts, conditions, and tools used or proposed for the development of modern managers who must function in the post-COVID-19 era. What makes this time special, apart from COVID-19 itself, is the combination of exponential changes in new technologies and services, dramatically increasing environmental problems, economic challenges, and global political tensions, including, in particular, the war in Ukraine. In general, many managers across the world need to make decisions faster than ever in conditions of increasing uncertainty, unpredictable competition, and often with employees they rarely or never meet in person. It requires a new work mindset and specific attitudes toward knowledge, and its acquisition. The situation also increases demand for skills: in using new technologies and analytical tools, and – somehow paradoxically – in so-called soft aspects of management, including building and maintaining trust in teams, supporting employees' resilience, distant motivating or engaging employees, accompanying others in development, reflecting and sharing narratives on organizational and individual purposes (especially while cooperating with generation Z employees).

The authors of this volume are either people who deal with the science of management on a daily basis or practitioners who have years of experience in managerial education. Some of them share dual experiences. This publication is written in a manner which is readable, understandable, and useful for a broader audience. At the same time, it meets the scientific rigors related to collecting and interpreting data they employ and providing references to the works of other authors. We are convinced that it can primarily be a source of material and inspiration for everyone who deals with the education of managers, in business schools, management faculties, or as consultants and trainers. Last but not least, we address this publication to managers themselves, especially in pandemic/post-pandemic Times, when self-education flourishes. Educational platforms such as Coursera, Udacity, or Udemy develop exponentially (Gaskell, 2018; Mahajan, Gupta, & Singh, 2019), as well as new learning environments and technologies (Martin, Dennen, & Bonk, 2020).

The publication deals primarily with micro (individual and interpersonal) and meso (e.g., organizations) perspectives relevant to managers' development. In turn, here we name its two macro contexts, that is, changes in learning and development practices (L&D) and the impact of national cultures on the development. Both constitute the framework or points of reference for all the chapters of this book.

Learning and development (L&D)

Firstly, it is important to explore changes taking place in learning and development functions in organizations. It is the field where most of the managerial professional development takes place. As CIPD (2022) states, learning and development (L&D) function is responsible for creating an organizational culture of learning and growth through programs that enable organizations to evolve permanently. L&D is to translate organisational strategy into learning priorities on all levels and help employees to fully develop.

Over the years, both theoretical concepts and relevant research on Learning and development have evolved from models where individuals were rather passive to more systemic approaches which consider an individual's goals, intentions, personal knowledge, or potential for development (Renninger et al., 2014). As a consequence, in managerial education Problem-Based Learning and informal forms of learning significantly gained importance (Delaney et al., 2017; Becker & Bish, 2017).

Already before the pandemic, Van Dam (2018) – McKinsey Chief Learning Officer – was writing on challenges faced by those who oversaw L&D function in organizations. A permanently rising competitiveness and complexity of the business coupled with the digital revolution are influencing the mix of employees. The situation is aggravated by growing overall uncertainty, cross-generational tensions, and last but not least, 'a shorter shelf life for knowledge.' All the above make reskilling and upskilling particularly important. Van Dam finds five of L&D's current strategic roles:

1. Attracting and retention of talent.
2. Developing employees' capabilities.
3. Creation of a values-based culture.
4. Building employer brand.
5. Motivating and engaging employees.

Besides a real L&D alignment with business strategy, there are three tasks and challenges ahead of the L&D domain in times of transition that are particularly relevant for this publication. The first is the necessity of **designing a learning journey:** 'a provision of continuous learning opportunities that take place over a period … and include L&D interventions such as fieldwork, pre- and post-classroom digital learning, social learning, on-the-job coaching and mentoring, and short workshops' (p. 9).

Secondly, Van Dam goes on to emphasize the importance of **Execution and scaling up**: 'The successful execution of L&D initiatives on time and within the budget is critical to build and sustain support from business leaders' (p. 9). And last but not least – there is **Assessment of capability**.

And then the time of the pandemic had come, followed – to some extent – by what can be called the post-pandemic period. Just as the war in Ukraine has shaken not only European politics and economy, making the world fundamentally different from the one we have known for the last decades, so the time of the pandemic has become a global watershed in the functioning of the organization, and thus also the L&D function. Above all, the pandemic sped up digital transformation, including learning.

Because the dynamics of change are overwhelming in many respects, regularly published reports from recognized consulting (sometimes training) companies are often a better source of knowledge than strictly scientific texts – not only for managers but also for others, including researchers. Scientific texts usually have a long metabolism of formation and are hermetic from the viewpoint of a broader audience. To some extent, the accuracy of the presented results and conclusions can be confirmed by comparisons with other thematically similar reports (transverse comparisons). The reports that appear periodically are of special value. They enable capturing long-term trends and juxtaposing them with specific, but relevant events. As editors of this volume, we believe that management science should be much more open to the use of such reports.

So let us have a look into the data collected in the recent reports on upcoming trends in (post) pandemic organizational L&D practices. The transformation of L&D, according to LinkedIn's (2022) global report, means that those who oversee learning in organizations are often dismantling today's prevailing silos-mentalities and – practices to build a new comprehensive vision for HR. Moreover, L&D has become more cross-functional, and the demand for L&D specialists surged. SHRM (2022) 'Workplace Learning & Development Trends' report revealed that more than 8 in 10 HR managers are convinced that training is favorable to attract (83 %) and retain (86 %) talented employees. Moreover, almost 50 % of employees admit that training opportunities were vital for choosing a company they work for. At the same time, around three-quarters of them declare to stay with a firm that offers continuous training. In turn, self-paced online courses proved to be the most popular, followed by online/instructor-led training, in-person learning with an instructor, and hybrid ones.

Business dramatically depends on employee engagement, which organizations can maintain and reinforce by providing enhanced career development and learning opportunities (Udemy, 2022). 'By seizing this unique moment, companies could gain an edge in the race to attract, develop, and retain the talent they need to create a thriving post-pandemic organization' (McKinsey, 2021, p. 2). Usually, however, firms have performed poorly in this respect. Employees tend to switch jobs (and even careers) more often than ever, looking for organizational cultures that promote flexibility and well-being (Qstream, 2022, LinkedIn, 2022). As PwC (2022) report – *Global Workforce. Hopes and Fears* – shows, globally younger workers are particularly concerned that technology will replace their roles (38 %) and about not having enough training in new technologies and digital skills (44 %).

Symonds Research (2022) report encapsulates significant new learning and development trends in post-pandemic organizations:

1. A steady increment of **online training** not suppressed by the return of employees to the offices. It seems that blending learning of online delivery combined with classroom or in-person training will prevail in a near future.
2. More focus on training around **Equality, Diversity, and Inclusion** challenges.
3. A growing number of more tailored out or **bespoke training**, coupled with **personalized** online learning.
4. Growing interest in training and education supporting **employee health and well-being** (including stress management and mindfulness). A healthier staff is generally more satisfied and happier, which translates into more overall productivity.

There are two trends mentioned directly relevant for managers:

5. Trend Towards Solving the 1st Time Manager Training Gap.

One significant skills gap that still exists in so many companies, from our experience, is the lack of training for first-time managers and new managers. From our own research, we have found that more than 55 % of new managers fail in their role as new manager, and it is not hard to see why. So many new and first-time managers have risen through the ranks of a business to then be promoted to a management role, and for this reason, they have never been trained in essential management skills such as:

- Inclusive Leadership skills – are essential to ensure that the people you manage are fairly treated.
- Managing Difficult People skills – as a manager, there will inevitably be situations when awkward situations need to be dealt with, and there are techniques to manage these situations.
- Topics such as Managing the Return-to-Work Process – can also be invaluable for understanding and learning effective methods for people management.

So many companies fail to provide new and first-time managers with the essential skills and training that they really need. In terms of trends, this is changing as greater awareness of such managers' skills gap is becoming better understood.

6. Training Trend to Help Managers Manage Virtual Teams and Employees

With so many workplaces now involving distributed teams (as discussed in point one), there is an increasing need to provide training to develop leadership skills to manage virtual teams. We are seeing a definite increase in the demand for team leaders, managers, and supervisors to manage staff on an everyday basis as staff WFA (Work From Anywhere) and WFH (Work From Home).

Culture and human development

According to Harkness and Super (2020) – outstanding international researchers – human development was extensively studied in the context of national cultures in the last decades of the twentieth century. This interest seems to have waned in recent years. Developmental agenda has long been dominated by Western cultural perspectives. Nowadays, we witness a dramatic shift in the opposite direction. Research of culture and human development is plagued by the 'conflict between different schools of thought, especially postmodernism, with its insistence on the utmost qualitative uniqueness of any given culture' (p. 111). Furthermore, there is another trend to be noted. Recently, **developmental studies** have begun to seriously consider the impact of globalization processes on local cultures. For ages, cultures were analyzed as rather static entities, despite all the ongoing changes in cultural practices (Maynard & Chaudhary, 2020).

Moving on to the domain of employee development, we can only reinforce the belief that a profound understanding of cultural contexts is as vital as it used to be, since even professionals are often unaware of how much human behavior is influenced by national cultures. Ali and Loon (2016) posit that the conscious consideration of differences between cultures allows L&D professionals to use L&D solutions in a proper and effective way. 'National culture influences the relative appropriateness of different learning methods, whether the employer or employee should take responsibility for training, what constitutes appropriate sources of "wisdom." The relationship between the "teacher" and the "pupil" and favored learning styles. For example, some Eastern cultures tend to advocate structured, instructive forms of training and passive learning. ... Alternatively, many Western cultures tend to emphasise education and training through facilitative, investigative techniques, teacher and peer interaction, active learning and debates' (Ali & Loon, p. 360).

Language and **culture** remain inseparable (Fang, 2022). And English is the prevailing language of education for managers worldwide – especially for those at higher organizational echelons. This phenomenon is combined with dominant implicit Western beliefs driving business schools both in terms of teaching content and style. It is not hard to see that local concepts and practices very often should be strongly taken into consideration while creating respective curricula. Business schools and management departments outside of the Anglo-Saxon world so rarely contextualize teaching subjects, even if they are strongly pre-defined by vernacular values or practices: business ethics, desirable leadership, crisis management of employees, or development tools like coaching or mentoring, just to mention a few. Especially coaching with its individualistic approach based on the assumption that the coach and coachee are equal partners and that full wisdom resides in the coachee's mind may easily prove to be completely inappropriate in more collectivistic countries, such as India or China, where learners' roles are clearly defined by traditional notions (Chatwani, 2015; Rosinski, 2010; Żylicz, 2015).

Managerial education in general, and business schools and management departments in particular, face increasing criticism for their **one-size-fits-all** approach (Bush, 2003; Benneworth, Pinheiro, & Sánchez-Barrioluengo, 2016; Mingers & Willmott, 2013; Zaar, Van Den Bossche, & Gijselaers, 2020). Zaar and associates (Zaar, Van Den Bossche, & Gijselaers, 2020) found that too much attention is paid to knowledge- and skills-building, but also the developmental needs of managers. At the same time, insufficient attention is given to both conscious, purposeful learner leadership development and learners' identities which are strongly related to their culturally determined **implicit leadership concepts**.

In the famous worldwide GLOBE research project (House et al., 2004) – based on Hofstede's six dimensions of culture – leadership is conceived as the ability of an individual to influence, motivate, and enable others to contribute towards the effectiveness and success of the organizations of which they are members. This conceptualization of societal cultures-based leadership models is strongly influenced here by implicit leadership theory (ILT). It assumes that group members of a given society share implicit expectations and assumptions about the desirable traits of a leader, making a kind of leader's prototype, against which real-life managers or leaders are compared. 'Implicit' means here they have not been explicitly named, while 'theory' refers to the assumption that people tend to systematically generalize expectations derived from previous experience with leaders (managers) to the new ones. Interestingly, referring to Hofstede's dimensions, women strongly support cultural individualism, while masculinity and uncertainty avoidance prevailing in national cultures are more detrimental dimensions for them than for men. In turn, for men power distance is more favorable than for women (Gitling, 2020).

And last but not least, considering managers' development also in terms of an interplay between social stratification and local cultures should be taken into account. As Angram and Joohyun (2022) convincingly showed, in the USA, individuals coming from lower social strata are significantly less likely to become managers. A critical factor behind this social class's negative effect is the education and deficits of cultural capital. They found similar unfavorable patterns in almost every country under investigation, patterns which were closely related to distinctive characteristics of local national cultures, such as individualism or materialism.

References

Ali, S. & M. Loon (2016). Developing and delivering L$D solutions for international markets. In M.Loon (Ed.), *Professional practice in learning and development: how to design and deliver plans for the workplace*. Kogan Page Publishers.

Becker, K., & Bish, A. (2017). Management Development Experiences and Expectations: Informal vs Formal Learning. *Education & Training*, *59*(6), 565–578.

Benneworth, P., Pinheiro, R., & Sánchez-Barrioluengo, M. (2016). One size does not fit all! New perspectives on the university in the social knowledge economy. *Science & Public Policy (SPP)*, *43*(6), 731–735. DOI: https://doi.org/10.1093/scipol/scw018.

Bush, T. (2003). Theories of Educational Leadership and Management. Third Edition. In *SAGE Publications (CA)*. SAGE Publications (CA).

Chatwani, N. (2015). A Cross-Cultural Approach in Coaching as Viewed Through the Guru–Śiṣya Paramparā. In Pereira, V., Malik, A. (Eds.), *Investigating Cultural Aspects in Indian Organizations. India Studies in Business and Economics*. Springer, Cham. DOI: https://doi.org/10.1007/978-3-319-16098-6_5.

CIPD (2022). Learning and development roles. Creating a culture of continuous learning and growth. https://www.cipd.co.uk/careers/career-options/learning-development-roles#gref.

Delaney, Y., Pattinson, B., McCarthy, J., & Beecham, S. (2017). Transitioning from Traditional to Problem-Based Learning in Management Education: The Case of a Frontline Manager Skills Development Programme. *Innovations in Education and Teaching International*, *54*(3), 214–222.

Fang, F. (2022). The Application of Diversified Blended Models in Teaching British and American Culture Based on Big Data Analysis. *Scientific Programming*, 1–9. DOI: https://doi.org/10.1155/2022/2190032.

Fey, C. F. (2022). A perspective on the potential of Chinese business schools: A call for greater attention to context, differentiation, and developing an indigenous model. *Management and Organization Review* *18*(5), 982–999. DOI: 10.1017/mor.2022.19.

Gaskell, A. (2018) The evolution and evaluation of massive open online courses: MOOCs in motion. *Open Learning: The Journal of Open, Distance and e-Learning*, *33*(1), 75–77. DOI: 10.1080/02680513.2017.1378571.

Gitling, M. (2020). The Significance of Organisational Culture in the Development of Human Capital. *Scientific Papers of Silesian University of Technology. Organization & Management / Zeszyty Naukowe Politechniki Slaskiej. Seria Organizacji i Zarzadzanie*, *148*, 189–201. DOI: https://doi.org/10.29119/1641-3466.2020.148.14.

Harkness, S., & Super, C. M. (2020). Culture and human development: Where did it go? And where is it going? *New Directions for Child and Adolescent Development*, *2020*(173), 101–119. DOI: https://doi.org/10.1002/cad.20378.

House, R., Hanges, P., Javidan, M., Dorfman, P., Gupta, V. (2004). *Culture, Leadership, and Organizations: The GLOBE Study of 62 Societies*. Newbury Park: SAGE Publications.

Ingram, P., & Joohyun, J. (2022). Mapping the Class Ceiling: The Social Class Disadvantage for Attaining Management Positions. *Academy of Management Discoveries*, *8*(1), 56–76. DOI: https://doi.org/10.5465/amd.2020.0030.

LinkedIn (2022). The Transformation of L&D Learning leads the way through the Great Reshuffle. https:///LinkedIn-Learning_Workplace-Learning-Report-2022-EN.pdf.

Mahajan, R., Gupta, P., & Singh, T. (2019). Massive open online courses: concept and implications. *Indian pediatrics*, *56*(6), 489–495. DOI:10.1007/s13312-019-1575-6.

Martin, F., Dennen, V.P. & Bonk, C.J (2020). A synthesis of systematic review research on emerging learning environments and technologies. *Educational Technology Research and Development*, *68*, 1613–1633. DOI: https://doi.org/10.1007/s11423-020-09812-2.

Maynard, A. E., & Chaudhary, N. (2020). Human Development at the Intersection of Culture and Globalization: Towards a More Inclusive Future. *Human Development*, *64*(4–6), 250–257. DOI: https://doi.org/10.1159/000513046.

McKinsey (2021). *Great Attrition' or 'Great Attraction'? The choice is yours.* https://www.mckinsey.com/capabilities/people-and-organizational-performance/our-insights/great-attrition-or-great-attraction-the-choice-is-yours.

Mingers, J., & Willmott, H. (2013). Taylorizing business school research: On the 'one best way' performative effects of journal ranking lists. *Human Relations*, *66*(8), 1051–1073. DOI: https://doi.org/10.1177/0018726712467048.

Pereira Sartori Falguera, F., Lima, M. A. F., Ferrari, V. A. S., Barriga, G. D. C., & Mariano, E. B. (2021). Human Development by Gender and National Culture: A Comparative Analysis. *Journal of Development Studies*, *57*(9), 1549–1570. DOI: https://doi.org/10.1080/00220388.2021.1919632.

PwC (2022). *Global Workforce Hopes and Fears Survey*: https://www.pwc.com/gx/en/issues/workforce/hopes-and-fears-2022.html.

Qstream (2022). *Workplace Learning Report.How more effective workplace learning opportunities can empower organizations to fight the labor shortage*: https://qstream.com/wp-content/uploads/2022/06/2022-Workplace-Learning-Report.pdf.

Renninger, K. A., Hidi, S., Krapp, A., & Renninger, A. (2014). *The role of interest in learning and development*. New York: Psychology Press. DOI: https://doi.org/10.4324/9781315807430.

Rosinski, P. (2010). *Global coaching: An integrated approach for long-lasting results*. London: Nicholas Brealey.

SHRM (2022). *Workplace Learning & Development Trends Research Report*: https://www.shrm.org/hr-today/trends-and-forecasting/research-and-surveys/pages/2022-workplace-learning-and-development-trends.aspx.

Symonds Research (2022). 7 Learning and Development Trends for 2023 and in the Future for the Training Industry: https://symondsresearch.com/learning-development-trends/.

Van Dam, N. (2018). Elevating Learning & Development: Insights and Practical Guidance from the Field.

Udemy (2022). *Workplace Learning Trends Report: Skills of the Future*: https://business.udemy.com/resources/5-workplace-learning-trends-2020/.

Zaar, S., Van Den Bossche, P., & Gijselaers, W. (2020). How Business Students Think about Leadership: A Qualitative Study on Leader Identity and Meaning-Making. *Academy of Management Learning*

& Education, *19* (2), 168–191. DOI: https://doi.org/10.5465/amle.2017.0290.

Żylicz, P.O. (2015). *Coaching Between Magic and Science*. Post-Conference Book of 5th Research Conference on Mentoring and Coaching by EMCC.

Richard Temperley-Little, Impact, UK/ WSB University, Poland

Management Education for Arsonists

Abstract: The world faces unprecedented disturbances – environmental, social, economic, and political – of such urgency and severity as to constitute a danger to all humanity. And yet the neoliberal market economy, fixated on profit and shareholder value and possessed by a narrow view of social efficiency, seems to have rendered all other possible economic arrangements unthinkable. Business education serves that economy, reflecting back to it its own sense of privileged entitlement and routinely presenting historically contingent and highly contested moral and ideological assumptions as if they were eternal truths. If catastrophe is to be averted, we need a new generation of 'critically imaginative' business managers, educated in the realities of the global problematique, whose instinct is for collaboration, who repudiate the fetishisation of leadership and who understand that heedless profit-making comes at huge social and environmental cost.

Keywords: Management education, Neoliberal market economy, Sustainable development

> *'The world's biggest polluters are guilty of arson of our only home ... Unchecked carbon pollution is forcing the world's most vulnerable on a frog march to destruction – now. ... Now is the time to turn rage into action. ... Delay means death.'*
>
> *Antonio Guterres. Remarks at the launch of IPCC Report, 28th Feb. 2022*

There is a moment in George Eliot's novel *Middlemarch*, when Dorothea, the central character, begins to understand that her much older husband, Edward Casaubon, has his own motives and peculiarities of character – that he is a separate human being and not merely an object of her interests. It is a moment of clear realisation in which she 'conceives with that distinctness which is no longer reflection but feeling – an idea wrought to the directness of sense, like the solidity of objects.' I was reminded of this by an encounter, pre-covid, with a student at my old university. It came about because, for several years, I was a volunteer mentor to final-year students: this one was about to complete a law degree and we arranged to meet at the university. It was a pleasant summer afternoon and I thought he might like to talk while we took a stroll through the campus. There cannot be a more beautiful university campus than Exeter's anywhere in the world, although, in the 50 years since I was a student, some of the woodland glades and hilltops that I remember have been buried under piles of brick and glass, mostly belonging to the business school. He seemed puzzled by my proposal and said that he had booked a meeting room. I was to learn that he had attended a 'neuro-linguistic programming' course on which he was advised to always take control of the location and form of any encounter. In the room, he pointed me to a carefully positioned chair. After satisfying himself that I was not an impostor, he laid out his career plan. He would complete his course, he said, then do an MBA. He had in mind Harvard Business School. After that, he would join a hedge fund, or possibly a private equity firm. This was impressive, if slightly alarming. He went on: when, after fifteen or twenty years of hedging, he had maximised his personal wealth, he would retire and 'give something back.'

Perhaps, he thought, he would become CEO of a major charity or NGO. And why not, I thought. When I mentioned the various threats and disturbances, not least amongst them climate change, that might shape events during that period, he dismissed the point out of hand: not his problem, and in any case, the future was green growth, the new hi-tech green economy was the biggest game in town, he would certainly consider investing in it. What troubled me that afternoon was not his unassailable confidence, or the improbable precision of his plan; it was not the fact that he had been posting on Instagram while we talked: what troubled me was how naturally he took it for granted that, in twenty years, the world of hedge funds and careers and 'giving back' would still exist just as it does now. I wondered whether this was a case of dissociation; whether the possibility of catastrophic changes in his way of life, partly caused by climate change, had, for him, not yet been *wrought to the directness of sense*. But he is not alone: it seems to me that when it comes to the 'global problematique,' it is not just my student acquaintance who is in a state of dissociation but just about everybody, including most governments and, my particular concern in this chapter, most of the global business system and its satellite business education.

The term 'global problematique' is associated with the Club of Rome report (Meadows, 1972) and rarely heard these days. Its scope has widened since then to comprise emerging problems that were not in the original report (Ruggie, 1980). Global warming was in there, on page 73, but mentioned only in passing as a 'side-effect' of energy use. I was brought up on Limits to Growth and the IPAT model (ibid; Commoner, 1972; York et al, 2003) and I have continued to think of the indivisible totality of malignant human impact on this planet as the glob-prob. But whatever you call it, it is incontrovertibly true that the world faces unprecedented threats and disturbances – environmental, social, economic, and political – of such a severity and scale as to call into doubt the continuing existence of humanity. Also incontrovertibly, a business system that largely abhors limits and regulation, that pursues growth at all costs, in which there is little room for compassion or conscience, has played a huge part in getting us into this mess, notwithstanding decades of environmental and social reporting and acres of greenwash. Business education is part of that system, reflecting back to it its own sense of privileged entitlement and routinely presenting historically contingent and highly contested moral and ideological assumptions as if they were eternal truths. The business schools supply that system with an annual cohort of administrators for whom 'capitalism seamlessly occupies the horizons of the thinkable' (Fisher, 2009). For too many of them, business ethics and sustainability are still, at best, marginal considerations or, at worst, are thought of as positive impediments to the pursuit of profit. They are caught in the machinery of a desacralising, deterritorialising global capital that reduces every human possibility to mere profit and morality to the narrowest pragmatic consequentialism; that searches out and monetises every last particle of human life and culture, selling it back to a globalised citizenry reduced to consumers, on the one hand, and fungible human resources, on the other. We face, as Wendell Berry puts it, 'the possibility of a world that the supranational corporations, and the … systems that serve them, will control entirely for their own enrichment – and, incidentally and inescapably, for the impoverishment of all the rest of us' (Berry, 2001). The all-pervading discourse of neoliberalism serves to naturalise these conditions and to make alternative arrangements almost unthinkable, even in the face of catastrophe. As Frederick Jameson put it, 'someone once said that it is easier to imagine the end of the world than to imagine the end of capitalism. We can now revise that and witness the attempt to imagine capitalism by way of imagining the end of the world' (Jameson, 2003).

Most businesses have not yet registered the full horror of the occasion, let alone risen to it. The longer that action commensurate with the scale of the problem is deferred, the less effective and the more draconian it will be and the more likely it will be that people everywhere, but especially in the global South, will suffer.

Procrastination thus brings about a triple danger: it compounds the environmental danger; it multiplies the cost and difficulty of mitigation; and it increases the likelihood of conflict associated with it. The likelihood of state and non-state eco- terrorism and revolution also increases (Work, 2019; Collins, 2019; Spadaro, 2020, Malm, 2021). And yet, too many business leaders still wait to be assured that there is a 'business case' for 'going green' or imagine that 'putting a recycling bin in the office is a start' (Bennet, 2021). Or they publish a CSR, or HSEC, or ESG report, the abbreviation varying with fashion, explaining that 'we have enhanced our governance structure by establishing a dedicated Environmental, Social and Governance committee of the Board to provide direction for the Group's sustainability policies and approach (and to) promote board-level engagement with an input into the Group's material ESG risks and performance.' No-one would doubt the sincerity and integrity of the authors of such material, but, as Greta Thunberg might put it, 'blah, blah, blah.' My example is taken from the ESG report of a huge commodities trading company (Trafigura, 2021). The same report goes on to say that the company is committed to transparency and disclosure, a declaration which sits ill with the firm's habit of taking out injunctions to prevent the press from reporting on its activities (Guardian, 2009; Spectator, 2009). Those activities include the egregious cost-cutting wheeze of dumping toxic waste in Africa to avoid paying European processing charges (Amnesty International, 2012).

Companies are not monoliths; they may commit egregious environmental crimes while carrying out laudable reclamation elsewhere; and they may say one thing while doing the opposite. In fact, they do not say anything: they are not entities capable of utterance and the 'we' and 'they' in the sample above are examples of the fallacy of misplaced concreteness, the same error that produces phrases like 'our people are our greatest asset' (or even 'we are experiencing unprecedented volumes of calls to customer service'). The claims of an imaginary corporate 'we' are often far ahead of a fragmented establishment that goes about its daily business unheedful of those claims. The same 'we' produces lists of company-specific 'values,' as if commonly agreed standards of business conduct did not already exist. This may be thought of as another kind of dissociation, a chronic state of corporate akrasia – a perpetually renewed disjuncture between the company and its members, the company and its social environment, and between its large moral claims and the claims of conscience and duty that may be felt by its employees. Consider Shell as an example of just how extreme this dissociation can become. In 1991, the company made a film that laid out the link between fossil fuels and the full horror of climate change ('Climate of Concern', The Guardian, 2017). The narrator warns that, unless carbon emissions are dramatically reduced, the world will suffer storm, flood, fire, famine, and mass migration. It notes that this is the view of 'a uniquely broad consensus of scientists.' And yet, the same company has continued since then to exploit fossil fuel reserves, open up new oilfields, and obstruct decarbonisation. If Shell had taken heed of its own film, it would have had a decades-long head start on that process. Instead, they have done what almost every other large company is doing – proclaiming the need for change, claiming even to be in the forefront of change, while making things worse. Shell is not a monolith – it is thousands of thoughtful and conscientious people, but, somehow, the terrifying facts of the climate catastrophe have not been *wrought to the directness of* collective *sense*. As long as such gaps persist between a deontic ideal and a pragmatic everyday, movement towards truly responsible and sustainable business conduct will remain glacially slow. It is rank and file managers who find themselves obliged to negotiate this gap between rhetoric and reality, not the Chief Sustainability Officers or PR spokespeople who produce the movies and communiques. To the extent that they are a collectivity, they are willing to put things off, or rely on someone else to make the necessary changes or wait for government to impose new regulation.

They are like heavy smokers who persist, despite knowing that the habit is killing them. They are Guterres' fire-raisers of my epigraph, careless of their victims. Blithely unaware that 'delay means death'.

Eighteen years ago, the European Federation of Management Development, in a sanguinary 'Call for Engagement' noted that 'Businesses ... have a tremendous opportunity to shape a better world for existing and future generations. Business schools ... can play a pivotal role, alongside business, in developing the present and future leaders required to ensure that business is a force for good' (EFMD, 2004). Eighteen years ago, it was merely urgent; now, it is a matter of life and death. In the rest of this chapter, I will list in more detail the factors that add up to a glob-prob and look briefly at some ways in which business and management education might do more to fulfil its 'pivotal role.' In particular, I will ask how it might cultivate a *critical imagination* that undermines the appearance of fixedness in present arrangements and encourages students to see the system they will enter as a social object like any other – historically and ideologically situated, contingent and liable to radical change.

Notwithstanding the EFMD call for engagement, and with honourable exceptions, too many business schools still see sustainability in wholly instrumental terms, something which, if it was neglected, might interfere with profit-making, or with a business' license to operate. It is something to be mentioned in passing, in terms that have been safely incorporated into the analects of neoliberal economics – the 'new planetary vulgate' of Bourdieu and Wacquant (1999). In the green vulgate, business – the pre-eminent institution – must be 'resilient' and 'agile,' 'innovative,' and 'disruptive'; evidence must be 'compelling,' and it is science that must do the persuading – rarely the job of the corporate world to persuade the rest of us of its legitimacy, 'the green economy will be where the sharpest leaders will place their chips' (BBC, 2007). New vulgate managers are told that they must be 'authentic' and 'visionary leaders' who focus on 'execution.' The word 'sustainability' appears as something to be 'embraced,' like 'diversity' – a choice, not a duty (Boltanski and Chiapelli, 2006; Davies, 2015). Or, if you prefer, it is something to be stolen: appropriated and instrumentalised in the service of profit. All such formulations rest on the assumption that the neoliberal market economy is natural and inevitable, and, crucially, that it is the only mechanism that can get humanity out of its predicament – a predicament in whose making that same mechanism played a disproportionately large role.

In the passages below, I list some of the elements of the glob-prob, as they occur to me – counting them off on my fingers, as it were. It is a lamentable catalogue. In making it, it is hard to know where to start; even harder to know what is fundamental and what follows from it – to understand the mereological relations of the multiple problems faced by humanity or to know which of several orders or taxonomies to apply. One might follow Felix Guattari, who argues that the crisis is manifest in three 'ecologies,' of subjectivities, social relations, and environment (Guattari, 1989). Or Raskin, who distributes effects across three realms, the *environmental*, *geo-economic* and *social* (Raskin, 2000). But it is difficult to sustain such categorisations when multiple causes are so profoundly interpenetrated. A probabilistic approach to the same question can be found in Toby Ord's recent book 'The Precipice' (2022). Other useful texts are Leslie (1996) and Bostrom (2011). Please note that, for ease of reading and to preserve your sanity, I have referenced only a few of the dozens of papers consulted for this *tour d'horizon*. A representative sample is listed at the end and all references are available on request. I mention only things about which there is a reasonable degree of consensus in the relevant literature. It is a rather gloomy exposition.

Others, like Stephen Pinker (2018) or Oded Galor (2022), a latter-day Edward Casaubon, might lay out a positive view of the state in which we currently remain, but my task here is to list the elements of a global problematique, and I would rather be Cassandra than Pollyanna. As would the UN Office for Disaster Risk Reduction, worried as it is about the dangerous effects of unduly optimistic accounts of the state of the world: '(increasing risk) is not reflected in surveys of individual risk perception. The prevailing perception of risk – in particular long-term threats – is one of optimism, underestimation and invincibility' (UNDRR, 2022).

First, in the environmental realm, global warming is the most salient of many dangers, though not necessarily the most immediately dangerous to humanity. Its effects are being felt sooner than had been predicted even a decade ago (IPCC, 2022). The most recent US National Climate Assessment states that 'more frequent and intense extreme weather and climate-related events, as well as changes in average climate conditions, are expected to continue to damage infrastructure, ecosystems, and social systems' (Fourth US NCA, 2018). As I write, in May 2022, the IPCC target (1.5°C above pre-industrial temperatures) is beginning to look unachievable (IPCC, 2018, 2022). The IPCC says that, to achieve that target, global carbon emissions must be halved this decade, but right now they are at an all-time high and rising. Total carbon dioxide emissions rose in 2021 to 36.3 billion tones, their highest ever level, as the world economy rebounded from the pandemic (International Energy Authority, 2022). That is the largest rise in history (I thought it was supposed to be going down – perhaps I have misunderstood). In any case, reducing emissions by half is widely asserted to be nowhere near enough. Even previously conservative analyses now register alarm at the social and economic consequences of a rise in temperature of more than 1.5°C. (Howard and Sylvan, 2021). However, popular perceptions of climate change have changed quite dramatically in the last decade, somewhat mitigating the effects of climate scepticism (Zhou, 2015; Kahan, 2011; UNDRR, 2022) and political pressure, not least from Greta Thunberg, has increased. A number of recent meta-studies, best-sellers and films (like 'Don't Look Up', 2021) have been both indicators of this and accelerators. While some accounts may seem to exaggerate the danger, like David Wallace-Wells 'The Uninhabitable Earth' (2018) and Jem Bendell's work on 'deep adaptation' (2018, 2021), the question is not whether social collapse will follow environmental disaster, but how long we have got (Weyhenmeyer et al, 2020).

Meanwhile, Biodiversity studies show that the extinction rate is now 1000 times faster than the background rate (the rate taken across the whole period of human existence); that large animal populations have declined by 60 %, insects by 40 % and pollinating insects by 60 % (multiple sources, including Natural History Museum, 2021).

Ironically (the glob-prob is a hotbed of ironies), while animals not yet known to science become extinct, science is creating new species in the laboratory, at uncertain risk. Many animals and plants are driven from their ranges, usually towards cooler latitudes or altitudes, and often towards extinction (Gunderson and Stillman, 2015; Gunn et al, 2021).

Drought, irregular weather, and flooding are already increasing significantly, especially in Africa and South Asia. Heat waves in 2021, in India and Saudi Arabia, Russia, California, British Columbia and even in the Arctic (Edwards, 2020) were a foretaste of what is likely to become more frequent and intense to the point that they become unsurvivable. The description of a deadly Indian heat wave in Kim Stanley Robinson's novel 'The Ministry for the Future' (2020) is a frightening fictional account of what will probably happen soon. It is a striking feature of these trends that they often turn out to be worse even than the most pessimistic predictions. Not only heating: topsoil is disappearing and ice melting faster than had recently been thought likely. The reinsurance industry publishes regular reviews of literature associated with climate change and other emerging risks: in one, Swiss Re reports that wildfires have increased seven-fold, incidents of flooding 15-fold, heatwaves 20-fold since 2005.

The company, not unnaturally, sees the global catastrophe in terms of insurable risk and challenges to business: 'A refusal to grasp the magnitude of the environmental challenge could cost reputations and even render business models obsolete' (Swiss Re, 2020). I would rather say that a refusal to grasp that those business models are already obsolete could cost a livable planet for generations to come.

Given all this, there is a strong likelihood that the number of *human* climate refugees will rise steeply; estimates range from 200 million to 1 billion by 2040. In the US alone, it is estimated that 50 million people will have been displaced internally by 2050, many from Florida (IPCC, 2019, USNCA, 2018 and multiple additional sources). Certainly, consideration of the movement of people displaced by climate takes us from Raskin's environmental realm to the social and geo-economic realms. The rate of global population increase is falling a little faster than had been expected, reduced by education and urbanisation. That might be good news generally, but not for those developed economies (including UK and Japan) where increased life expectancy and declining birth rates combine to increase the dependency ratio and drive global competition for migrant labour and tax-payers.

Next, the pandemics. The current pandemic had long been predicted; there had been several near-misses in the previous decade and there will be more to come. Global warming materially increases the risk that harmful viruses will cross between species: 'the coming decades will not only be hotter, but sicker' (Carlton et al, 2022). Climate change has extended the ranges of many diseases including malaria, dengue fever and lyme disease.

Urbanisation, mass-travel, pet ownership and bush-meat consumption all increase disease transmission. Habitat loss, population pressure and changes in the ranges of species increases the likelihood of new pathogens. Thus, pandemics are associated with global warming; global warming is associated with carbon dioxide emissions; carbon dioxide emissions are associated with economic growth; pandemics and global warming affect economic growth: a longer account of the glob-prob might make more careful distinctions than I have between such first and second order effects and between environmental, social, and geo-economic forces. One might say that the world itself does not make those distinctions: brute reality does not divide itself into neat categories, and has a habit of cohering in unexpected ways. I will continue, as best I can, in the social and geo-economic realms.

Amongst the more egregious social conditions, inequality is deepening, within and between countries; wealth is increasingly sequestered, untaxed, and unavailable for socially useful investment (Piketty, 2014, 2020); wages, for all but a tiny minority, are stagnating, even in the wealthiest countries (CIA, 2021 – note that the CIA is, perhaps unexpectedly, a reliable source for data on inequality). Lowest wages in the USA in 2017 had 30 % less buying power than in 1968. 'Net (US) productivity grew 72.2 percent between 1973 and 2014. Still, inflation-adjusted hourly compensation of the median worker rose just 8.7 percent over the same period' (Bivens & Mishel, 2015). The broader picture of global inequality, including the equivalence recently claimed between the wealth of the poorer half of the world's population and the richest 25 or so individuals, is well known. Gross inequality may be thought of as an evil, but links between inequality and poor social outcomes has been laid out, somewhat contestably, by Pickett and Wilkinson (2009). They showed that in unequal societies physical and mental health, educational attainment, teenage pregnancy, drug abuse, crime and imprisonment, obesity, social trust, and civic engagement were all worse than in less unequal societies. Employment conditions are deteriorating for all but a tiny minority. Working conditions in many developing countries and in China are worsening, despite increased oversight and attempts by large corporations to supervise supply-chains. After it had been falling for two decades, the number of children in labour and hazardous work has begun to rise again (Unicef, 2021).

Work-related deaths and injuries are rising worldwide: 2.3 million people are killed at work every year and 317 million are injured according to the ILO (2021). Millions more are indirectly affected by accidental or environmental exposures. Work-related mental health problems and employer demands on non-work time are all increasing in white collar jobs worldwide. These trends have been sometimes exacerbated, sometimes mitigated by the coronavirus pandemic. In the US and UK, large numbers of companies are now owned by private equity firms that have little interest in improving employee conditions. In a notorious recent case, a British ferry company, part-owned in Dubai sacked 800 sea-going employees, replacing them on the same day with contract workers paid as little as £5 an hour (the minimum wage in the UK is £9.50). Employees on 'zero-hours contracts' have little or no job security and, in general, are stripped of their autonomy. The availability of surveillance technology has taken 'scientific management' to previously unimaginable lengths of intrusion and control so that, in many organisations, and indeed in at least one entire society, people must assume that every move they make is supervised (Gownder et al, 2015; Martella, et al, 2016; Solomon, 2001; Wirz et al, 2012). It so happens that I was shown a document this morning in which a company notified employees that they must provide it with evidence that their domestic finances are well-managed, on the basis that private debt might affect their 'wellbeing' and thus their work performance – an egregious and once-unthinkable encroachment by the corporate into the private sphere. The pace at which combined surveillance technologies are developing constitutes a threat to the global polity that has so far been grossly underestimated; if we have not already been subject to it unawares, we will soon see the realisation of George Orwell's 'facecrime' (Little, 2016/2; Alegre, 2022).

Corporate profits and executive salaries are soaring (multiple sources, including US Dept. of Commerce, 2014, 2019) corporate profits in the US rose to a record high of $2.53 trillion in the last quarter of 2021. Corporate interests can be seen everywhere to displace and distort democracy; public space is privatised, civic freedoms destroyed, and public goods appropriated for profit (especially in the UK, where successive governments have privatised practically everything, absent any concern for the morality of markets – even where it is obvious that profit-seeking has perverse consequences, as in social care and regulatory bodies). The negative externalities of business corporations continue almost unchecked, despite decades of social impact reporting. In effect, those externalities amount to theft from the global commons: a broad social accounting shows that business is, in effect, taking more than it gives back (Estes, 1995; Hofrichter, 2000 etc.). The reckless, relentless growth of a fossil-fuelled global economy is scarcely dented by the determinations of 26 successive COP meetings. See Carleton and Hsiang (2016) for an overview of the economic impacts of climate change and a guide to the literature.

As if all that were not enough to worry about, the nuclear clock stands at 100 seconds to midnight, marking the highest risk of nuclear war since 1953 (Bulletin of the Atomic Scientists, 2022). Threats about the use of tactical nuclear weapons and even of large-scale nuclear exchanges have been thrown about with abandon recently by one gangster-dictator, while another one seems to be developing hypersonic ICBMs in his North Korean fortress. The post-war consensus about nuclear proliferation is in jeopardy and emerging nuclear powers North Korea and Iran are volatile and unbiddable ('proliferation optimists' argue that nuclear weapons can be regionally stabilising but I'm not sure it is an experiment one would wish to see). Destruction is still mutually assured, but the balance that it once implied is increasingly doubtful. Mutually assured destruction, in another form, characterizes the possible use of cyberweapons. Russia, the USA, and China already have the capacity to interfere with one another's infrastructure: nuclear power, energy, water, and finance (Perlroth, 2020). Soon, too, they will have militarised space. It has been evident for some time that the post-war supranational institutions (ILO, IMF, UN, WB, WTO) are no longer adequate defences against trade wars, real wars or the rise of nationalism and nativist populism, so that those with irredentist ambitions feel emboldened to act. It gives me no pleasure to say that, in 2016, I, (and many others), predicted that 'revanchist war in Europe – in Ukraine or the Baltic States – is probable within a decade' (Little, 2016/1). I wish I had been wrong. Naturally, there are other flash points – in the Arctic, Middle East, the South China Sea, Kaliningrad, Korea, and Taiwan, all further complicated by the climate crisis.

Twentieth-century confidence in a post-war *Pax Americana*, liberal hegemony, and globalised trade has given way in the new century to increased security competition between the large trading blocs, the rise of authoritarian governments and, in China, a dirigiste alternative to Western capitalism (which, in an uncomfortable irony, may prove to be better adapted for decarbonisation). These challenges to liberal democracy have echoes in Europe and America, where inequalities in campaign spending and voting rights are aggravated by institutional rearrangements that include blatant gerrymandering, where legitimate political discussion is distorted, and the public sphere corrupted by social media and a naïvely absolutist insistence on freedom of speech. And now, as I write, there is outright war in Europe. This war and the pandemic should be reminders to corporations that they are always vulnerable to political *force majeure* but they have done little to slow the creeping political incursions of rentier oligarchs. The economic stranglehold of neoliberalism may seem to be weakening; another global recession might finally put paid to a discredited idea that only survived the last one by the skin of its teeth. But I would not bet on it. On top of the recessionary forces already mentioned, a conservative estimate of global public debt puts it at $220 trillion (IMF, 2022 and multiple other sources). The richest economies are host to multiple asset and debt bubbles, including property, student loans and car loans, while the long-term effect of crypto-currencies (ponzi schemes without a Ponzi) remains unknown. Despite all this, Toby Ord, in his probabilistic assessment of global risks (2022), argues that the most pressing danger facing humanity is not global warming, but runaway artificial intelligence. It is beyond my biological intelligence to do more than mention his concerns. Nor have I discussed overfishing, water and other resource shortages and conflicts, disappearances of indigenous cultures, deforestation, or unsustainably extended and vulnerable food supply chains (the last of these thrown into relief by the war in Ukraine). I like to think that you, the reader, having your own compendium of global risks, will fill in these and anything else that I have omitted.

The mereological and categorical dilemmas that arise when making a list like this are acute but, whatever the relations between the elements in the glob-prob, they add up to a supreme predicament and an urgent danger for humanity. I would argue that this is no time for debate about the viability of the precautionary principle – at least to the extent that it requires us all to stop and consider the consequences of any course of action. At a minimum that principle 'imposes a duty of planetary care on the human will. It seeks to deepen, to widen, and to lengthen all manner of so-called impact assessments. Above all, it provides a basis for public discussion and deliberation over what kind of society and moral accountability we collectively should choose to adopt' (Read and O'Riordan, 2017). Surely, that duty of planetary care extends to business and business owners and devolves to business managers taking every-day decisions. Read and O'Riordan go on to assert that 'such (deliberations and) decisions must be collective. It is conceptually impossible for a society to leave it up to individuals or corporations to choose what technology to select when there may be all manner of consequences for others' (ibid). Whether or not it is conceptually possible, the power to make many of those decisions has been arrogated by a tiny number of people whose only distinction is wealth. It seems to me, for example, that it is dangerous for one man with a shaky grasp of political philosophy to decide on a whim that content controls on the social network Twitter should be relaxed in the name of a jejune version of free speech. The same man and some of his peers are proposing that, having made a mess of one planet, humanity should decamp to another and become an 'interplanetary species'. It is worth noting that space entrepreneurialism is largely financed from the public purse and constitutes a covert militarisation of space (Space Angels, 2019). But sending people to another planet or galaxy is a non-starter. For one thing, who wants to live in a place with pink skies and giant flesh-eating marmots? The game is not worth the candle. More to the point, that fantasy – a demented Turner's Frontier Hypothesis – may be said to create moral hazard to the extent that it encourages people to suppose they can ignore merely terrestrial problems when they can simply rocket away from them. This is the world, the world is everything that is the case, and this is where we must learn to live sustainably.

Furthermore, other planets and their inhabitants might object to being used as lifeboats by billionaire narcissist earth-people. To close this necessarily brief survey of the glob-prob, I go back to one of the starting points of environmental consciousness – the book *Silent Spring*, published in 1962. Its author, Rachel Carson, had been alarmed by reports of fish and bird deaths in America, apparently associated with industrial pollution. Her research was exhaustive and systematic and her findings horrifying.

Eventually, in what she called 'a synthesis of widely scattered facts' she proved that the effects of chemicals in the landscape were profound and deadly. Her work led directly to the founding of the Environmental Protection Agency in the USA. Last month, a major study showed that '... the increasing rate of production [of polluting chemicals and plastics] and higher numbers of novel entities with diverse risk potentials exceed societies' ability to conduct safety related assessments and monitoring' (Persson et al 2022). The insects that were the target of all those chemicals, including DDT, quickly developed resistance. They are not doing so well now – more effective pesticides and the destruction of insect-friendly habitats has brought about a rapid decline in their numbers since the 1970s, shrinking the base of the global food chain. So important is their role in that food chain, in pollinating and in breaking down waste material, that the loss of insects might be, for humanity, 'an agonising ordeal eclipsing any war and rivalling the looming ravages of climate breakdown' (Milman, 2022).

If the greenhouse effect did not exist and global heating was not happening, then chemical, particulate and plastic pollution would be at least as acute a public health crisis without it. And poverty, inequality, war, and oppression would still be there too. We may, at the end of this rehearsal of risks, ask what the point would be of saving the world from global warming if, afterwards, it was still grossly unequal, violent, and fixated on material goods. Inversely, if the world paid as much attention to these egregious harms as it does now to climate, the global warming problem might be solved *en passant*. If, instead of the prevention of climate disaster, the primary purpose of COP talks was the achievement of a just and peaceful global polity and a sustainable form of capitalism – if it was focused on social justice first, including reparation to the victims of historic harms (much of the global South); if it was seeking to create a system of laws and regulation that gave labour greater protection and involvement in governance; if it sought to moderate the unconscionable and relentless demand that capital produce an unfeasible rate of return – if all of that were to be hammered out in a global citizens' assembly, we might find that many of the geo-economic conditions that sustain global warming had been weakened. Social and economic justice would be given a chance to underwrite climate justice and we might be able to enjoy the blessings of industrial modernity untroubled by existential risks: the world described by Stephen Pinker (2018), with its science, humanism, and progress, might become real rather than a liberal fantasy. To put it another way, what is the point of 'going green' if you continue to track employees visits to the lavatory, or conceal profiteering behind impenetrable pricing? Going green would be a stunted moral impulse that left intact the more fundamental dishonesty that allows organisations to do harm. As illustration, the ferry company P&O, whose unprincipled HR practices are mentioned above, says on its website, 'we want to do all we can to reduce our carbon footprint and protect the environment.' What about protecting their staff? When the boss of P&O was asked at a Parliamentary enquiry whether he understood that what he did was wrong he replied: 'we had no alternative' (BBC, 2022). So much for a Kantian ethics of business.

Discourse, saturated by ideology, naturalizes a way of talking, thinking and being and occludes the conception of other arrangements; the discourse of neoliberal capital leads many people to think that there could never be any other way of ordering the world – 'it's just the way it is,' but, on the contrary, there is *always* an alternative to any and every social or economic arrangement. In the term 'sociological imagination,' C. Wright Mills was referring to that understanding, and to the capacity to imagine those alternatives. It was, he wrote, a capacity that 'enables its possessor to understand the larger historical scene in terms of its meaning for the inner life and the external career of … individuals' (Mills, 1959). A little sociological imagination goes a long way to extend the horizon beyond the ideological constraints of capitalism (Fisher, 2009). Jane Jacobs gives us an example of Mills' concept in her study of the Chicago heatwave of 1995 (Jacobs, 2004). An official inquiry attributed excess deaths to individual failures to seek help, or secure enough water. Jacobs showed that the inquiry had failed entirely to take into consideration wider questions of social solidarity, socio-economic structures and 'environmental racism' (Helfland, 2004). In its unreflecting individualism, the inquiry failed to recognise the narrowing effect of ideology on its collective imagination. 'Sociological imagination' reverses the assumption that the individual is the locus and initiator of social phenomena, seeing it instead as the site on which large social processes are realised (Gergen, 1994). It is a starting point for a habit of critical inquiry that holds business as one social institution amongst many – adaptive, mutable, contingent, and accountable to the commonwealth. With its help, one can see management as a historically situated and ideologically shaped practice whose legitimacy should depend upon whether it can reconcile the interests of an organisation with the wider good, efficiency with compassion, 'performance management' with love and care. If, as I believe, the possession of sociological imagination is a necessary accomplishment for a business manager, then its cultivation should be an intrinsic element of business education. It was conspicuously absent from the thinking of my student mentee. When, a few years ago, my colleagues and I made a survey of business education institutions (Little and Melling, 2016), we were struck by the monotony of curricula: the same phrases, evidence of the same assumptions, rarely any hint of critical thinking about business. In a more recent survey of the literature of several large business schools I found similar repetitions of the same anodyne tropes, but with a new overtone of muscularity – language for which Giacalone and Promislo (2013) have coined the word 'potensiphonic,' expressive of power and supremacy. A corpus analysis showed that the most commonly occurring adjectives were 'deep,' 'strong,' 'robust,' 'expert,' 'dynamic,' 'tough,' 'passionate,' and, improbably, 'creative' (unpubl., 2019). 'Sustainable' was the twelfth most frequently occurring word, but it was often used to refer to profitability (even the first of the UN Principles for Responsible Management Education supports this interpretation). The words 'compassion,' 'love,' 'social,' and 'emotion' appeared not at all in the corpus. Martin Parker notes this monoculture in his critique of business education (Parker, 2018). He argues that 'if we want those in power to become more responsible, then we must stop teaching students that heroic transformational leaders are the answer to every problem, or that the purpose of learning about taxation laws is to evade taxation, or that creating new desires is the purpose of marketing. In every case, the business school acts as an apologist, selling ideology as if it were science'. One might add, *pace* Swiss Re, 'teaching students to think of responsible, ethical, green business merely as a means to avoid reputational harm.' Naturally, there are many honourable exceptions.

A business and management education fit for the global crisis might be directed to the same ends as my imaginary climate-free COP talks: it would start and finish with the idea that the pre-eminence of business as a global institution brings with it colossal responsibilities that go far beyond mere duty to shareholders. It never was true that 'The Social Responsibility of Business is to Increase Its Profits' (Friedman, 1970); The 'open and free market' on which Friedman's title is predicated did not exist then and certainly does not now; business risk-taking then and now went egregiously beyond fair limits; many businesses then and now have been happy to maximise profits despite knowing that they are doing harm to the commonwealth (the US opioid crisis a current example of murderous profit-making); it was not true then, and it certainly is not now, that government always acts on a democratic mandate, that regulators intervene to bust cartels or that auditors (become profit-making enterprises themselves) expose dishonesty. It was not true then, and it is not true now that business trespasses on the province of government when it considers its social impact: doing so is a duty, not a costly supererogation. Socially *ir*responsible business is still pushing the world towards disaster. Business is a global institution whose responsibilities are commensurate with its pre-eminence; business owners, investors, executives, managers, and non-managing employees all carry that responsibility, and the first duty of business education should be to prepare people to exercise it.

One name for the public exercise of private duty is 'leadership'. If only one element of business education was to be changed, it should be the way leadership is taught. The conventional view, repeated to the point of tedium in the manifestos and curricula of business schools (Little and Melling, 2010), is that students are leaders-in-embryo, who in their future roles must inspire 'followers' by their vision and authenticity, doing the five, six or eleven things a leader must do and being the three, seven or nine things a leader must be. A search on duckduckgo shows that there is a list for every number between two and fourteen. IMD, picked at random, settles for eight, in a 'six-minute read' (IMD, 2022). It is a monotonous refrain entirely innocent of the relevant critical or scholarly literature; it tells us that 'leadership is about being yourself, following your dream, finding your passion, defining a compelling vision and inspiring your people …' (it is always 'your people,' as if employees were possessions, and they are always on the receiving end of 'inspiration'); it tells us that 'authentic and visionary leaders are ferociously humble and impeccably ethical' (Collins, 2001); 'unrealistically persistent and wildly courageous' or that they 'employ encouraging ... positive words that provoke others into dazzling action' (Shah, 2010). The dominant tone in many leadership case studies is bathos: in one, the CEO of a large IT firm has exercised 'heroic leadership' in 'service-oriented architecture' (Sheth et al, 2010); in another 'focus is an important element of leadership in oral care products' (Nightingale, 2008). Jack Welch is a favourite of the genre, endlessly telling us that 'leadership is not just about you. It's about them.'

Carlos Ghosn and Jack Dunlap remain stars despite revelations of criminality and incompetence. Turning with relief to a leadership case study based on Greta Thunberg I am dismayed to find that I am invited to emulate her habits of 'holding eye contact with her audience' and 'displaying contagious emotions'. Five leadership lessons from Malala Yousafzai's include the usual injunction to be yourself: 'a true leader knows that they'll be more compelling, persuasive, and inspiring to others if they express all parts of their personality' (Sweeney and Gosfield, 2013). It turns out that even the characters of Ghandi and Wangari Maathai have been ransacked for leadership recipes. Thus, the sublime is commodified, principle is instrumentalised and human achievement reduced to a single function. When, after having been enjoined to 'be themselves,' 'find a compelling story,' and 'leverage the passion of your followers,' MBA students encounter organisational reality, the collision can produce cognitive dissonance. Their education as managers ought, as Stephen Segal puts it, to have begun 'with the murkiness, contingency and uncertainty of experience' rather than with the *de haut en bas* thinking that characterises the case method (Segal, 2010). In a celebrated study, Alvesson and Sveningsson (2003) showed that 'initial claims about leadership values and style tend to break down when managers are asked to expand on how they perceive their leadership and account for what they actually do in this respect'. They argue 'that thinking about leadership needs to take seriously the possibility of the nonexistence of leadership as a distinct phenomenon'. When we allow this possibility, we admit, or restore other possibilities, including the possibility that the most valuable leadership is encouraging collaboration and dialogue, not from a pedestal, but from the floor, stepping up then stepping back.

The popular discourse of leadership emphasises individual exceptionalism and requires infantilised, intransitive followers who wait patiently to be inspired; it anoints and elevates what might otherwise be an unassuming managerial class and encourages it in moral posturing and magical thinking; the same discourse marginalises labour power, collaboration, democratic deliberation and dialogue in a community of presumed equals. Simultaneously, in a branch-discourse the leadership literature stigmatises and pathologizes 'resistance to change' as the failure of non- leaders to be moved by their authentically inspiring betters. An article published in HBR fifty years ago provides the essential tropes of this refrain (much of the piece is regularly reproduced without acknowledgement or attribution, as if it were holy writ). The author complains that 'employee resistance to change is one of the most baffling and recalcitrant problems business executives face' (Lawrence, 1969). It goes on to list the symptoms, including 'sullen hostility … and … the expression of a lot of pseudological reasons why the change will not work' and to advise against employee participation, on the grounds that it 'may lead to trouble' (ibid). These mutually articulated conceits – that managers must be visionary leaders and that non-leaders resist change – obscure the irony that it is managers and capital, overwhelmingly, that is, resisting the order of change needed to avoid climate disaster.

These conceits join a broader aggregation of false claims, amongst them the idea that business is the pre-eminent institution, and that profit is the only source of wealth. They spring up like Japanese knotweed, outfacing more delicate plants like cooperatives, democratic and social enterprises, activist capitalism (as opposed to capitalist activism, see Berruti, 2017) and grassroots organisations, which are characterised as well-meaning but naïve – places you go to 'give something back' after you have 'maximised your personal wealth' in the real world. But those alternatives are growing in strength and scale. The rump of management education that does not take this into account is already redundant – a dead system walking, preparing people, including my student mentee, for a future that is not going to happen. Management education can be, and sometimes is, the opposite – higher learning to equip the people who will provide organisational and administrative services in the transition to a socially just, low carbon world. Certainly, some of the things that can bring management education back to life are already happening in dozens of business schools, including many that have subscribed to the UN Principles for Responsible

Management Education. There is not space here to do more than glance at some possibilities and texts that support the reform of curricula in those schools that have not yet got to grips with the new reality. To some extent, the discussion of management education for sustainability takes place within the wider debate about the role of higher education in general. A recurring suggestion is that universities, in general, and management education, in particular, should cultivate 'critical reflexivity.' (Schatzki, 2001; Cunliffe, 2004; Segal, 2010; Waddock et al, 2010). The critical part, in my own definition, is the cultivable habit of recognising the ways in which language and discourse frame, distort and constrain thinking about social and organisational relations and conditions and especially the ways they sustain power relations and the privileges of a class or interest. The reflexive part refers to the turning of that critical scrutiny back upon oneself, on one's own theoretical assumptions and beliefs and to the requirement that action is informed by this critical awareness. This is not 'thinking outside the box,' beloved of management away-days, it is recognising, understanding, and dismantling the larger social, economic, and political effects of the box. It is not 'blue sky thinking': it is a kind of thinking informed by awareness that the box and the blue sky – and the connected ideas of innovation and entrepreneurialism – are themselves constraining metaphors drawn from the closed discourse of neoliberal economics. Planning the processes involved in teaching students to think in this way and the institutional arrangements in which they are carried out may also be critically reflexive. For example, at my own establishment (Institute for Leadership and Sustainability), we expect postgraduate students to be involved in planning and critique of the curriculum and teaching and even in faculty appointments, to the extent that these things are allowed by the host university.

IFLAS, and Impact, a closely associated commercial management development, have developed critically reflexive pedagogies at different scales, from short courses to master's programmes. Learning takes place as students encounter people and organisations quite different from their own, reflect systematically on those differences and are taught formally about ethical partnerships and developments in sustainable business practice. Between IFLAS and Impact we enjoy a network of hundreds of organisations of every imaginable shape and size, from small NGOs working in the favelas of Mumbai to huge social media corporations and special needs schools in Japan (the *quid pro quo* varies from place to place). We might assign students to these organisations for an hour, days, or weeks to become participant observers. In one instance, students worked with the representatives of indigenous people displaced from their homes in Orissa by mining. Students might make conventional records of their experience and observations; sometimes they make movies or photographic records, in any case, they are involved in the real-world actions of their hosts. Those records are studied as texts in themselves alongside formal exercises in textual analysis. The effect of this combination is what Paulo Freire calls 'conscientisation' (Freire, 1993). It may take the form of an epiphany about the way that organisations, including teaching organisations, are historically, socially, and economically constructed. At every point in a critically reflexive management education, students are encouraged to deal with dilemmas of principle and expediency, deontological and consequentialist implications of action, local practice, and global context: it is a process that constantly emphasises and develops moral imagination. Students get used to shifting their focus from the content of a claim, image, or description to the text *qua* text. In mini deconstructions, they come to recognise the sentence forms that emphasise the subjectivity and transitivity of management and the objectification of non-managers. Bakhtin (1981) and Nicolini (2010) have been especially useful in helping us understand practice while holding in mind theoretical perspectives. The latter author's use of the metaphor 'zoom in' and 'zoom out' allows us to switch registers, for example, from a deontological to a consequentialist reading, or from ideal type descriptions to real-world. This is not to be confused with the idea as (mis)represented by Rosabeth Moss Kantor (2011).

These two abstractions – critical reflexivity and moral imagination – become practicable habits of thought and action. Taken in combination, they may be thought of as 'critical imagination,' something which, in turn, is the precondition for moral and intellectual growth through what Otto Rank called 'unlearning' (Rank, 1936). Critical imagination is a paradoxical capability: a kind of *verfremdungseffekt* or distantiation whereby one can see a particular organisation and all organisations as contingent social objects suspended in discourse, and, at the same time, an awakening to the possibilities for transformation: invisible social, moral, and ideological conditions become tangible to thought. Their apperception has *that distinctness which is no longer reflection but feeling – an idea wrought to the directness of sense.*

This is a process of opening up thought, the opposite of the convergence associated with the case method as it is usually deployed. It is the necessary preliminary for the development of managers who understand the significance of their own agency – able to hold in mind the organisation and its responsibility in the totality of a global predicament while dealing collaboratively with daily micromanagement and problem solving. It is a necessary preliminary for the development of managers who know that it is not just the technicalities of, say, a closed loop manufacturing process that matters, but its place in the totality of social and institutional relations. The late industrialist Ray Anderson reported making this discovery in his carpet tile company Interface Flor. He had been moved to transform the company after reading 'The Ecology of Commerce' (Hawken, 1993). Interface was to change from a careless polluting giant to a zero-carbon and restorative exemplar. He told me, in a private conversation, that the change became possible not because the company mastered technicalities of sustainable production, but because he and his fellow executives realised that it could not happen without the active participation of every single person in the organisation, something that could not happen so long as they themselves clung to executive privilege; the symbolic leadership of the process had been symbolising the wrong things: unfeasible individual agency and control, centralisation of power and exclusivity of know-how, Ludwig Wittgenstein described the moment of learning as being 'struck' – a sudden, vertiginous change of perspective that leads someone to see that the assumptions that have previously governed their thinking and conduct are unsafe (Wittgenstein, 1980). Sometimes, what strikes us is the tangibility of something that had been abstract and distant. For many of us, the moment when the *idea* of death becomes the *fact* of our own death is one such epiphany – the idea is wrought to the condition of sense. It is the case that the world we live in is being torn apart by our reliance on fossil fuels. Our only hope of deliverance lies in huge and rapid institutional change. Businesses can get ahead of a too-slowly emerging political mandate, but not those that wait for a conclusive business case to be made, not if they have PR departments declare that they 'are committed to reducing our carbon footprint' (or, as a fast-food giant recently said, they 'take the welfare of chickens extremely seriously'). Mere reduction is actual arson.

'Sustainable innovation,' going green because it attracts customers, or because 'the hi-tech green economy is the biggest game in town' as my student mentee put it, is not enough. A new generation of critically imaginative business managers, educated in the realities of the global problematique, whose instinct is for collaboration and who repudiate the fetishisation of leadership and profit might bring about that revolution in time to avert catastrophe. That will need a business education system devoted to producing fire-fighters, not fireraisers.[1]

References

Abrams, F. W. (1951). Management's responsibilities in a complex world. *Harvard Business Review*, 29(3), 29–34.

Alegre, S. (2022). *Freedom to Think*. London: Atlantic.

Alvesson, M., & Sveningsson, S. (2003). The great disappearing act: difficulties in doing 'leadership.' *Leadership Quarterly*, *14*(3), 359. DOI: https://doi.org/10.1016/S1048-9843(03)00031-6.

Amnesty International (2012). *Report Slams Failure to Prevent Toxic Waste Dumping*. https://www.amnesty.org/en/latest/news/2012/09/report-slams-failure-prevent-toxic-waste-dumping- west-africa/.

Bakan, J. (2004). *The Corporation*. London: Constable.

Bakhtin, M. (1981). *The Dialogic Imagination: Four essays*. Austin: University of Texas Press.

BBC Radio 4 (2007). *In Business*.

BBC Radio 4 (2022). *News report*, 24th March 2022.

Bendell, J. (2018). Deep Adaptation: A Map for Navigating Climate Tragedy. *IFLAS Occasional Paper*.

Bendell, J. (2021). *Deep Adaptation: Navigating the Realities of Climate Chaos*. Oxford: Polity Press.

1 It would not be feasible to list the very large number of reports consulted for the section of this chapter that deals with the global predicament. A few are included here as representative samples.

Bennet, J. (2021). Opinion:The Business Case for Going Green. *First Voice*. https://firstvoice.fsb.org.uk/opinion-the-business-case-fr-going-green.html.

Berry, W. (2001). Conserving Communities. In Jerry Mander (Ed.), *The Case Against the Global Economy, and for a Turn Towards Localization* (pp. 254–263). London: Routledge.

Beyes, T., & Michels, C. (2011). The production of educational space: Heterotopia and the business university. *Management Learning*, *42*(5), 521–536. DOI: https://doi.org/10.1177/1350507 6114000.

Bivens, J., Mishel, L. (2015, Sept.). *Understanding the Historic Divergence Between Productivity and a Typical Worker's Pay.Why It Matters and Why It's Real*. Economic Policy Institute.

Boltanski, L., Chiapelli, E. (2006). *The New Spirit of Capitalism*. London: Verso.

Bostrom, N. (2011). *Global Catastrophic Risks*. Oxford: Oxford University Press.

Bourdieu, P., Wacquant, L. (2000, May). The New Planetary Vulgate. *Le Monde Diplomatique*, 554, 6–7.

Bowie, N. E. (1999). *Business Ethics, A Kantian Perspective*. Oxford: Blackwell.

Brookfield, S. (1987). *Developing Critical Thinkers*. San Francisco: Jossey-Bass.

Buchholz, R. A., & Rosenthal, S. B. (2001). A Philosphical Framework for Case Studies. *Journal of Business Ethics*, 29(1/2), 25–31.

Bulletin of the Atomic Scientists (2022). https://thebulletin.org/doomsday-clock/current-time/.

Carleton, T. A., & Hsiang, S. M. (2016). Social and economic impacts of climate. *Science (New York, N.Y.)*, *353*(6304). DOI: https://doi.org/10.1126/science.aad9837

Carlson, C. J., Albery, G. F., Merow, C., Trisos, C. H., Zipfel, C. M., Eskew, E. A., Olival, K. J., Ross, N., & Bansal, S. (2022). Climate change increases cross-species viral transmission risk. *Nature*, *607*(7919), 555–562. DOI: doi.org/10.1038/s41586-022-04788-w.

Carson, R. (1951). *Silent Spring*. London: Staples.

Central Intelligence Agency (2022). *The World Factbook*. US Government Publication. https://www.cia.gov/the-world-factbook/.

Collins, J. C. (2001). *Good to Great*. New York: Harper Collins.

Collins, C. (2019). *Climate Change and Global Security: Planning for Potential Conflict*. Washington DC: Climate Institute. http://climate.org/wpcontent/uploads/2019/09/Climate-Change-and-Global- Security-Planning-forPotential-Conflict.pdf.

Commoner, B. (1972). The Environmental Cost of Economic Growth. In *Population, Resources and the Environment*. Washington DC: Government Printing Office.

Conley, R. (2012). *Leading with Trust*. Blog post. https://leadingwithtrust.com/author/rconley/.

Cooper, A. (2016). *Images from a Warming Planet*. Ambleside: GWI Publishing.

Cunliffe, A. L. (2004). On Becoming a Critically Reflexive Practitioner. *Journal of Management Education*, *28*(4), 407–426.

Davies, W. (2015). *The Limits of Neoliberalism*. London: Sage.

Dietz, S., Bienkowska, B., Jahn, V., Hastreiter, N., Scheer, A., & Sullivan, R. (2022). *TPI Sectora Decarbonisation Pathways* February 2022. Transition Pathway Initiative https://www.transitionpathwayinitiative.org/publications/100.pdf?type=Publication.

Dobbin, M. (1999). *The Myth of the Good Corporate Citizen*. Toronto: Stoddart.

Donaldson, T., Werhane, P. H., Cording, M. (1988). *Ethical Issues in Business: a Philosophical Approach*. New Jersey: Prentice Hall.

Douglas, M.(1986). *How Institutions Think*. New York: Syracuse University Press.

Edwards, T. (2020). *The Arctic Heatwave*. The Guardian, 25th June. https://www.theguardian.com/commentisfree/2020/jun/25/arctic-heatwave-38c-siberia-science.

EFMD (2004). *Globally Responsible Leadership: A Call For Engagement.*

Eliot, G. (1871). *Middlemarch*. London: William Blackwood.

Estes, R. (1995). *Tyranny of the Bottom Line*. San Francisco: Berrett-Koehler.

Fisher, M. (2009). *Capitalist Realism*. Winchester: Zero Books.

Freire, P. (1993). *Pedagogy of the oppressed*. New York: Continuum.

Galor, O. (2022). *The Journey of Humanity: The Origins of Wealth and Inequality*. London: The Bodley Head.

Gergen, K. (1994). *Realities and Relationships: Soundings in Social Construction*. Cambridge, Mass.: Harvard University Press.

Giacalone, R. A. & Promislo, M. D. (2013). Broken When Entering: The Stigmatization of Goodness and Business Ethics Education. *Academy of Management Learning & Education*, *12*(1), 86–101. DOI: https://doi.org/10.5465/amle.2011.0005a.

Gownder, J. P., Voce, C., Johnson, D. K., Shey, H., Mueller, P., Hewitt, A., Mills, A. (2015). *Brief: Smart Body, Smarter Workforce: How to Drive Worker Productivity by Quantifying the Workforce*. Forrester Consulting.

The Guardian (2009, Sept. 16). *How UK oil company Trafigura tried to cover up African pollution disaster*. 16th September 2009. https://www.theguardian.com/world/2009/sep/16/trafigura-african-pollution-disaster.

The Guardian (2017, Feb. 28). *Shell Knew: oil giant's 1991 film warned of climate change danger*. https://theguardian.com/environment/2017/feb/28/shell-knew-oil-giants-1991-film-warned-climate-change-danger.

Guattari, F. (1989/2000). *The Three Ecologies*. London: Continuum.

Gunderson, A. R., & Stillman, J. H. (2015). Plasticity in thermal tolerance has limited potential to buffer ectotherms from global warming. *Proceedings. Biological Sciences*, *282*(1808), 20150401. DOI: https://doi.org/10.1098/rspb.2015.040.

Gunn, R. L., Hartley, I. R., Algar, A. C., Niemelä, P. T., & Keith, S. A. (2022). Understanding behavioural responses to human-induced rapid environmental change: a meta-analysis. *Oikos*, *2022*(4). DOI: https://doi.org/10.1111/oik.08366.

Guterres, A. (2022). *Remarks by António Guterres, Secretary-General of the United Nations, to the press conference launch of IPCC report*. United Nations. https://media.un.org/en/asset/k1x/k1xcijxjhp.

Hawken, P. (1993). *The Ecology of Commerce*. New York: Harper Collins.

Helfland, J. (2004). *Cooked: Survival by Zipcode*. https://www.cookedthefilm.com/.

Hofrichter, R. (Ed.) (2000). *Reclaiming the Debate: the politics of health in a toxic culture*. Cambridge: MIT Press.

Howard, P., Sylvan, D. (2021). *Gauging Economic Consensus on Climate Change*. Institute for Policy Integrity, New York University School of Law.

Hsiang, S. M., Miguel,E. & Burke, M. (2013). Quantifying the Influence of Climate on Human Conflict. *Science*, *341*(6151), 1235367.

IMD (2022). *The 8 key leadership strengths you should learn today*. Lausanne: IMD https://www.imd.org/imd-reflections/reflection-page/leadership-strengths/.

International Energy Agency (2021). *Net Zero by 2050. https://www.iea.org/reports/net-zero-by-2050.*

International Labour Organisation (2021). *Child Labour: Global estimates 2020, trends and the road forward*. https://www.ilo.org/wcmsp5/groups/public/---ed_norm/---ipec/documents/publication/wcms_800278.pdf.

International Labour Organisation (2021). *Global database on occupational safety and health legislation*. ILO/LEGOSH https://www.ilo.org/safework/info/publications/WCMS_217849/lang-- en/index.htm.

International Monetary Fund (2022). *World Economic Outlook*. https://www.imf.org/en/publications/weo.

International Panel on Climate Change (2018). *Special Report: global warming of 1.5* °C. https://www.ipcc.ch/sr15/.

International Panel on Climate Change (2022). *Climate Change 2022 Impacts, Adaptation and Vulnerability* https://www.ipcc.ch/report/ar6/wg2/downloads/report/IPCC_AR6_WGII_SummaryForPolicymakers.pdf.

Jacobs, J. (2004). *Dark Age Ahead*. New York: RandomHouse.

Jameson, F. (2003). Future City. *New LeftReview*, *21*, 65.

Jones, C., O'Doherty, D. (2005). *Manifestos for the Business School of Tomorrow*. Dvalin Press of Finland. https://research.manchester.ac.uk/en/publications/manifestos-for-the-business-school-of-tomorrow.

Kahan, D., Wittlin, M., Peters, E., Slovic, P. (2011, Jan.). *The Tragedy of the Risk-perception Commons. Culture Conflict, Rationality Conflict and Climate Change. SSRN Electronic Journal*. DOI:10.2139/ssrn.1871503.

Korten, D. (2001). *Creating a Post-Corporate World*. E. F. Schumacher Lecture.

Krabbe, O, Linthorst, G., Blok, K., Crijns-Graus, W. (2015). Aligning corporate greenhouse-gas emissions targets with climate goals. *Nature Climate Change*, *5*(12). DOI:10.1038/nclimate2770.

Lawrence, P. R. (1969). How to deal with resistance to change. *Harvard Business Review*, *47*(1), 4–176.

Leslie, J. A. (1996). *The End of the World: The Science and Ethics of Human Extinction*. London: Routledge.

Little, P. R. T., Melling, N. (2010). *Leadership in the Business School Curriculum, an international comparative study*. Restricted publication. Ambleside: Impact International/University of Cumbria.

Little, P. R. T. (2016/1). *The Consulting Industry and Global Social and Political Predicaments*. Restricted publication. Ambleside: Impact.

Little, P. R. T. (2016/2). *John Ruskin and Panoptic Managerialism*. Public Lecture, University of Cumbria.

Malm, A. (2021). *White Skin, Black Fuel*. London: Verso.

Martella, C., Miraglia, A., Cattani, M. & Van Steen, M. (2016). *Leveraging proximity sensing to mine the behavior of museum visitors*. IEEE International Conference on Pervasive Computing and Communications (PerCom). DOI: 10.1109/PERCOM.2016.7456513.

McDonald, Duff (2017). *The Golden Passport: Harvard Business School, the Limits of Capitalism and the Moral Failure of the MBA Elite*. New York: Harper.

McKay, A. (Director/producer) (2021). *Don't Look Up*. Hyperobject Industries/Bluegrass Films.

Meadows, D. H. (1972). *The limits to growth A report for the Club of Rome's project on the predicament of mankind*. London: Pan.

Mezirow, J. (Ed.). (1990). *Fostering Critical Reflection in Adulthood*. San Francisco: Jossey-Bass.

Mills, C. W. (1959). *The Sociological Imagination*. New York: Oxford University Press.

Milman, O. (2022). *The Insect Crisis*. London: Atlantic.

Moss, K., R. (2011). *Managing Yourself: Zoom In, Zoom Out*. Harvard Business Review, 89(3), 112–116.

National Climate Assessment (USA), (2018) https://nca2018.globalchange.gov/.

Natural History Museum (2021). *Biodiversity Trends Explorer*. London: Natural History Museum. DOI: https://www.nhm.ac.uk/our-science/data/biodiversity-indicators.html.

Nicolini, D. (2009). Zooming in and out: Studying practices by switching theoretical lenses and trailing connections. *Organization Studies*, *30*(12), 1391–1418. DOI: https://doi.org/10.1177/0170840609349875.

Nightingale, F. P. (2008). *Leadership Style of Reuben Mark*. IBS Case Repository.

Nordhaus, W. D. (1993). *Reflections on the Economics of Climate Change*. Journal of Economic Perspectives, 7(4), 11–25. DOI: https://doi.org/10.1257/jep.7.4.11

Nordhaus, W. (2014). Estimates of the Social Cost of Carbon: Concepts and Results from the DICE- 2013R Model and Alternative Approaches. *Journal of the Association of Environmental and Resource Economists*, *1*(1/2) (Spring/Summer 2014). 273–312.

Ord, T. (2021). *The Precipice: Existential Risk and the Future of Humanity*. Hachette.

Orwell, G. (1949). *Nineteen Eighty-Four*. London: Secker and Warburg.

Parker, M.(2002). *Against Management*. Cambridge: Blackwell.

Parker, M. (2018). *Why We Should Bulldoze the Business Schools*. The Guardian website: https://www.theguardian.com/news/2018/apr/27/bulldoze-the-business-school.

Perlroth, N. (2021). *This is How They Tell Me The World Ends: The Cyberweapons Arms Race*. London: Bloomsbury.

Perrow, Charles (2002). *Organizing America: Wealth, Power and the Origins of American Capitalism*.Princeton, NJ: Princeton University Press.

Persson, L., et al (2022). Outside the Safe Operating Space of the Planetary Boundary for Novel Entities. *Environmental Science & Technology*, *56*(3), 1510–1521. DOI: https://doi.org/10.1021/acs.est.1c04158.

Pickett, K., Wilkinson, R. (2009). Th*e Spirit Level: Why More Equal Societies Almost Always Do Better*. Allen Lane.

Piketty, Thomas. (2014). *Capital in the Twenty First Century*. Harvard University Press.

Piketty, Thomas. (2020). *Capital and Ideology*. Harvard University Press.

Pinker, S. (2018). *Enlightenment Now*. London: Allen Lane

Rank, O. (1936). *Truth and Reality*. New York: Knopf.

Raskin, P. D. (2000). Bending the Curve: Toward global sustainability. *Development*, *43*(4), 67. DOI: https://doi.org/10.1057/palgrave.development.1110199.

Raskin, P., Electors, C., Rosen, R. (2010). *The Century Ahead: Searching for Sustainability*. Sustainability, 2(8), 2626–2651. DOI: https://doi.org/10.3390/su2082626.

Read, R. & O'Riordan, T. (2017). The Precautionary Principle Under Fire. *Environment.Science and Policy for Sustainable Development*, 59(5).

Robinson, K. S. (2020). *The Ministry for the Future*. London: Orbit.

Ruggie, J. G. (1980). On the Problem of 'the Global Problematique': What Roles for International Organizations? *Alternatives*, 5(4), 517–550. DOI: https://doi.org/10.1177/030437548000500404.

Schatzki, T. R. (2001). *The Practice Turn in Contemporary Theory*.

Schon, D.A. (1983). *The ReflectivePractitioner*. London, Maurice Temple Smith.

Schumacher, E. E. (1973). *Small is Beautiful*. London: Blond and Briggs.

Segal, S. (2010). A Heideggerian approach to practice-based reflexivity. *Management Learning*, 41(4), 379–389. DOI: https://doi.org/10.1177/1350507609346367.

Shah, R. (2010). *The Leader Who Had No Title*. New York: Simon and Schuster.

Sheth, P. (2010). *Leadership Transition at SAP*. IBS Case Repository.

Solomon, L. (2001). *Understanding and Overcoming Agent Resistance to Monitoring*. Call Centre Management Review.

Space Angels (2019). *U.S. Government Support of the Entrepreneurial Space Age*. Space Angels, for NASA JPL/California Institute of Technology.

Spadaro, P. A. (2020). Climate Change, Environmental Terrorism, Eco-Terrorism and Emerging Threats. *Journal of Strategic Security*, *13*(4), 58–80. DOI: https://doi.org/10.5038/1944-0472.13.4.1863.

The Spectator (2009). *British Press Banned from Reporting Parliament*. Seriously. 13th October 2009.

Sweeney, C., Gosfield, J. (2013*) The Art of Doing: How Superachievers Do What They Do and How They Do It Well.* New York: Penguin Putnam.

Swiss Re (2020). *Special Report: Climate Change.* https://corporatesolutions.swissre.com/dam/jcr:071c5173-84d0-43d2-8038-0e287e6f3306/climate-change-report.pdf.

Trafigura (2021). *Sustainability Report.* https://www.trafigura.com/brochure/2021-trafigura- sustainability-report/.

Turner, G. (2014). *Is Global Collapse Imminent.* MSSI Research Papers.

United Nations Office for Disaster Risk Reduction (2022). *Global Assessment Report on Disaster Risk Reduction.* www.undrr.org/GAR2022.

US Dept. of Commerce Bureau of Economic Analysis (2014). *Corporate profits with inventory valuation adjustment.* Reports, 2012–14.

Waddock, S. et al (2010). The Principles for Responsible Management Education – where do we go from here? In D. Fisher and D. Swanson (Eds.). *Assessing Business Ethics Education.* Charlotte: Information Age Publishing.

Wallace-Wells, David (2019). *The Uninhabitable Earth.* London: Allen Lane.

Weisbord, M. (1992). *Discovering Common Ground.* SanFrancisco: Berrett-Koehler.

Weisbord, M., Janoff, S. (2000). *Future Search: An Action Guide.* San Francisco: Josset-Bass.

Weyhenmeyer, G., et al, (2020, Dec, 6th). Open letter to the press. The Guardian website: https://www.theguardian.com/environment/2020/dec/06/a-warning-on-climate-and-the-risk-of-societal-collapse.

Wirz, M., Franke, T., Mitleton-Kelly, E., Roggen, D., Lukowicz, P., & Tröster, G. (2013). Coenosense: A framework for real-time detection and visualization of collective behaviors in human crowds by tracking mobile devices. In *Proceedings of the European Conference on Complex Systems 2012* (pp. 353–361). Springer International Publishing.

Wittgenstein, L. (1980). *Remarks on the Philosophy of Psychology.* Oxford: Blackwell.

Work, C. (2019). *Climate change and conflict: Global insecurity and the road less travelled. Geoforum,* 102, 222–225. DOI: https://doi.org/10.1016/j.geoforum.2018.11.004.

York, R., Rosa, E. A., & Dietz, T. (2003). *STIRPAT, IPAT and ImPACT: analytic tools for unpacking the driving forces of environmental impacts*. Ecological Economics, 46(3), 351. DOI: https://doi.org/10.1016/S0921-8009(03)00188-5.

Zhou, M. (2015). *Public environmental skepticism: A cross-national and multilevel analysis*. International Sociology, 30(1), 61–85. DOI: https://doi.org/10.1177/0268580914558285.

Adrianna Nizińska, University of Gothenburg, Sweden

Ewa Kurantowicz, DSW University, Poland

Shifts in the Perspectives on Adult Education and Workplace Learning: An Overview of Trends in the Discipline

Abstract: Human development concerns an individual's life course with its developmental stages and tasks involved in each of them. The andragogical perspective engages with development by mobilizing the processes of learning and teaching to support adults as they carry out their tasks in life. The effective dissemination of andragogical perspectives across environments and sites of adult lifelong learning is premised on grasping how new theories, research findings, and social practices have been and still are recasting the notion and understanding of adult education. In this chapter, we seek to offer an overview of the andragogical perspective on adult development by depicting the so-called classical model of factors in adult learning/ teaching, its current perceptions and the effects of the theoretical-empirical transgression associated with adult workplace learning. We offer a brief survey of shifts in conceptualizations of adult learning, including workplace learning, prompted by selected learning theories and an examination of workplace culture in terms of its expansive and restrictive learning environments. In conclusion, we make a case for understanding the adult education perspective on adult development as a dual social practice.

Keywords: Adult education, andragogical perspective, workplace learning, adult learner

The Adult-Education Perspective

As a scholarly discipline, adult education (andragogy) examines the social world through the lens of its fundamental concepts and principles. The central ideas that inform the adult-education perspective can be encapsulated as the belief 'that all adults can learn; that all persons need education periodically throughout life, that it is their right, and that it is the duty of society to make lifelong education possible for everyone' (Titmus, 1996, p. 14). If this view reverberates with the echoes of Enlightenment, this is because the practice of adult education emerged in the eighteenth century and was formatively shaped in the twentieth and the twenty-first centuries by critical participatory research, collaborative and community-based learning, engaged research perspectives, and transformative learning.

Three fundamental concepts have been pivotal to the development of adult education/andragogy as a discipline. They are adulthood/maturity, learning/teaching and learning environments/contexts. All these concepts have demonstrated 'duality' in the way they have been adopted in some of the major studies conducted in this field over the recent years (see works by Alheit et al., 1996; Field, 2000; Murphy & Fleming, 2010; Malewski, 2010; Bainbridge et al., 2021; etc.).

The adult-education perspective can be understood and depicted in various ways, and the approach we propose results from the horizontal analysis of these three central ('dual') concepts, driven by the question: How does adulthood/maturity condition learning/teaching processes so that they become multidimensional processes in a given social environment/context?

In psychological models, adult development tends to be portrayed as a linear sequence of periods of adulthood, for example, from the entry into the adult world, to the novice period, to old age (Levinson et al., 1978), or from pre-reflective to reflective stages in an individual's life course (Pietrasiński, 1990), or by listing developmental tasks typical of respective phases of adulthood. In this perspective, learning is regarded as one of the many activities supporting adults as they carry out their tasks in life (learning in the life course). In our view, today's adult education/andragogical perspective regards adult learning as even more critical to individual and social life. The significance and relevance of adult learning are associated both with the development of adult education as a scholarly discipline and with the diversification of social practices, including solutions in educational policy (e.g., lifelong/lifewide learning). Today, as the adult education/andragogical perspective on adult development encourages moving beyond the linear concept of the adult life course, it invests in expanding its another dimension and aspires not only to support the fulfillment of people's tasks in life ('how to achieve') but also capitalize on the emancipatory potential and transformative power of learning in individual and collective life. For these reasons, if not for any other ones, people's individual and collective activities in social life course deserve to be examined from the adult education/andragogical perspective.

Factors in adult education have classically been defined based on six assumptions depicted in the literature as the 'andragogical model' (Knowles et al., 1998). These include the need to know, the learner's self-concept, the role of experience, readiness to learn, hinging on the relevance of content, orientation to learning, and motivation. Frequently criticized by subsequent generations of adult-education researchers, Malcolm Knowles' traditional andragogical framework was forged in opposition to the long-entrenched pedagogical model, which ascribed to the teacher 'full responsibility for making all decisions about what will be learned, when it will be learned, and if it has been learned' (Knowles et al., 1998, p. 55). However, in terms of the adult education perspective, this opposition, which historically underpinned the disciplinary self-definition and training of adult education professionals, no longer sounds as convincing as it did some decades ago, since both pedagogy and andragogy/adult education itself, as well and the changing contexts of education, work, and social life, have called for substantial shifts, a reshuffling of foci, and the inclusion of new aspects and views.

Shifts in the Adult Education Perspective

From cognitive to emotional reasons for learning

As cited by classic adult education handbooks, Knowles' model is informed by the principle that an adult learner must know why s/he engages in learning. 'The need to know/of knowing' assumption reminds adult learners and organizers of adult education that it is expedient for adult learners to realize *why* they should undertake to learn something. Becoming aware that knowledge is replete with benefits and that its lack comes with unpleasant ramifications is supposed to prompt adults to engage in learning. Sometimes, it is just the basic responsibility of the educator to make adult learners aware of this need and to rationalize their learning. However, recent social-scientific and cultural research urges reflection on whether the 'need' has indeed such an important part in motivating people's educational pursuits in contemporary global culture. Today, researchers of social reality tend to recognize desires or even 'whims' as fueling people's behavior (including learning) more powerfully than rationally grounded needs (Bauman, 2007). This observation certainly has a bearing on the efforts of organizers/facilitators/teachers of adult education in various spheres of life. Until recently, most providers of educational offers for adults shared the belief that educational needs could be fostered by playing up the benefits of cultural, occupational, and/or financial promotion. Still, adult learning/education is obviously not immune to the pressures of a culture dominated by the triune consumerist principle of acquiring-using-discarding, poignantly discussed by Bauman (2007, p. 36). In education, this principle appears to be ousting the concept of knowledge as a socially ennobling good accumulated by individuals with a view to their further development. At least, such a conclusion is suggested by recent and current solutions in adult education, where short-term educational programs, crash training courses, and online instructional tutorials on how to do things (to sew on a button or to fix a bike wheel) proliferate, and quite unsurprisingly, too. While the application of the consumerist principle in adult education can be effective and verifiable, it also curtails the chances of nurturing learners' identities, social relations, and existential learning outcomes, all of which are highlighted by contemporary andragogical theories (e.g., Jarvis, 2010; Mezirow, 2007). Given the disparity between 'needs' and 'whims,' the management and organization of education in various institutional and non-institutional settings considerably depart from the previously implemented approaches. While needs are long-term, purpose-oriented, plannable, and verifiable, 'whims' are temporary, fleeting, contextual, and situational. Intriguing insights are bound to be yielded by new observations of researchers studying the behavior of adult learners and educators, as they relinquish the tenet that 'an adult must know' why s/he is engaging/is being engaged in learning.

From (reliable) self-knowledge to questioning (one's own) identity

The adult learner's self-concept, that is, self-knowledge coming from the inquiry into one's own identity ('Who am I?'), represents another classic premise of the andragogical model. Self-concept, self-knowledge, and self-attitude as components of identity are difficult to modify and often defy inner negotiations. In the sequence of psychological adult development stages, individuals develop a deep belief that they are 'self-directed and independent.' This belief is of key relevance to the conditions, course, and outcomes of adult learning. That is why the organizers of educational environments repudiate pedagogical 'tricks' that spark behaviors conditioned by learners' prior school experiences, with adults putting on their 'dunce hats of dependency' and passively expecting 'to be taught' (Knowles et al., 1998, p. 44). The set of 'tricks' avoided by adult educators also includes (i) manipulating the assessment of learning outcomes, competence acquisition evaluation, and/or employee appraisal (e.g., 'Only God deserves the highest grade, perfection, and brilliance'); (ii) organizing space so as to keep 'order' and elicit authoritative and transmissive behavior (knowledge transfer) from teachers; and (iii) infantilizing learning environments through spatial arrangements (e.g., holding adult education classes in pre-school and early school education classrooms), language (e.g., addressing adult learners by unwarranted diminutives), and/or teaching methods (e.g., relying solely on play-based methods). Adult learners are reluctant to modify their self-concepts and believe that they are self-directed in their pursuits in life (including learning). Whether this indeed is the case and to what extent individual feelings of self-direction depend on cultural contexts are empirical questions that must be posed in university research projects.

Adult education research on the benefits of learning has identified-: human capital (skills, knowledge, competencies), adults' identity capital (the image of one's self, that is, self-concept, goals, motivations, attitudes, and values), and social capital (social participation, social networks) (cf. the concept of three capitals in Schuller et al., 2004). The interplay of these three capitals causes changes in all the elements listed above. The critical trends in today's andragogical research are even more robustly engaged in the debate on the mutability of adult learners' self-concept (cf. Murphy & Fleming, 2010). This direct investment stems not only from the assumptions of critical philosophy but also from the experiences of scholarship/research involved in everyday social and political issues. In its group/collective dimension, education is dedicated to improving the quality of life, empowering disadvantaged groups and communities, and social recognition through education (teaching/learning). In the individual dimension, education entails adults acquiring competencies in various life environments to consciously construct and redefine their identities and to sustain openness to change. At the same time, these competencies are supposed to sensitize learners to manipulation, enable them to deconstruct reality and the limitations it involves, and equip them to discover latent individual, social, occupational, consumerist, and other entanglements (Brookfield, 2005). This means that the major mission of critical adult educators/teachers consists in making adult learners question their self-concepts and identities (Malewski, 2010). This shift in andragogy/adult education exemplifies moving away from the normativity of what seemed permanent and unchanging in Knowles' model (the self-concept including the belief in adults' self-determination) and towards embracing openness to changes in self-identity. The decision of whether it is worthwhile to risk abandoning the well-known territory of their identities lies with adult learners, but so-called critical moments in their lives depicted in developmental psychology and andragogy which enforce such decisions.

From expert knowledge to people's knowledge

Knowles' model and today's approaches appreciate adult learners' experiences in life. Individuals are what they have experienced, and their experiential knowledge is important and useful in the learning process. This emphasis in Knowles' conception draws on a salient epistemological shift in conceptualizing where knowledge is located. If knowledge is indeed deposited in adult learners' experiences, it should be brought out (for example, by employing activation methods, case studies, and role-playing in the education process) and then incorporated into the education process, which asserts its relevance to and significance in learning.

Adults' experiences are somewhat differently approached in the well-known scheme of learning proposed by Kolb (1984), the founder of the experiential learning concept, where experience is the source of learning and development and a rather common learning mode in adults. According to Kolb, the reiterated learning cycle comprises four stages: (i) concrete experience, (ii) reflective observation, (iii) conceptualization, and (iv) experimentation. Kolb identifies two kinds of learning associated with these stages: active learning resulting from concrete experience (concrete and active learning) and reflective learning resulting from abstract conceptualization (abstract and reflective learning). Kolb's concept is essentially founded on the idea that learning is not an outcome of experience, but a process based on experience. This is an essential distinction, as it insists on the necessity to complete all the stages of the cycle: only if 'concrete experience' is processed through 'reflection' does it result in the production of knowledge ('conceptualization'), which is then used in practice ('experimentation'). If any phase of the cycle is omitted, adult learners are deprived of the opportunity for change and development. As Kolb pithily puts it, 'learning is the process whereby knowledge is created through the transformation of experiences' (Kolb 1993, p. 155). Kolb's model is attractive not only because it spotlights the role of experience but also because it identifies learning styles and learner types, which contributes to streamlining the organization of learning processes in non-school settings, such as work and voluntary service.

Interest in adults' life experiences was greatly boosted by the biographical turn in adult education (Alheit et al., 1996). Learning from life stories and biographies narrated by adult learners has become an inspiring research and educational practice. Biographical learning is premised on specific skills, such as storytelling, narration, interpretation of events, the discovery of meanings, and reflection on (one's own) life history. At the same time, biographical learning invariably unfolds in relations and communication with others. When describing his work with students at the University of Geneva as based on 'educational biography,' Dominicé (2000, p. 15) explains: 'Educational biography makes adult learners partners in an inquiry process. It involves adults in a collaborative inquiry, a partnership akin to action research that deepens their understanding of the process and impact of learning activities.' In the practice of adult education, life experiences serve as the content of learning rather than merely as an inspiration for the educational process. As narratives are also endowed with social and integrative power, they lay the foundation for adult identities and reinforce self-understanding. Sometimes, they may trigger the opposite process of adult learners' 'unlearning' old habits and attitudes. Recounting one's life experiences is also a path to restoring one's social bonds, as argued by Bainbridge (2021) in a succinct observation that 'stories are ways to reconnect' (p. 25).

From school to the University of Life

In Knowles' model, readiness to learn indicates that learning is a response to new occurrences in life. The coincidence of learning and the emergent developmental task makes for an ideal situation for adult learners. Educators are expected to be well versed in the developmental phases of adulthood, their nuances and critical moments and attitudes bound up with respective developmental stages turn to develop a relevant educational offer and a set of suitable methodologies for adult learners.

Today, the value of learning tends to be understood as correlated with the skillful transfer of learning outcomes from one space of life to another, from work life to social relations, or from civic engagement to the workplace (Field et al., 2009). This capacity of transitioning learning outcomes, in conjunction with the principle of 'perpetual non-satisfaction,' which Zygmunt Bauman (2007) considers axial to consumerism, is well aligned with the andragogical concept of lifelong/lifewide learning (LLL/LWL) of both individuals and communities or groups, where the 'perpetual educational non-satisfaction' of collectives is at play. Contemporary discourses on LLL/LWL expound on why adults learn throughout their lifetimes (Jarvis, 2010; Jarvis, Rabušicová & Nehyba, 2015, p. 112). These strong statements not only work as humanistic calls to undertake lifelong learning but also function as political appeals urging states, societies, and humankind to treat LLL/LWL as a political challenge, less in terms of its economic impact (human capital) and more in terms of its transformative/emancipatory potential in socio-civil pursuits and relations (Alheit, 2002).

John Field (2000, p. 133) depicts the new educational landscape with LLL as its prominent feature and observes that 'Lifelong Learning is an uncertain business. It can be joyous, fruitful, and deeply satisfying. And it can be painful, exhausting and deeply disturbing. Still, whatever we think of it, we live in a world where it is pervasive.' Consequently, even those who are not involved in learning at a given moment or are part of the group of non-learners and non-believers in the benefits of learning cannot help but be steeped in the world of learning.

From practicality to reflectivity

In Knowles' model, orientation to learning is a response to the urgency to imbue adult curricula with practical relevance by explicating how learning outcomes can be implemented to solve occupational and/or social problems at hand. This insight is directly linked to American pragmatism and utilized in all forms of adult learning. Nevertheless, recent studies on culture and society indicate that to cope in and with the world, adults must understand, explain, and anticipate, tapping into their knowledge and competencies (cf. Giddens, 2001). The adult education perspective accommodates critical and radical andragogy, which results in a heightened interest in conceptions such as transformative learning (Mezirow, 2007). Drawing on J. Habermas' critical theory, this framework is founded on two types of learning: (i) instrumental learning, which involves problem-solving, action, and a task-oriented approach; and (ii) communicative learning, which is essentially about the search for and pursuit of coherence through constructing proper meaning perspectives. In both types, learning becomes transformative if adult learners develop critical reflection and a capacity for self-reflection, involving scrutiny of their presuppositions. In Mezirow's (2007) definition, transformative learning is 'the process by which we transform our taken-for-granted frames of reference (meaning perspectives, habits of mind, mindsets). To make them more inclusive, discriminating, open, emotionally capable of change, and reflective so that they may generate beliefs and opinions that will prove more true or justified to guide action' (Mezirow, 2000, p. 7).

From individualism to integration

According to Knowles and associates (1998), two types of motivation guide adults in the education process. They are external motivation (e.g., promotion, better pay, etc.) and internal motivation (e.g., self-esteem, gratification, etc.). Disputes over which of these motives is more beneficial to development and learning are still rife in research discourse, but there is a tendency to appreciate both kinds of motivation in adult education as equal.

Today, adult educators are more attentive to the genesis of adults' motivations to learn, and they examine them not only in relation to individuals but also in their social dimension. Learning motivations can ensue from shared values (e.g., care for the climate), common civil attitudes and/or social solidarity (e.g., minority rights), an increased sense of belonging, and inclusion in the community. Hence, learning motivations can be situationally, contextually, relationally, and/or collectively inflected (cf., e.g., Lave & Wenger, 1991). This very interesting shift in adult education increases the opportunity for learning and teaching.

***

Table 1 below concisely brings together insights into the shifts in the andragogical/adult education perspective on adults' development. It displays six basic factors identified in Knowles' model and the vector of their change as implied by the selected contemporary concepts of andragogy/adult education. The Table is followed by an introduction to analyses of adult workplace learning.

Table 1. Shifts in the andragogical/adult education perspective

From the assumptions of the traditional andragogical/adult education perspective	To the challenges of today's andragogical/adult education perspective
Need to know and need of knowing	Educational desires and whims
Self-concept	Questioning self-concept
Life experiences	Expanding learning and transitions
Readiness to learn	Readiness for lifelong learning
Orientation on tasks in life	Orientation on understanding
Motivation	Responsibility, sensitivity, and engagement

A brief overview of changes in approaches to workplace learning

The idea of workplace learning has been transforming along with changes in thinking about adult learning. The conceptual evolution and theoretical development of adult learning and education, as outlined above, are mirrored by parallel processes in reflection on adult workplace learning as its specific sector. The andragogical perspective itself builds on several disciplines and fields and, as emphasized by Fenwick (2010), is by nature multidisciplinary, conflictual, and elusive. Andragogical explorations of the workplace necessitate an even greater enlargement of this framework and entering at least into circumscribed dialogue with other fields and disciplines – such as HRD, management studies, VET, and the sociology of work – that are committed to investigating the workplace. Researchers tend to forget that even though the various disciplines share an interest in workplace learning, their entry points, goals, and meanings ascribed to learning are different. This makes the study of workplace learning considerably complicated and any simplifying generalizations highly risky. Fenwick (2010) argues that workplace learning should be accepted for what it is, namely, a 'messy and multiple objects.'

Emphatically, changes in theories of workplace learning have been formatively affected not only by epistemological shifts in thinking about adult learning but also by the mutating nature of work and its new forms spawned by broader developments, such as globalization, growth of the service sector, and digitalization. Fenwick (2010) points out that these processes have bred new needs and expectations related to workplace learning and lent special relevance to learning as such:

> The nature and organization of work have changed so rapidly in the past decade with the effects of globalization that *learning has become a lightning rod*, attracting all sorts of new attention outside educational debates. All the emphasis on the so-called knowledge economy has created a *demand for innovation*—people learning to be creative and entrepreneurial—as a way to stay competitive. New technologies and environments have fundamentally changed *what and how people learn at work* (Fenwick, 2008, p. 18; emphasis added).

Because the andragogical perspective and the study of workplace learning coexist and compete with other disciplines, theories of workplace learning are often borrowed and interpreted in terms of the goals and interests of these fields. This may both contribute to innovative re-drawing of theory and cause its instrumental simplification and shriveling. Applying the adult education perspective, we present a survey of workplace learning theories as surveyed by Paul Hager, who relied on the educational perspective and took changes in understanding adult learning as a starting point of his investigations.

According to Hager, three trends in workplace learning theory are identifiable in the history of disciplinary development over the last decades. These trends have been informed by a) psychology, b) the socio-cultural approach, and c) postmodernism, respectively (Hager, 2011). This sequence helps trace how the evolution of ideas of adult learning has promoted new models of understanding challenges inherent in modern workplace learning and produced new responsibilities both for an organization as a whole and its members, from management to rank-and-file workers. In a somewhat different approach, a group of researchers affiliated with educational psychology and corporate learning (and, thus, located at the intersection of psychology, business, and education), has largely rehashed Hager (2011) notion of the three major trends in workplace learning theory (behavioral, cognitive, and socio-cultural) to propose complementing this typology with two new theoretical approaches: connectivism and hybrid expansionism, where connectivism corresponds to some extent to Hager (2011) and his ideas of postmodernism and emergent concepts (Segers et al., 2022).

Hager (2011) accounts that the oldest theories, which are still deeply attached to the notions of effective workplace learning, have been shaped by psychology, in particular behaviorism, since the 1930s. On this take, workplace learning is a rational process of mastering a repertory of codifiable behaviors observable in a given occupation or position. Workers can be trained to execute these behaviors, and suitable stimuli can later be applied to reinforce the desirable ones, while at the same time eliminating the undesirable ones. In this account, learning is first and foremost an individual endeavor and an activity undertaken by respective workers. The fundamental role – and aim – of learning is to bolster employees' on-the-job work performance, mainly through properly selected techniques, means, and instruments geared to reinforcing desirable behaviors and eliminating those that can compromise work efficiency. Conceived of as instrumental, learning is reduced to an object (learning as a thing) and a product, while the context, culture, organization, and motivation – factors deemed central in today's approaches to workplace learning – are not thought to matter. It did not take long for such an approach to workplace learning to be denounced as limited and ineffective. As Hager (2011) relates:

> ... behaviourism requires that the job be specifiable as a series of behaviours that can be minutely codified and workers trained to perform correctly. The implication is that the required learning can be acquired in training rooms in advance of joining the workplace. Trainers merely need to set up the appropriate stimuli and reinforcement schedules for prospective workers to learn the specified behaviours. The major problem here is that most work is not minutely codifiable

or predictable as required by the theory. This has become increasingly apparent as social, economic and technological changes have accelerated in recent decades.

Consequently, attempts at redeeming and refining classical behavioral theories of workplace learning were undertaken, with one important contribution coming from Chris Argyris, who discussed the previously ignored mental dimensions of the learning process, such as thinking, understanding, and reflection. He insisted that workplace learning was not only reactive but also reflective and proactive. The now classic study *Organizational Learning: A Theory of Action Perspective* (1978) co-authored by Argyris and Donald Schön, introduced an important distinction between two kinds of knowledge coexisting in all organizations. Specifically, espoused theory, which is external, codified in procedures, and usually simplified, depicts the formal organizational layer, while what Argyris and Schön dubbed theory-in-use is the practiced knowledge of the organization and the subjective understanding of processes that take place in it, rules that govern it, and 'the way things are done' in it. Theory-in-use refers to the loose, flowing, and social way that employees solve problems and learn.

According to Argyris and Schön (1978), workplace learning is founded on action and problem-solving, whereby theory-in-use offers a catalogue of strategies and tried-and-tested solutions. Depending on a given problem, learning will either involve a reactive adjustment of strategies to the changing working conditions (single loop learning) or require a reflection-based transgression beyond the readily available set of strategies and developing new ones, which may trigger a change in theory-in-use itself (double loop learning). Argyris and Schön called on organizations not to frown on theory-in-use for the sake of consolidating espoused theory but rather to promote workers' free and unstructured contact with their work environment to facilitate their insight into a routine, adaptive strategies of single loop learning and at the same time, augment space for reflection and out-of-the-box thinking for the sake of generating double loop learning. In the long run, this is expected to create a third loop called deutero-learning, that is, a higher-order learning type, producing a change in the learning system itself.[1]

1 Several adult education researchers complain that Argyris and Schön's use of the term deutero-learning, borrowed from Gregory Bateson, is rather unclear and

Another theoretical approach that emerged in opposition to the cognitive model comprises socio-cultural theories of workplace learning, in which learning is thought of as participation rather than an object or a product. The participation process means involvement in contextually embedded activities that are meaningful to a given organization, intimately inscribed in its culture, bound up with the values cherished by its members, and relevant to the shared self-image of the profession. In this approach, workplace learning and effective work performance are not simply determined by rationality but encompass a complex ensemble of human pursuits, motivations, and values. One of the most important contributions to this field was made by Wenger and Lave (1991); Wenger, (1998), who founded situated learning theory based on the concept of the community of practice (COP), a notion which has garnered considerable popularity over time. In this framework, workplace learning is a social practice, always situated in a concrete context, where participation in a community of practice lies at the core of learning. Practitioners form a community by engaging in a given domain in which their practice is founded on shared and jointly negotiated values. Thus, workplace learning covers not only mastering a set of behaviors but also constructing a communal professional identity underpinned by a shared understanding of the work domain and its values. Therefore, learning is never independent of the context; on the contrary, the context determines essential dimensions of learning in ways that may be imperceptible to the learner and the organization alike. Critics of the situated learning theory claim that it heavily relies on the undertheorized concept of participation and pictures a one-directional process in which novices learn from full participants. Importantly, this model pays attention to the increasing role of incidental and informal learning in the workplace. These ideas have been picked up and further developed by Hager (2011).

The third trend identified by Hager (2011) includes postmodernist theories, which argue that the metaphors of learning as knowledge acquisition proposed by psychologically grounded theories and as participation

---

inconsistent. In Argyris' later, post-2000 studies, the term is dropped altogether, making room for the concept of meta-learning. For a more thorough discussion, see Visser (2007).

fail to adequately capture the complexity of learning processes in contemporary workplaces because they ignore the temporal factor. Instead, postmodernist theorists of organization, such as Tsoukas and Vladimirou (2001), propose the metaphor of emergence, which gives justice to workplace learning as a dynamic phenomenon anchored in ever-changing value systems and, consequently, constructed and reconstructed time and again. In Tsoukas and Vladimirou's (2001) view, workplace learning results from an individual's involvement in a continual refashioning of meanings, practices, and values and is essentially contingent, with all its findings and conclusions always being merely temporary. Tsoukas and Vladimirou (2001) propose conceptualizing today's workplace as a threefold phenomenon that operates at once as a) a *concrete* setting within which individual action takes place; b) a set of *abstract* rules in the form of propositional statements; and c) a *historical* community. So learning in the workplace is the members' capability to carry out their work, in concrete contexts, by applying sets of rules whose application depends on historically evolved collective understandings and experiences (Tsoukas & Vladimirou, 2001, p. 973).

In brief, Hager (2005) points out that the multiplicity of approaches to workplace learning makes the strivings to establish a universal and general theory unfeasible. He also emphasizes that theories that seek to identify a single factor providing a complete and thorough explanation of workplace learning are bound to fail because they offer fragmentary and selective perspectives that cannot but produce reductive and superficial accounts of the complex problem field of workplace learning.

Table 2. An overview of workplace learning theories, based on Hager (2005, 2011)

Workplace learning theories influenced by	**Concept of learning**	**Metaphor of learning**	**Representatives**	**Focus**	**Organizational knowledge**
Psychology	Learning as a product	Thing	Argyris, Schön	On the individual (learners).	The knowledge of the organization is the sum of individuals' rational, cognitive workplace performances.
Socio-cultural theory	Learning as a process	Participation	Lave and Wenger, Engeström, Fuller and Unwin	On the conditions and frameworks in the workplace (**context**).	Organizational knowledge is about sustaining the interconnected communities of practice through which an organization knows what it knows and thus becomes effective and valuable as an organization.
Postmodernism	Learning as a co-emergent phenomenon	Engagement	Tsoukas, Fenwick, Usher and Edwards	**on learners in context** (individuals and conditions are seen as a transactional process; **a relationship** between the individual and his/her experiences and the external conditions).	Organizational knowledge is the members' capability to carry out their work in concrete contexts, by applying rules whose application depends on historical understandings and experiences.

The multidimensionality of workplace learning: Learning as a 'messy object'

According to Fenwick (2010), workplace learning is essentially a blurry concept. The term *learning* is used, for example, to refer to skill development, information access, and personal consciousness-raising for individuals. Furthermore, it also serves to designate system processes ranging from innovation and organizational change to knowledge management. Fenwick (2010) argues that the question that should be core in any discussion of learning is: learning *what*, exactly? learning *for what*, because *why*? In the arena of work, 'learning needs to be appreciated as a messy object, existing in different states, or perhaps a series of different objects that are patched together through some manufactured linkages' (Fenwick, 2010, p. 79).

Tara Fenwick (2008) argues that today, adult educators' interest in workplace learning is focused on two fundamental issues or areas: a) How people solve workplace problems through learning; and b) How particular groups of workers learn. Further in our argument, we examine the former issue to show how workplace learning researchers perceive learning as a method for solving workplace problems. Fenwick (2008) emphasizes that as the nature of work changes, today's workers are confronted with an array of challenges, ranging from simple and adaptive ones to complex ones concerning organizational culture and value conflicts. Her list of the most frequent issues faced by employees includes integrating new technologies and improving the flow of work processes, getting interdisciplinary teams to work together, stopping inequities and prejudices in the workplace, and making people aware of their own power to change the conditions of their work.

Various forms and dimensions of learning can broaden a worker's repertoire of effective actions and strengthen his/her professional expertise. However, as the above overview of workplace learning theories indicates, in order to meaningfully discuss learning, it is indispensable to recognize the multifacetedness of learning and specify what is meant by learning in the first place, for example, by drawing as basic a distinction as individual learning versus group learning understood as a collective form determined by an organizational culture or a community of practice (COP).

An interesting model of investigating workplace learning cultures along with the varied learning environments and learning opportunities they produce for workers has been proposed by Fuller and Unwin (2004, 2003). Taking Engeström (2001) activity theory as their starting point and inspired by Lave and Wenger's studies, Fuller and Unwin have used empirical data from English companies in various industries and sectors to argue that workplace learning stretches over a continuum spanning the poles of expansive vs. restrictive organization-generated learning cultures. All such cultures produce their specific opportunities for and barriers to workplace learning.

Expansive cultures promote transformative, reflective, bottom-up, and unconstrained learning, which Engeström (2001) refers to as third-order learning. Restrictive cultures spawn closed, top-down designed learning pathways for workers by defining the area, content, and scope of access to organizational knowledge for respective worker positions, curtailing workers' autonomy and putting in place institutional barriers to learning, narrow specializations, and obstacles to skilling transfer and mutual learning. As Fuller and Unwin (2003) observe:

> factors such as organizational culture and history, the way jobs are designed, and work is organized, and the way people are managed and their performance is judged help explain the lived realities of workplace learning and provide messages for enhancing workforce development. ... contrasting forms of work organization and approaches to managing employees are likely to generate different learning environments and opportunities for workplace learning. (Fuller and Unwin, 2005, p. 21).

This means that workers' effectiveness in workplace problem-solving and their capacity to learn largely depend on the culture fostered by the organization, rather than on workers' capacities and skills alone. This insight corresponds to the interpretative understanding of workplace competencies and the claim that 'People do not have competencies independent of context' (Fischer et al., 1993). As distinct from rationality-based approaches, this model does not endorse the notion of competence as 'independent of the social and task-specific context in which we perform our job' but perceives it as 'a function of the context in which it is applied, where **worker and work form one entity** through the lived experience of work' (Sandberg, 2000, p. 11; emphasis added).

Table 3. Organizational learning cultures (adapted from Fuller and Unwin, 2003, p. 52)

Expansive learning culture	**Restrictive learning culture**
Widely distributed skills	Polarized distribution of skills
Technical skills valued	Technical skills taken for granted
Knowledge and skills of whole workforce developed and valued	Knowledge and skills of key workers/groups developed and valued
Teamwork valued	Rigid specialist roles
Cross-disciplinary groups/ communication encouraged	Bounded communication and work
Manager/supervisor as enabler	Manager as controller
Pursuit of formal qualifications valued/supported	Pursuit of formal qualifications not valued or supported/or seen as tangential to business needs
Chances to learn new jobs/skills	Lack of workplace mobility
Expanded job design	Restricted job design
Bottom-up approach to innovation	Top-down approach to innovation
Formative approach to evaluation	Summative approach to evaluation
Strong internal labor market	Weak internal labor market

The context is crucial in grasping the nature of workplace learning. The needs and challenges involved in workplace learning are to a considerable degree sparked by, for example, particular organizational models. From Ford's model of work as a series of repetitive routines to Weber's bureaucracy and work as regulated by and demanding a firm grasp of procedures, to the currently prevalent vision of work as problem-solving and managing unpredictable situations, learning is significantly shaped by the nature of tasks employees carry out and the needs of the organization. This results from the precedence given to work performance over learning. As Fuller and Unwin (2005) underscore, 'learning is not the primary goal of the workplace but a by-product of engagement in the activities and relationships involved in the production of goods or services. ... any analysis of learning at work should be located within a wider analysis of the organizational context within which it is embedded' (p. 25). Workplace learning is deeply anchored in the context and given the multiplicity of these contexts, it tends to be highly diversified. This raises the question of whether it is at all possible to construct a universal model of workplace learning and, further, whether individual organizations are based on one operative model and one type of learning. The complexity of modern organizations implies that workplaces may require workers to be able both to perform routine activities regulated by expert procedures and to solve problems as they arise.

An interesting theoretical framework sensitive to the multidimensionality of workplace learning has been put forward by Ellström (2005, 2012), who has identified two kinds of organizational logic that breed two types of workplace learning. One of them is the *logic of production* (*performance or routine*), which focuses on how the explicit work process is reproduced and realized in actual practice. It covers activities that aim to implement and maintain the *officially prescribed work* processes/tasks in practical action. The logic of production puts a strong emphasis on goal consensus, *standardization*, stability, and the avoidance of uncertainty. Consequently, the logic of production generates *adaptive or reproductive learning*. As noted by Ellström (2005):

> the predominance of routine action becomes a way to manage the daily flow of events, problem situations and contradictory demands and at the same time, maintain a feeling of security and stability ... A problem, of course, is that excessive routinization can play devastating tricks by placing on us blinkers, which impede our detection and management of changes (p. 37).

The other type of logic is called the *logic of development*. It focuses on moving beyond and challenging the status quo. It covers activities that aim to *change*, develop, and transform the organization. The logic of

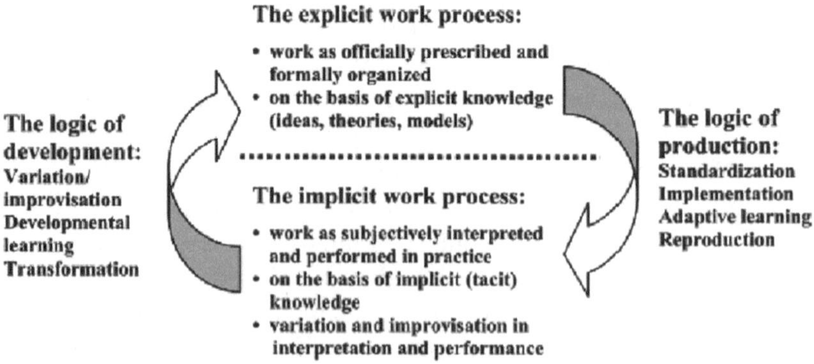

Figure 1. Two logics of learning (Ellström, 2012, p. 32)

development puts a strong emphasis on creativity, experimentation, and improvisation, and it seeks to produce variations and diversity rather than reducing differences. Additionally, it accepts risk-taking and failures as a part of the process. It generates developmental learning and involves 'movement away from a routinized level of action towards a knowledge-based or reflective level of action' (Ellström, 2005, p. 37).

Either of these logics presupposes a different type of workplace learning. Adaptive learning is focused on establishing and maintaining *routinized action patterns*. Instances of adaptive learning are easy to find in working life (e.g., the mastering of *new tasks or situations*, or learning to follow certain *instructions*). Adaptive learning is also central to the *socialization* of individuals to an organization: people in an organization acquire 'the code' and thereby learn how one 'should' or 'must' think and act in different situations. As opposed to adaptive learning, developmental learning moves *beyond the existing patterns*, experiments with new solutions, and in this way, develops an organization. It may eventually lead to transformation. It shares some central premises and features with Argyris' 'double-loop learning' and Engeström's 'expansive learning.' As most contemporary workplaces are steered by both logics, learning in the workplace tends to move from routine to reflection and back again, like a pendulum (Ellström, 2001, 2012). As pithily explained by Ellström (2005, p. 41): 'While ambiguity and conflicts regarding objectives are obstacles to reproductive learning, they are at the same time potential catalysts for developmental learning.'

Conclusion

As demonstrated by our analysis, a series of incisive changes have unfolded in the andragogical perspective over recent years. While our survey of these developments is neither exhaustive nor comprehensive, but rather selective and correlated with our research foci, we hope that it will prove useful and inspiring to practitioners whose daily work gives shape to adult education realities in social spaces and, particularly, in workplaces.

References

Alheit, P., Bron, A., Brugger, E., & Dominice, P. (Eds). (1995). *The Biographical Approach in European Adult Education.* Verband Wiener Volksbildung.

Alheit, P. (2002). Podwójne oblicze całożyciowego uczenia się [The 'double face' of lifelong learning] (trans. A. Nizińska). *Teraźniejszość-Człowiek-Edukacja, 28*(2), 55–78.

Argyris, C., & Schön, D. A. (1978). *Organizational Learning: A Theory of Action Perspective. Reading*, Addison-Wesley.

Bainbridge, A. Formenti, L., & West, L. (2021). *Discourses, Dialogue and Diversity in Biographical Research.* Brill Sense.

Bauman, Z. (2007). *Consuming life.* Polity Press.

Brookfield, S. (2005). *The Power of Critical Theory for Adult Learning and Teaching.* Open University Press.

Dochy, F., Gijbels, D., Segers, M., & Bossche, P. (2022). *Theories of workplace learning in changing times* (2nd ed.). Routledge.

Dominicé, P. (2000). *Learning from our lives.* Jossey-Bass.

Ellström, P- E. (2001). Integrating learning and work: Conceptual issues and critical conditions. *Human Resource Development Quarterly, 12*(4), 421–435.

Ellström, P-E. (2005). Two logics of learning. In P. E. Antonacopoulou (Ed.), *Learning, Working and Living Mapping the Terrain of Working Life Learning.* Basingstoke: Palgrave Macmillan.

Ellström, P-E. (2012). Practice-based innovation: a learning perspective. *Journal of Workplace Learning, 22* (1/2), 27–40.

Engeström, Y. (2001). Expansive Learning at Work: Toward an Activity Theoretical Reconceptualization. *Journal of Education and Work,* 14(1), 133–156.

Erikson, E. (2004). *Tożsamość a cykl życia* [Identity and the life cycle] (transl. M. Żywicki). Wyd. Zysk i S-ka.

Fenwick, T. (2008). Workplace Learning: Emerging Trends and New Perspectives. *New Directions for Adult and Continuing Education, 119*, 17–26.

Fenwick, T. (2010). Workplace 'learning' and adult education. Messy objects, blurry maps and making difference. *European Journal for Research on the Education and Learning of Adults*, *1*(1–2), 79–95.

Field, J. (2000). *Lifelong learning and the new educational order*. Trentham Books.

Field, J., Gallacher, J., & Ingram, R. (Eds.) (2006). *Researching Transitions in Lifelong Learning*. Routledge.

Fischer, K. W., Bullock, D. H., Rotenberg, J.E., & Raya, P. (1993). The Dynamics of Competence: How Context Contributes Directly to Skill. In R. Wozniak & K. Fischer (Eds.) *Development in context: Acting and thinking in specific environments* (pp. 93–117). The Jean Piaget symposium series. Hillsdale, N.J.: Erlbaum.

Fuller, A. & Unwin, L. (2003). Fostering workplace learning: Looking through the lens of apprenticeship. *European Educational Research Journal* EERJ, *2*(1), 41–55.

Fuller, A. & Unwin, L. (2004). Expansive Learning Environments: Integrating Organisational and Personal Development. In H. Rainbird, A. Fuller & A. Munro (Eds.), *Workplace Learning in Context* (pp. 126–144). Routledge.

Fuller, A., & Unwin, L. (2005). Older and wiser? *International Journal of Lifelong Education*, *24*(1), 21–39.

Giddens, A. (2001). Nowoczesność i tożsamość [Modernity and self-identity] (trans. A.Sulżycka). PWN.

Hager, P. (2005). Current Theories of Workplace Learning: A Critical Assessment. In N. Bascia, N. Cumming, A. Datnow, K. Leithwood & D. Livingstone (Eds.), *International Handbook of Educational Policy* (pp. 830–846). Springer International Handbooks of Education.

Hager, P. (2011). Theories of Workplace Learning. In M. Malloch, L. Cairns, K. Evans & B. N. O'Connor (Eds.), *The SAGE Handbook of Workplace Learning* (pp. 17–31). SAGE Publisher.

Illeris, K. (2004). *Adult Education and Adult Learning*. Krieger Publishing Company.

Jarvis, P. (2010). *Adult Education and Lifelong Learning*. Routledge.

Jarvis, P., Rabušicová, M., & Nehyba, J. (2015). Adult learning as a life-long concern: Interview with Peter Jarvis. *Studia Paedagogica, 20 (4)*, 109–122. DOI 10.5817. SP2015-4-7.

Knowles, M. S. (1990). *The Adult Learner*. Houston: Gulf.

Knowles, M.S., Holton III E., & Swanson R.A. (1998). *The Adult Learner: The definitive classic in adult education and human resource development*. Burlington: Elsevier.

Kolb, D.A. (1984). *Experiential Learning – Experience as the source of learning and development*. Prentice Hall.

Kolb, D.A. (1993). The process of experiential learning. In Thorpe et al (eds), *Culture and Processes of Adult Learning*. Routledge.

Lave, J., & Wenger, E. (1991). *Situated Learning*. Cambridge University Press.

Levinson, D.J. (1978). *The seasons of a man's life*. Knopf.

Malewski, M. (2010). *Od nauczania do uczenia się. O paradygmatycznej zmianie w andragogice* [From teaching to learning: On the paradigmatic change in andragogy]. WNDSW.

Mezirow, J. (2007). Adult education and empowerment for individual and community development. In B. Connolly, T. Fleming, D. McCormack & A. Ryan (Eds.), *Radical learning for liberation* (pp. 9–18). MACE.

Murphy, M. & Fleming, T. (2010). *Habermas, Critical Theory and Education*. Routledge.

Pietrasiński, Z. (1990). *Rozwój człowieka dorosłego* [Adult development]. Wiedza Powszechna.

Sandberg, J. (2000). Understanding Human Competence at Work: An Interpretative Approach. *Academy of Management Journal*, *43*(1), 9–25.

Segers, M., Endedijk, M., & Gijbels, D. (2022). From Classic Perspectives on Learning to Current Views on Learning. In F. Dochy, D. Gijbels, M. Segers, & P. Van den Bossche, P. (Eds.) *Theories of workplace learning in changing times* (pp. 3 – 14). Routledge.

Schuller, T. Preston, J., Hammond, C., Brasset-Grundy A., & Bynner, J. (2004). *The Benefits of Learning*. RoutledgeFalmer.

Titmus, C.J. (1996). Adult Education: Concepts and Principles. In A.C. Tuijnman (Ed.), *International Encyclopedia of Adult Education and Training* (pp. 9–17). Pergamon.

Tsoukas, H. & Vladimirou, E. (2001). What is organizational knowledge? *Journal of Management Studies*, *38*(7), 973–993.

Visser, M. (2007). Deutero-Learning in Organizations: A Review and a Reformulation. *The Academy of Management Review*, *32*(2), 659–667.

Leesa Soulodre, R3i Ventures, Singapore

Are We Ready for the Friction-Free and Risk-Driven Economy?

Abstract: The transition from the industrial to the information age has placed us in a paradigm-changing business environment where 'labor, information, and money move easily, cheaply, and almost instantly.' New skills for digital times are needed. Their systematic development is to become a shared goal and a core competency of early childhood and adult education systems worldwide alike. New leadership is to emerge, adopting paradoxes of a digital mindset underwritten by active investment capital, accelerated technological transfer, education, and policy reform; we can take transformative action toward a more sustainable, post-pandemic world.

Keywords: Friction-free economy, digital leadership, twenty-first-century skills

Bill Gates (1996) in his book *The Road Ahead* described **a friction-free economy** where labor, information, and money move easily and almost instantly with transaction costs reduced to the bare minimum. To succeed in the friction-free economy, long-established companies must form new and more fluid relationships with customers, workers, and owners. Those that do not will either struggle to maintain market share or fail. As such, we have seen the rise of companies like Slack, Paypal, and Airbnb, where 'capital-light' upstarts can compete with and surpass far more established companies. This new risk-driven friction-free economy is an ongoing mega-shift that is completely transforming the very nature of our societies and businesses. A transition where we are operating no longer in silos but in systems. A shift where mobility, the Metaverse, social media, the cloud, cybersecurity, and big data are mere manifestations of technological evolutions. Success in a friction-free economy requires digital management and digital leadership in particular. Authentic digital leadership requires developing a twenty-first-century competency and an entirely new growth mindset.

However, we have lived in a global pandemic, and as humans often do, we turn to the worst of which we can recollect for comparison, the Bubonic Plague. In the mid-1300s, almost seven centuries ago, the first significant outbreak of the Bubonic Plague forced Europeans into some of the harshest social distancing measures in history. As Boccacio wrote in *The Decameron* in 1353, the hysteria was so extreme that 'brother abandoned brother ... fathers and mothers refused to see and tend their children as if they had not been their own.'

People slowly came out of their homes when they sensed the worst was over. However, there was no grand re-opening of the economy, like some department stores suddenly under new management. People remained highly mistrustful of one another, avoiding even the most basic interactions with their loved ones. The economy remained depressed for years. Commerce was slow, and just when it seemed that the situation was finally starting to improve, the plague struck again in 1360 and again in 1374. People quickly realized in medieval Europe that if just a single disease-ridden rat was left on the planet, another wave of the pandemic could begin anew. That fact alone made it almost impossible for anything to return to normal.

People still needed to eat, so agriculture did well. Nonetheless, only a handful of industries flourished after the plague. Most industries suffered immeasurably. Commercial trade dwindled. The textile industry in Italy practically ceased to exist. Many prominent banks in Europe collapsed, and even government debt defaulted. It took the lives of more than 200M people. Its arrival in Europe in 1348 led to the death of around one-third of the human population, and even today, bubonic plague kills people in many areas of the world (Keeling & Gilligan, 2000).

While the impact of **COVID** continues, like the plague, this pandemic has also left us all afraid to leave our homes, afraid to hug one another, to connect physically, and to engage with one another (Malik, Mihm & Reichelt, 2021; Lund, 2020; Porcelli, 2020; Philippe, Schiavio & Biasutti, 2020). One highlight was that as more people remained in lockdowns and isolation in medieval Europe, science advanced at a pace never seen in Western Europe. Today, the same trend is underway. The world has some of its brightest minds working to eradicate this pandemic. They have already demonstrated their excellent track record through their vaccines' rapid development and global distribution (Le et al., 2020). Nevertheless, our circumstances are also very different on other fronts. While there are undoubtedly many challenges to deal with (Ozili & Arun, 2023), we can still produce goods and services, ship them internationally, and order online for home delivery.

There is no doubt that this global pandemic has shocked the world. COVID-19's silent weapon has already stolen millions of our loved ones from our lives. Soon the same description may fit another global crisis: climate change in just a few decades (Van Lange & Rand, 2022). As awful as this pandemic is, **climate change** could be worse. Climate change could present an even more significant economic and health threat.

Janson Yap, Chief Risk Officer from the Office of Risk Management and Compliance (ORMC) at the National University of Singapore (NUS), and Peck Thian Guan partnered with R3i to identify what students perceive as the most important lifelong learning and career stage challenges that they face. Understanding this is critical for any higher education institute to meet the needs of current and future students, parents, employers, alumni, and the nation not only for the ASEAN region over the next 5–10 years.

During February-August 2022, over 2,104 students in Singapore, Malaysia, Indonesia, Vietnam, and Thailand shared their opinions through an anonymous online survey on a broad range of potential risks to higher education. To provide a more in-depth understanding of the greatest risks, focus group discussions also took place over Zoom in each country. As many foreigners responded to the Singapore and Malaysia surveys, a follow-up analysis determined that the conclusions from the survey remained the same when foreigners were excluded. To provide a more in-depth understanding of the greatest risks, focus group discussions also took place over Zoom in each country. Finally, an additional in-depth survey involving 305 (mutually independent) respondents discussing personal issues of retrenchment, financial concerns and more from across the region of ASEAN. The findings can be clustered into 6 domains:

1. **Skills Development.** The top concern is that students are not well prepared for life after graduation. The key findings are that students do not learn the soft skills needed in the workforce, such as teamwork, how to make a good presentation, and creative problem-solving. They

do not feel ready to address major societal problems, such as climate change, poverty, sustainability, and instability; or confident that they have mastered the technical skills that they will need in the digital workplace. Respondents often commented that students do not know how to apply their classroom learning to real-world problems, are unaware of the career path options for their major, and do not know what the work is like beyond its average starting salary.

2. **Career Advancement.** Based on career stages, all across ASEAN, the top concern is that individuals may lose interest in their chosen careers. This has ties to the Great Resignation. Other key concerns include poor employment conditions or career advancement opportunities. A lack of relevant skills was ranked 4th out of 9th as a concern but was the risk that respondents felt they had the most control over. In 5–10 years, a majority of respondents expect that they will be in the next phase of their careers. However, a minority think they might be back to exploring again, demonstrating that career stages are not linear, but rather cyclical.
3. **Job Turnover.** Across ASEAN, respondents enjoy relative job security, with more than 50 % of all respondents changing roles, most of their own volition in the past 3 years; and 80 % of them landing a job within a year after leaving their old role, despite 92 % of them have left their company at the same time. The following top reasons for voluntary turnover were provided: (1) search for more meaningful or (2) enjoyable work or (3) to be self-employed or at a startup; (4) higher pay, (5) more responsibilities; and finally (6) better working conditions.

For those that left involuntarily, which was significantly the case for those stepping back from work, it was a story of downsizing or outsourcing of roles by their companies. Interestingly, job exits to go back to school were associated with those who aspire to be in the establishment stage over the next 5 years. Furthermore, underemployment was noted by only 20 % of respondents, with job title, responsibilities and skills cited as equally as important as monetary perks in considering themselves underemployed.

4. **Top Risks for the Career.** Across ASEAN, the top three concerns – cited by over half of the respondents – were poor advancement opportunities, too low income, and poor working conditions or workplace

culture. 15 % cited not being able to live in their country of choice as a core concern. Over the next 5 years, the risk concerns remained the same with little variation. 60 % expect to be focused on exploration and establishment, while one-third of respondents – Late Career – expect to be focused on mentoring others, as opposed to cementing more power or influence in their careers.

Nearing peak productivity and upgrading skills was a concern to Explorers, Establishers, and Mid-Career with the focus on exploring options for careers and establishing themselves in their selected careers. Across the board, over the next 5 years, those upskilling were more likely to select short courses, job-specific courses, or digital online certifications over MBAs or PhDs.

5. **Lifelong learning.** Around half of the respondents expressed concerns regarding continuous and lifelong learning, especially in terms of its format and affordability. In Singapore and across ASEAN, respondents think that they are not prepared enough for life after graduation mainly because they are not satisfied with continuous learning and lifelong learning opportunities, hence the need for the coursework to be broken down into smaller blocks with generous time. It was expected that coursework needs to be broken down into shorter or individual modules that do not require committing to an entire degree/certificate.

Lifelong learning risks triggered discussions around talent concerns and the need for experience within agile startup ecosystems and COVID lockdowns. Discussions did not spontaneously touch on the probability of experiencing mental health problems or the vulnerability of certain groups or types of individuals to mental health risks, but rather the focus was on hard rather than soft skills and the role of the school in developing them.

Given the aforementioned, it is a small wonder why most of the respondents opted for short course training in soft skills in the future. In a world where automation is on the increase, having a wide array of soft skills will certainly make a progression of a career faster and even career change easier.

6. **Networks.** In Singapore and across ASEAN, it is common knowledge that 'guan xi' matters most. (This phenomenon in Chinese culture is

> understood as a person's social network of mutually beneficial personal and business relationships). Unfortunately, respondents think that they are not prepared enough for life after graduation mainly because they are unable to build ties with other students and alumni. Hence the need for more alumni programs to sustain relationships and build connections.

This lack of connectivity has been exacerbated by the global immobility of the COVID-19 pandemic, adding pressure to both perceptions of returns on investment of degree and price sensitivity, and the value of the University as a platform for their development of personal 'guan xi.' In addition, respondents want more career counselling and job/internship placement services, stronger connections to alumni and practitioners inside and outside of the classroom, and ways to build stronger connections among themselves both while in School and after graduation.

Despite the risks, we at R3i feel very safe today (Soulodre, & R3i Ventures, 2020). **Artificial intelligence** has our back, changing our lives for the better. We are scaling breakthrough innovation for impact through our House of MedTech and House of DeepTech accelerators in the Metaverse. The Metaverse is a digital universe that allows users to interact with each other and with virtual objects and experiences. It is a growing platform with immense potential, and women are more likely than men to engage in it (Xu et al., 2022). At R3i, our Metaverse plays a role in helping us to get to net zero climate impact as a small business. It provides a platform for our R3i ecosystem (businesses, partners, investors, and founders) to unite, connect, engage, and trade, but also take action on climate change together. Indeed, we are making it the core of our education and awareness-raising. There are many reasons why the R3i Metaverse holds much promise for our ecosystem, particularly our female founders. The metaverse is a level playing field, with no physical barriers to entry or obstacles to success and new opportunities for women to explore and participate in it in a safe space for self-expression and creativity. Most importantly, our R3i Metaverse is an inclusive community; it welcomes all users, regardless of gender, race, or background.

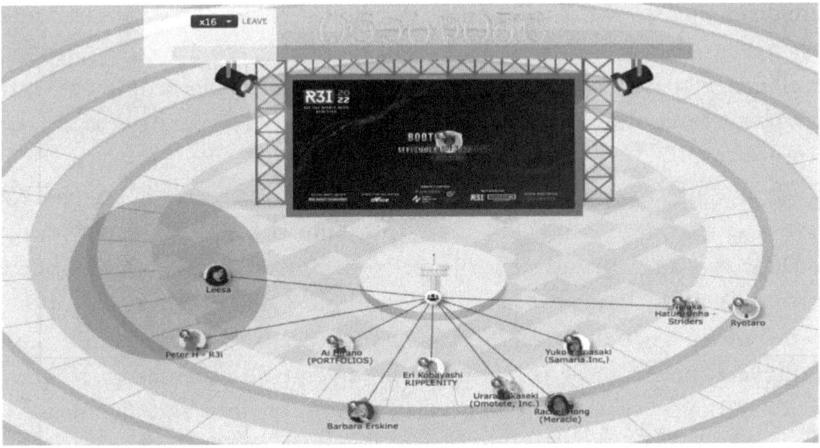

Exhibit 1. 'She Loves Tech X' R3i Bootcamp

In the Metaverse, women are more likely to engage with other users and participate in activities than men. This is because women were more likely to use social networking sites and chatrooms than men. Finally, the Metaverse provides an excellent way for women to network and build professional relationships in a more psychologically safe environment. The Metaverse also offers a variety of educational and entertainment options for women. This could have implications for how virtual reality is designed in the future. If designers consider women more social in virtual worlds, they can create better experiences for everyone.

When working from our office or home, smart devices can enable us to connect to our doctor to refill a prescription. It monitors our facial recognition to give us entry to our building and order lunch online. All this while monitoring our temperature throughout the day and sanitizing our workspace. Driven by a voice assistant, it reads out the calendar appointment for this editorial deadline and alerts us if anyone experiences health anomalies throughout the day. As we left the house for our office today, contact tracing beeped to 470 other phones within this city. It maps if we come into contact with anyone who is ill, it registers when we enter our building, and it will register exactly when we leave. A Boston Dynamics robot, 'Spot' patrols the parks, telling us when we are not observing the safe distancing protocols. A remote-controlled robot plays a pre-recorded message to visitors. 'Spot' is also fitted with cameras driven by Artificial Intelligence to tell when more than a set number of people are gathering and to run anomaly detection via people's temperature and facial expressions.

We live in an age of extraordinary immobility. Once a US passport gave a citizen access to more than 150 countries on the planet, during COVID, it was the equivalent of one from Botswana. Whether public or private, small or large, every organisation must find new ways to operate cross-border. They must do this to meet the needs of their customers and employees, particularly as our countries emerge and then again return to national lockdowns and protectionism to preserve jobs and incomes. As a result, **Machine Learning technology** plays an essential role in enabling that shift by providing the tools to support remote communication, promote telemedicine, and protect food security (Chatterjee, Gerdes & Martinez, 2019; Suith et al., 2022).

Once pledged to Montessori and a non-digital education, our children in lockdown now spend their days logging into their digital devices and Zoom® rooms everywhere. Today children across the planet log into their Miko®, a children's new companion – a robotic brain with loads of heart who chats to children about the world's facts. They log into Reading Eggs to deliver their phonics education, and they log into their TIMO™ app – the time and money management app for our children that allows them to self-regulate their day and manage their money for the future (Ahessy, 2021; Saxena et al., 2021). Out of this, the pandemic arises the opportunity to reimagine education and more effectively empower our children (Polizzi, 2021). It allows us to reinvent our complex global supply chains and recognise and mitigate the burdens of care disproportionately faced by women. Moreover, it also allows us to better supply today's generations with the skills to meet the demands of an ever more rapid and risk-driven global economy. That is how our economies can increase productivity, flow on supply chain and consumption effects, and facilitate and empower economic participation.

With 85 % of the brain growth thought to be developed by age three and up to 1M new neural networks created per second, it is, in fact, during the first five years that we have a unique ability to develop these **twenty-first-century skills**. These scientific facts provide the ideal foundations for hardwiring young brains with critical competencies even more intentionally. Ultimately, we must intentionally develop this foundational toolkit that our children need to survive and thrive in this new twenty-first-century friction-free world (see Gotschalk, 2019).

Authentic **digital leadership** requires us to not only develop a twenty-first-century set of competencies but to respect the development of an entirely new growth mindset (Petrucci & Rivera, 2018; Brett, 2020; Sheninger, 2019). Around the world, business leaders, economists, futurists, venture capitalists, teachers, and parents are all asking the same question: 'What skills will our children need to succeed in a digital and interconnected global future?' Estimates are that two-thirds of the children alive today will work in jobs that do not exist yet. Therefore, what skills should they have, and how should those competencies be most effectively developed?

The World Economic Forum (2016) released a report after looking at the future employment, skills, and workforce strategy. This report, *The Future of Jobs*, Employment, Skills and Workforce Strategy for the Fourth Industrial Revolution, was launched during the 2016 Annual Meeting in Davos. It asked chief human resources and strategy officers from leading global employers what the current shifts mean, specifically for employment, skills, and recruitment across industries and geographies. In the list, skills considered as 'soft' are clearly gaining prominence in boardrooms, playrooms, and classrooms worldwide rather than IQ skills. What remains more interesting is that children can develop these skills far earlier than most people realise. A second report, entitled *New Vision for Education: Fostering Social and Emotional Learning through Technology* (World Economy Forum, 2016 A), determined that students need more than traditional academic learning. They must be adept at collaboration, communication, and problem-solving, skills developed through Social and Emotional Learning (SEL). Coupled with mastery of traditional competencies, the authors believe that social and emotional proficiency will equip students to succeed in the swiftly evolving digital economy (see also Chin, 2016).

Extensive research by Gerald Ferris and associates (2005) reports that people with stronger political skills received higher performance evaluations and were rated as more effective leaders. He defines political skill as 'the ability to understand others at work effectively and to use such knowledge to influence others to act in ways that enhance one's personal and/or organisational objectives.' Ferris and his team's research has been confirmed through multiple studies and led to the development of the Political Skills Inventory, which includes: Networking ability, Social astuteness, Apparent sincerity, and Interpersonal influence. For instance, a longitudinal study by Wolff and Moser (2009) showed that networking positively affects career success and salaries. This lends further credence to Ferris' finding that networking ability is a critical component of political skills, a crucial driver of future success in a reputation economy.

In 2015, the World Economic Forum (2015) published a report that focused on the pressing issue of the twenty-first-century skills gap and ways to address it through technology. In that report, the authors defined a set of 16 crucial proficiencies for education in the twenty-first century. Those skills include six 'foundational literacies' and ten skills that were labeled either 'competencies' or 'character qualities.' **Foundational skills** determine how students cope with everyday tasks. In turn, **Competencies** enable students to approach complex challenges. Finally, effectively, **Character qualities** are how students come to their changing environment (see Exhibit 2).

The newer report, *New Vision for Education: Fostering Social and Emotional Learning through Technology* (World Economic Forum, 2016), explored how these competencies and character qualities do more than just deepen twenty-first-century skills. Together, they lie at the heart of Social and Emotional Learning (SEL) and are equally important as the foundational skills required for traditional academic learning.

Laura Jana (2017, 2018), the spokesperson for the Academy of Pediatrics, outlines 7 QI skills for the future (named after the Chinese concept of *qi* – which relates to positive life force or energy). Jana believes that social and creative skills are the key competency for development. These competencies include **creativity, curiosity, communication, collaboration, critical thinking, grit, leadership**, and **adaptability**.

She uses the analogy of comparing the brain's electrical wiring to that of a house. It is possible to rewire an old house, but it always takes longer, is more expensive, and never turns out quite as good compared to having done it when the wiring goes in – before the walls go up.

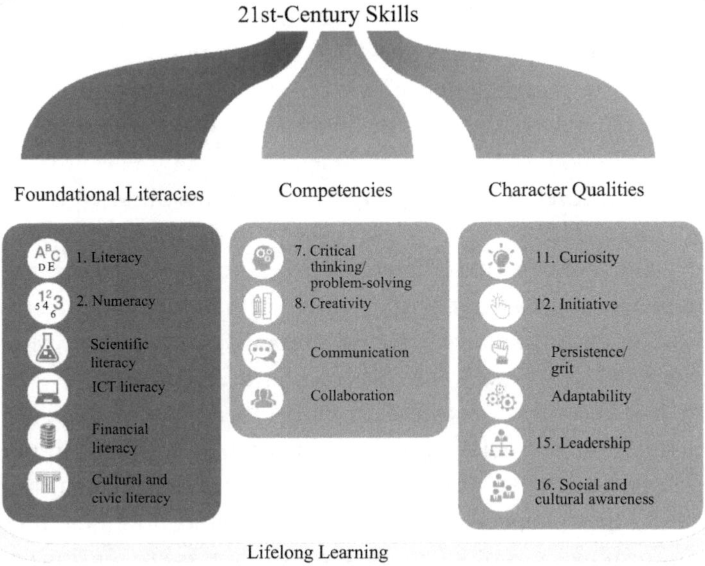

Exhibit 2. Sixteen Skills Expected from Students in the Twenty-First Century (adapted from World Economic Forum, 2015)

Regarding the wiring of a baby's brain, adults play the role of chief architects because neurons do not just connect, and babies do not just learn what they need to know on their own. Unlocking children's early learning potential is deeply dependent on social interactions, which explains why cultivating critical skills involves talking, cooing, singing, playing, and reading books to babies.

Her self-defined 7 QI skills begin with the core '**me**' skills. These include five core competencies: **self-awareness, self-control, impulse control, focus,** and **attention.** Such skills allow us to control our thoughts, feelings, and actions.

The pandemic has ushered in an era of Corporate Wellness which includes Corporate Mindfulness – where leaders worldwide have empowered their teams with Mindfulness apps, such as 'Calm' and 'Fabulous', mindful breathing, and even the introduction of chief mindfulness officers into their corporate culture. While the twentieth century was the era of business management, in the twenty-first century, we are witnessing the transition to a period of **self-management.** While a good self-management day in the life of a toddler is when no one bites their friends, this is because the ability to resist one's impulses is dependent on impulse control. It is also one of the three defining features of neuroscientists called executive function skills. Research now tells us about these all-important executive function skills that they develop most rapidly between three and five years of age (see Andersen, 2010).

After producing 'me' skills, the next is the development of the '**we**' skills. '**We**' are people skills – relationship skills, including **communication, collaboration, teamwork, active listening, empathy**, and **perspective-taking** – all skills needed to play well with others. Our skills are precious in a world where it has become as essential to read other people as it is to read. These highly coveted social-emotional skills can be nurtured in preschool and developed early in a child's life. Toddlers can learn empathy, i.e., to understand other people's perspectives. Children at only nine months of age begin to show signs of heart. Very young infants are sensitive emotion detectors, readily able to sense others' emotions even before walking or talking.

In congruence with Daniel Goleman's (2011) approach, Jana proclaims that the combination of '**me**' skills and the '**we**' skills fit the formal definition of **emotional intelligence.** The core skill is recognised worldwide as fundamental and critical to thriving in all aspects of twenty-first-century life.

The following critical competency is the '**why**' skill which prioritises asking her to identify the root cause of a problem. In this respect, the skills we are looking to develop include exploration, curiosity, inquisitiveness, and asking all sorts of questions to understand better how the world works. A core competency taught in Singapore Management University's creative and critical thinking classes to post-graduates is a skill that has often been long forgotten and needs more positive reinforcement to retrain. Creative and critical thinking have become the bedrock of any Masters' degree programme. As academics in this domain, we have aimed to ensure that the process of discovery – that ability to ask good questions, is far more valued than simply knowing the correct answer. Fueled by technology and the avalanche of data, including the advent of social media and fake news, the

Information Age has now put all the world's answers right at our collective fingertips. The critical question is how to move through the realms of the data, curate it, and tell a story accurately. Curiosity has its reason for existing.

These formal critical thinking and mental model training techniques ironically leave one fundamental question unanswered. Why should we go to such great lengths to train adults to do something that comes so naturally to a toddler? Unfortunately, as parents, careers, or teachers, so much time is spent to train this skill 'out of children' to ensure rapid conformity or efficiency in the mass approach to education. While it is natural for young children to question the world around them, making sure that they continue to see the world as a question mark very much depends on our commitment to encouraging rather than squelching their natural sense of wonder.

When we go on to think of '**will**' skills, we can be reminded of when our children first began school, and they became members of a club called the can-do Club, which recognised young students not just for their grades but their **drive** and **determination** – both critical aspects of 'will' skills. 'Will' is also about grit and perseverance. Research by Carol Dweck (2015) at Stanford and Angela Duckworth (2016) at the University of Pennsylvania illustrate that those with a 'growth mindset' and 'grit' – those who see problems as opportunities, who are willing and believe they can put in the energy and learn what is needed to advance, tend to fare much better than those with a 'fixed mindset,' who believe they are born with a set of skills.

It is highly evident in entrepreneurs, as illustrated by the team at the human analytics company, Fingerprint for Success (F4S), whose founder (Duval, 2013) delivered the most extensive longitudinal study on entrepreneurs that the world has ever tracked. Using the F4S people analytics tool, in only 10 minutes, it assesses attitudes and focuses. These 'exemplars' can be curated and include founding teams. These are people who get the job done and stick with it. Attitudes at the heart of ***will*** are core ***motivations*** – both extrinsic and intrinsic.

1. **Extrinsic motivation** involves rewards and punishments.
2. **Intrinsic motivation is** an activity derived from inherent satisfactions rather than separable consequences (see Staff, 2021). When **intrinsically**

motivated, a person is moved to act for the fun or challenge rather than because of external products, pressures, or rewards. Simply relying on rewards has been shown to kill creativity and, in the long run, decrease intrinsic or self-motivation. While approaches based on extrinsic motivation may work in the short run and for relatively simple tasks, the complex challenges of the twenty-first century will demand a lot more from our children. Therefore, in the world of adults, venture capital and employers search foremost for intrinsic motivation and focus from within.

At R3i Ventures, we use Fingerprint for Success to measure individual founders' and team members' specific focus and motivation. Here we are looking to ascertain cognitive, motivational, and skills-based diversity benchmarks on a team around the core critical success factors of successful entrepreneurs who have the intrinsic motivation to exit a company between USD6M and USD1.2.To foster this kind of self-motivation, we may need to rethink how we parent in the earliest years when even the most routine tasks of brushing teeth and peeing in the potty are all too often rewarded with sweets and treats rather than praise and pride.

We may not be accustomed to thinking of **wiggling** as a skill, but the best way to understand 'wiggle' skills is to recognise that physical and intellectual restlessness go hand in hand. Just think about how we commonly describe successful adults as movers, shakers, and go-getters who set stretch goals, spring into action, and reach for the stars. They are all about action. In innovation literature such as the F4S research, which benchmarked over 20 years, the core success factors in early-stage vs. late-stage entrepreneurs and their teams find that innovators are more highly motivated to focus on initiation and action rather than reflection and patience. We actively seek those on the spectrum of big-picture thinking or breadth – systems and concepts, rather than only depth. At work, this trend is demonstrable in the new 'walking meetings,' 'treadmill desks,' and 'manipulatives on tables,' all meant to enhance our ability to think, create and innovate actively.

Now think about the words we use to describe active young children – fidgety, antsy, restless. Those words are rarely used in a positive sense, whether out of fear for their safety or our convenience; we tend to favour the calm, quiet child who does not reach, touch, grab, poke, or demonstrate their curiosity about the world around them. Instead of giving young children the wiggle room they need, we strap them in instead. We insist they sit still and tell them to look but not touch. Still, especially young children, learn about the world by physically interacting with it instead of working their own '**wiggles**' out. Instead, our children need us to help them learn how to put their wiggles to work.

After wiggle comes '**wobble,**' a set of skills defined by agility and adaptability and the ability to face adversity and learn from failure, the word 'wobble' comes from 'weebles' toys that 'wobble,' but they do not fall.

This reference to a trendy, classic toy called 'weebles' – little eggs shaped with weight at the bottom so they could wobble back and forth but ultimately remain standing – is depicted as the skills needed to adapt to a rapidly changing world. '**Wobble**' skills have gained prominence in most college applications. Job interviewers routinely ask when a candidate failed and what they did about it. Silicon Valley's unofficial motto is said to **fail early, often fail and fail forward** – a slogan that we should be applying to raise young children.

The matter is that milestones only represent successes, not failures. Above quoted, Jana believes that if we want to raise resilient children, we need to celebrate their milestone moments and their ability to fall, brush themselves off, and get back up again.

The combination of critical skills is '**what if**' or '**possibilities**' skills defined by innovation, imagination, creativity, and out-of-the-box thinking. To reimagine the world, not only as it is but also how it could be, we deploy the 'what if' skills to clarify. The 'green hat' in de Bono's (2017, 2021) six thinking hats is a classic creative and critical thinking to achieve this objective.

In the World Economic Forum (2019) global survey of over 1,500 CEOs, researchers identified **creativity** as the most crucial factor for future success. Futurist Peter Diamandis (Diamandis & Kotler, 2020) describes children as some of the most imaginative humans around. Young children excel at imagining new worlds, from make-believe and superheroes to imaginary friends and fanciful stories. However, the creative adult is the child that survived our efforts to teach our children how we see the world.

We run the genuine risk of convincing them that there is only one right way to do or see things.

We know that what happens in early childhood does not stay in early childhood. By applying what we now know about all critical skills and applying it early to the development of '**me**,' '**we**,' '**why**,' '**will**,' '**wiggle**,' '**wobble**,' and '**what if**' skills, we can achieve success in our shared goal of giving all children access to a world of possibilities. At the same time, leaders and managers should integrate these principles into the curriculum design to develop creative and critical thinking skills in adult education.

IESE (2013) scholars discovered after more than 500 interviews with senior business leaders that five core competencies determine our ability to adopt a **digital mindset:**

1. Provide Vision Yet Empower Others

Digitally minded leaders need to step up and share a vision for how the company should evolve in this new age of digital transformation while at the same time supporting the grassroots initiatives of employees to translate this high-level vision into on-the-ground action.

A digital mindset requires adopting an organisational environment of psychological and emotional safety, where all employees can experiment with their ideas. It should also systematically capture the learnings from these experiments, including the data-driven insights in the analysis, for execution.

2. Give up control, yet architect choices

Servant Leadership and Empowering employees by giving up control do not mean leaders stop leading. Instead of sticking to rigid rules, leaders should seek to influence outcomes more by designing and presenting the choices to those best suited to make the decisions and carry out the tasks.

In their book *Nudge*, authors Richard Thaler and Cass Sunstein (2008) describe this approach as leaders becoming 'choice architects.' Based on psychology and behavioural economics research, the book presents a method which makes leaders offer the desired option as the outcome and the default choice. Hence, people must opt out of doing something instead of opting in. A 'choice architecture' that promotes social media use minimises reputational and operational risks and generates value for the company. One example is the blue-chip approach organisations like AXA and FedEx used to institutionalise social media policies across their complex corporate hierarchies of licensed entities, joint ventures, and company-owned operations. Instead of outright banning specific digital social behaviours, digitally minded leadership provides policy guidelines, offering positive advice on what content should be shared and where it makes the most sense to distribute the content.

3. Sustain yet disrupt

For most organisations, digital transformation is a multi-step progression. Digital transformation initiatives are designed under transformational change management to enhance and extend a company's existing capabilities, moving them over time from one market position to another. Other initiatives deliver transactional change management, rapidly moving the company from one competitive market position to another. In contrast, disruptive initiatives can create internal rifts and undermine core organisational skills and competencies. Digitally minded leaders need to mitigate conflicts and serve as a bridge between the old and the new.

Sustaining the 'Old' ensures ongoing operations and profitability and provides a foundation for the future blended business model. Sustaining the old brings a sense of stability, which can help employees cope with uncertainty as they develop the required new skills and capabilities. The 'New' needs to be protected, as it can be susceptible to traditional metrics and evaluation criteria. Shutting down an idea for a disruptive digital transformation initiative due to a lack of direct ROI is a common tactic by those who do not wish to support the necessary changes.

4. Rely on data, yet trust intuition

As digitally minded leaders, the IESE Professors argue, they must lead with a managerial discourse based on situational intelligence and critical thinking. Data-driven use cases can serve decision-making based on facts and experimental measurements derived from processes that remove unconscious biases.

However, the digital mindset does not rule out the use of professional judgment or intuition. The risk is that our corporate data is often historical and may only sometimes serve as an accurate predictor of the future, especially in rapidly changing environments. Intuition plays a role in creatively envisioning the future. Intuition can help leaders formulate hypotheses and define assumptions that decide which data types and resources to focus on and how to combine, analyse, and interpret them amidst the avalanche of information.

5. Be sceptical yet open-minded

Leaders are encouraged to adopt a 'try it and see' approach in the context of experimenting with the broader business objective – the exercise of active sense-making. This approach can empower leaders to forge new meanings of what technology affords us to do across contexts, generations, gender, cultures, and experiences. As well as encouraging experimentation throughout the organisation, digitally minded leaders are encouraged to embrace experimentation in their personal and professional career development.

The authors encourage digital leaders to be sceptical and curious and to explore actively if only to see and prove it for themselves. However, just as blending the physical and digital worlds does not respect boundaries, neither does the imperative for digitally minded leadership reside in one individual. Leaders must step out of their comfort zones and embrace their opposites. And not just the leaders and managers but everyone needs to step out of their comfort zones and embrace the opposites: short-term vs. long-term, old vs. new, control vs. empowerment. In some cases, the need to manage all these paradoxes may warrant the full-time attention of a dedicated individual empowered to lead digital transformation across the entire corporate value chain, necessitating the appointment of a Chief Digital Officer.

Conclusions

However, we are going to transform the way we live, work, learn, and play in our Smart Nations. In that case, stakeholders across all levels of society must work together to ensure that the development of these new twenty-first-century soft skills becomes a shared goal and a core competency of early childhood and adult education systems worldwide. Active consultation must occur across a broad spectrum of non-market and market stakeholders, including policymakers, economic developers, educators, futurists, business leaders, researchers, technology developers, venture capitalists, early childhood teachers, pediatricians, journalists, and NGOs. Children's voices and young adults must also be at the table, core contributors and co-developer in the conversation.

Industry changes are rapid and will not wait for us. As business leaders, managers, educators, and governments, we all need to be proactive and participatory in the lifelong learning commitment for up-skilling and retraining to adapt and thrive in our Smart Nations and this Fourth Industrial Revolution.

For the first time in history, the whole world has faced the pandemic – the same 'single' challenge simultaneously. Changes happened instantly and everywhere, yet this crisis has given us an extraordinary opportunity to pause, reflect, think, and transform together to build a better world. Now all of us, everywhere, are in the same conversations at every level. With our founders and our decade-long commitment to transforming the flows of capital for responsible business and responsible investment and impact, we are proud to be empowering these conversations and underwriting our founders with breakthrough ideas through the delivery of creative and critical thinking training, in-country market immersions, acceleration, and venture building. By applying leadership that adopts the paradoxes of a digital mindset through the development of the additional Jana's 7 QI's in both early childhood and adult education, together, underwritten by active investment capital, accelerated technological transfer, education, and policy reform, we can take transformative action towards a more sustainable, post-pandemic world.

References

Ahearn, K. K., Ferris, G. R., Hochwarter, W. A., Douglas, C., & Ammeter, A. P. (2004). Leader Political Skill and Team Performance. *Journal of Management*, *30*(3), 309–327. DOI: 10.1016/j.jm.2003.01.004.

Ahessy, B. (2023). 'Boom Boom in the Zoom Zoom Room': Online music therapy with children and adolescents with visual impairment. *British Journal of Visual Impairment*, *41*(1), 143–161. DOI:10.1177/02646196211029342.

Anderson P. (2002). Assessment and development of executive function (EF) during childhood. *Child Neuropsychology*, *8*(2),71–82. DOI: 10.1076/chin.8.2.71.8724.

Black, S. (2020, April 23). *They'll Wreck The Currency If They Have To*. Dinar Recaps. https://dinarrecaps.com/our-blog/theyll-wreck-the-currency-if-they-have-to.

Brett, J. (2020). *Evolving digital leadership*. Ascent Audio.

Chatterjee A., Gerdes M.W., & Martinez S. (2019). E-Health initiatives for the promotion of healthy lifestyle and allied implementation difficulties *International Conference on Wireless And Mobile Computing, Networking and Communications*. IEEE Computer Society.

Chin, M. (2016, August 11). *Private Schools: Social and Emotional Learning*. Melissa Chin's Blog for Education News. Https://sjamypchin.wordpress.com/2016/08/10/private-schools-social-and-emotional-learning/.

De Bono, E. (2017). *Six Thinking Hats: The multi-million bestselling guide to running better meetings and making faster decisions*. Penguin UK.

De Bono, E. (2021, Jan.1). *Six Thinking Hats – De Bono Group*. https://Www.Debonogroup.Com/Services/Core-Programs/Six-Thinking-Hats/. Retrieved December 28, 2021. https://www.debonogroup.com/services/core-programs/six-thinking-hats/.

Diamandis, P. H., & Kotler, S. (2020). *The future is faster than you think: How converging technologies are transforming business, industries, and our lives*. Simon & Schuster.

Duckworth, A. (2016). *Grit: The power of passion and perseverance*. New York, NY: Scribner.

Duval, M. (2013). *The Success and Failure, Attitudes and Motivations of Australian Entrepreneurs and Business Builders*. MA. The University of Derby.

Dweck, C. (2015). Carol Dweck revisits the growth mindset. *Education Week*, *35*(5), 20–24.

Ferris, G. R., Treadway, D. C., Kolodinsky, R. W., Hochwarter, W. A., Kacmar, C. J., Douglas, C., & Frink, D. D. (2005). Development and Validation of the Political Skill Inventory. *Journal of Management*, *31*(1), 126–152. DOI: 10.1177/0149206304271386.

Gates, B. (1995). *The road ahead*. New York: Penguin.

Goleman, D. (2011). *The brain and emotional intelligence: New insights*. More than Sound.

Gottschalk, F. (2019), 'Impacts of technology use on children: Exploring literature on the brain, cognition and well-being', *OECD Education Working Papers*, No. 195, OECD Publishing, Paris. DOI: https://doi.org/10.1787/8296464e-en.

IESE (2014, March 12). The 5 Keys To A Digital Mindset. *Forbes*. https://www.forbes.com/sites/iese/2014/03/11/the-5-keys-to-a-digital-mindset/?sh=54c3ad062ee0

Jana, L. (2017). *The toddler brain: Nurture the skills today that will shape your child's tomorrow*. Hachette UK.

Jana, L. (2018). *Skills Every Child Will Need to Succeed in the 21st Century*. TedTalk. https://www.ted.com/talks/dr_laura_a_jana_skills_every_child_will_need_to_succeed_in_21st_century.

Kahneman, D. (2011). *Thinking, fast and slow*. New York: Farrar, Straus and Giroux.

Keeling, M., & Gilligan, C. (2000). Metapopulation dynamics of bubonic plague. *Nature,* 407, 903–906. DOI: 10.1038/35038073.

Le, T. T., Andreadakis, Z., Kumar, A., Román, R. G., Tollefsen, S., Saville, M., & Mayhew, S. (2020). The COVID-19 vaccine development landscape. *Nature Reviews Drug Discovery, 19*(5), 305–306.

Lund, E. M. (2020). Interpersonal violence against people with disabilities: Additional concerns and considerations in the COVID-19 pandemic. *Rehabilitation Psychology, 65*(3), 199–205. DOI: 10.1037/rep0000347.

Malik, S., Mihm, B. & Reichelt, M. (2021). The impact of face masks on interpersonal trust in times of COVID-19. *Scientific Reports*,11, 17369. DOI: 10.1038/s41598-021-96500-7.

Ozili, P. K., & Arun, T. (2023). Spillover of COVID-19: Impact on the Global Economy. In *Managing Inflation and Supply Chain Disruptions in the Global Economy* (pp. 41–61). IGI Global.

Petrucci, T., & Rivera, M. (2018). Leading growth through the digital leader. *Journal of Leadership Studies*, *12*(3), 53–56.

Philippe, R. A., Schiavio, A., & Biasutti, M. (2020). Adaptation and destabilization of interpersonal relationships in sport and music during the Covid-19 lockdown. *Heliyon*, *6*(10), e05212.

Polizzi, Gianfranco (2021) *Children flourishing in the digital age: redesigning and regulating the online environment. Parenting for a Digital Future* (27 Jan 2021). Blog Entry.

Porcelli, P. (2020). Fear, anxiety and health-related consequences after the COVID-19 epidemic. *Clinical Neuropsychiatry*, 17 (2), 103.

Saxena, R., Gupta, V., Rakheja, V., Dhiman, R., Bhardawaj, A., & Vashist, P. (2021). Lifestyle modification in school-going children before and after COVID-19 lockdown. *Indian Journal of Ophthalmology*, 69 (12), 3623.

Serguei, N. (2014). *The Risk-Driven Business Model: Four Questions That Will Define Your Company*. Harvard Business Review Press.

Sheninger, E. (2019). *Digital leadership: Changing paradigms for changing times*. Thousand Oaks: Corwin Press.

Soulodre, L., R3i Ventures (2020, December 24). *What an extraordinary year of impact it has been*. R3i Ventures. Retrieved December 27, 2021, from https://www.r3iventures.com/blog/what-an-extraordinary-year-of-impact-it-has-been.

Staff, T. (2021, December 7). *The Definition Of Intrinsic Motivation*. TeachThought. https://www.teachthought.com/learning/a-definition-of-intrinsic-motivation/.

Sujith, A. V. L. N., Sajja, G. S., Mahalakshmi, V., Nuhmani, S., & Prasanalakshmi, B. (2022). Systematic review of smart health monitoring using deep learning and Artificial intelligence. *Neuroscience Informatics*, 2(3), 100028. DOI: 10.1016/j.neuri.2021.100028.

Thaler, R. H., & Sunstein, C. R. (2008). *Nudge: Improving decisions about health, wealth, and happiness*. Yale University Press.

Van Lange, P. A., & Rand, D. G. (2022). Human cooperation and the crises of climate change, COVID-19, and misinformation. *Annual Review of Psychology*, 73, 379–402.

World Economic Forum (2015). *New Vision for Education Unlocking the Potential of Technology*. https://en.unesco.org/icted/content/new-vision-education-unlocking-potential-technology.

World Economic Forum. (2016, March). *New Vision for Education: Fostering Social and Emotional Learning through Technology*. World Economic Forum. https://www3.weforum.org/docs/WEF_New_Vision_for_Education.pdf

World Economic Forum (2019). Five things you need to know about creativity. https://www.weforum.org/agenda/2019/04/5-things-you-need-to-know-about-creativity/.

Wolff, H., Mose,r K. (2009). Effects of networking on career success: a longitudinal study. *Journal of Applied Psychology*, 94 (1), 196–206. DOI: 10.1037/a0013350.

Xu, M., Ng, W. C., Lim, W. Y. B., Kang, J., Xiong, Z., Niyato, D. & Miao, C. (2022). A full dive into realizing the edge-enabled metaverse: Visions, enabling technologies, and challenges. *IEEE Communications Surveys & Tutorials*.

Luděk Stehlík, People & Data Scientist, Czech Republic

Lea Jakob, Assessment Systems, Czech Republic

Rostislav Benak, Assessment Systems, Czech Republic

Measuring and Evaluating the Development of Managers

Abstract: When we embark on a journey of management or leadership competency development, it is important to define what is a 'good' or 'successful' manager or leader. Once we know how to differentiate between those that perform desirably, we can identify appropriate developmental goals in those who do not reach this criterion. Competency is understood here as a universal construct that considers the individual as the owner of their skills situated within the knowledge acquired over time. The latest approaches to modeling managerial competencies consider the requirements of the post-industrial age, taking into consideration the requirements set in front of the leaders by the globalized workforce and the digitalization of the workplace. The real-life complex case of leadership development supported by extended competency measurements is presented toward the end of the chapter.

Keywords: Models of competencies, Assessment of development, Managers & leaders

What does it mean to be a good leader or manager?

In a previous book, we covered the concept of *failed leadership*: what happens when a leader does not perform well (Kasianiuk, Szklarski, & Żylicz, 2021). Just as with any other active system, leaders can also fail. The problems with performance can stem from doing the wrong things (e.g., making mistakes, causing conflicts) or the lack of action (e.g., being ignorant of the issues within the team or company, not communicating, and lacking skills; Patterson, 2016). A dysfunctional leader will not only underperform on their own, but will also disrupt employee engagement, cause dissatisfaction and lower engagement in followers, and cause a cascade effect of lower performance (Leary et al., 2013). While no one wants to be led by someone less smart, Furnham (2016) points out that: 'by ignoring, downplaying or not assessing leaders, cognitive ability or intelligence they get elected, chosen or promoted only to fail at a later point' (p. 199). This ability can be crucial in the leader's competencies to understand the intricacies of business plans, and strategies, and to make high-level informed decisions. Overall, we can consider the performance of a leader to be determined by their abilities, competencies, motivation, and environment.

A good (successful) leader or manager is considered as a person who is able to communicate a vision, set and uphold values, and create a supportive environment that drives the subordinates or followers to perform and bring profit. At the core of this success is *communication* (Patterson, 2016). Goleman (2000) emphasizes the *emotional intelligence competencies* of a leader as one of the key determinants of leadership success. Other theories focus on the three key competencies of leaders: creating and maintaining relationships, collecting and sharing information, and making decisions (Dai, Tang, & De Meuse, 2010). For each one of these abilities, different competency levels lead to different success outcomes. Surprisingly, some studies imply the existence of different requirements for the same competencies based on seniority level. For example, Kaiser and Craig (2004, as cited in Dai, Tang, & De Meuse, 2010) levels of interpersonal warmth expected from middle managers were significantly higher than for those workers who were in the role of a supervisor, and the opposite was found for being action-oriented and focusing on work-life balance. Does it mean that some individuals are fit to stay in a certain position or is there space for growth? To be able to avoid career stagnation, the motivation to pursue self-development becomes the key differentiator between those who excel and those whose careers show slow progress. The perception of some professionals that they have learned enough is often a dangerous path to follow and can lead to personal and organizational derailment (Dai, Tang, & De Meuse, 2010).

The historical context of manager selection and development

In its first forms, selection processes were focused on identifying key tasks and evaluating skills to execute those tasks successfully. This turned out not to be the best approach to predicting success on the job. Consequently, the idea of assessing competencies (instead of hard skills) emerged in the USA in the late 1960s. The time was represented by the idea that personality is a poor predictor of job performance, which made organizational psychologists abandon the idea that selection should be solely based on personality assessments. Similar conclusions were drawn for the assessment of aptitude, specific domain knowledge, and school performance. The latter was found to be heavily biased based on the individual's socioeconomic status, gender, and age. With the focus being shifted to the competency-based selection, the aim was to predict superior job performance which is not affected by race, gender, age, or demographic bias.

What is competency?

In a 1973 paper, McClelland shifted the focus of psychological assessment in the organizational context from intelligence tests (which he concluded were biased and did not provide the desired prediction of future job performance) to the assessment of competencies (Spencer & Spencer, 1993). This approach became known as *The new approach to measurement*, as it was based on behavioral event interviews. A list of competencies, their level (how well is the competency developed), and frequency (how often does the individual apply the competency in their work) were shown to be relatively strongly related to the performance of individuals in executive roles (McClelland, 1998). Based on this approach, McClelland identified the existence of tipping points that differentiate leaders that are outstanding performers from those that are typical executives. This approach to competencies also makes it possible to provide feedback clearly, as the descriptive language of the competency is familiar and based on the organizational language.

When defining a competency, Spencer & Spencer (1993) defined 20 generic competencies which can be used and combined to describe any job position and level:

1. Achievement orientation
2. Concern for order
3. Initiative
4. Information seeking

5. Interpersonal understanding
6. Customer service orientation
7. Impact and influence
8. Organizational awareness
9. Relationship building
10. Developing others
11. Directiveness
12. Teamwork
13. Team Leadership
14. Analytical thinking
15. Conceptual thinking
16. Expertise
17. Self-control
18. Self-confidence
19. Flexibility
20. Organizational commitment

For each of these competencies, they defined five distinct competency characteristics, (1) motives, (2) traits, (3) self-concept, (4) knowledge, and (5) skill. These characteristics can be organized in the so-called Iceberg Model, wherein Skills and Knowledge are very visible to the outside observer and can be developed, while Motives, Traits, and Self-concept remain hidden from the direct view and tend to be difficult to assess and develop. However, not all competencies are equal. There are different dimensions each can assume, depending on the organization or job position, such as the size of impact, complexity, or uniqueness (Spencer & Spencer, 1993).

In general, competency is a universal construct that considers the individual as the owner of their skills situated within the knowledge acquired over time. It provides the flexibility of adaptation of behavior beyond the bounds of the job requirements, enabling the person to grow within the role and the role itself as time progresses (Capaldo, Iandoli & Zollo, 2006). Another view is the situational view, which considers competencies to be idiosyncratic constructs highly connected to the organization's culture and the individual meaning of one's work (Capaldo, Iandoli & Zollo, 2006).

Management and leadership competency models

Standardized codebooks describing competency profiles were created to help HR specialists navigate the necessary competencies for different job profiles. However, this approach can have practical limitations (the same job position may require different competencies in different companies) and relies on a top-down identification of key competencies (Capaldo, Iandoli, & Zollo, 2006). Alternatively, a situational approach to competency management considers that one is to be perceived as competent not only based on their skills, abilities, and performance but to consider the situations in which they apply their competency and the competency-situation fit. This encourages organizations to use their language and corporate culture to define and describe competencies and competency levels required to be considered successful (Capaldo, Iandoli, & Zollo, 2006).

What does it mean to be an effective leader in the twenty-first century? A *Harvard Business Review* article by Gilles (2016) presents a study of 195 leaders around the world and their perception of which competencies matter the most. Being highly ethical, moral, and safety oriented was the most important for two-thirds of the leaders. Unsurprisingly, the ability to lead with value and a strong sense of safety in a tumultuous economy can motivate the workforce and align with universal human values of trust and transparency. Feeling like we know what to expect and that we will play by the same rules creates a sense of safety and alleviates the anxiety which may hinder productivity. The other key competencies identified were Self-organization (clarity of goals and objectives), Efficient learning (adaptability), Nurturing growth (a highly relevant value of continuous self-learning has been emphasized in the Millennial generation), and the ability to foster the feeling of Connection and belonging was the top competencies for leaders. Another study (Hill, Le Cam, Menon & Tedards, 2022) conducted on more than a thousand executives around the world found that they perceived adaptability to be the key quality of a successful leader. The authors were faced with a daunting realization that the leaders themselves felt that the executives of today were not in the right mindset needed to succeed as a leader in the digital age, highlighting the importance of situational aspects of competency application (on competencies of the twenty-first century see also the chapter in this volume: 'Are We Ready for the Friction-Free and Risk-Driven Economy?').

The latest approaches to modeling managerial competencies have grown to include the requirements of the post-industrial age, taking into consideration the requirements set in front of the leaders by the globalized workforce and the digitalization of the workplace. In a furry logic model, developed by Dzwigol, Dzwigol-Barosz, Miskiewicz, and Kwilinski (2020), the four key competency groups they envision the modern leader to have relied on (1) experience and term of work, (2) education, cognitive, and creative potential, (3) effective goal setting and development, and (4) communicative, leadership function and managerial orthobiosis (p. 2633). The emergence of digital tools to map leadership and managerial competencies through these types of models is on the rise. Nowadays, with the digitalization of the workforce which was especially prominent during the COVID-19 pandemic, appropriate focus also needs to be given to leadership competencies related to international work and collaboration (Jokinen, 2005). In the global setting, the leader is expected to understand the needs of a multinational workforce and effectively communicate the vision and direction. As diversity and inclusion become more visible and important, leaders must adapt to the new requirements and foster an inclusive workplace.

The ability to grow and transform is becoming even more pronounced with the faster digitalization of the workplace, the challenges of managing remote workers, and the emergence of new roles within the industries. By the same token, the new challenge for modern leaders is not just to adapt their competency levels to the new requirements, but to also build and foster a new leadership mindset. For example, in a digital leader survey, four key mindsets were identified by Ready, Cohen, Kiron, and Ping (2020): Producers (focused on executing and customers), Investors (focused on the community, development, and sustainability), Connectors (focused on networks and sense of belonging), and Explorers (focused on curiosity, finding meaning, and understanding the bigger picture). Through these archetypes of leadership, the new leaders can not only pursue organizational goals, but reflect the corporate culture and authentically lead the workforce with a unified vision.

A key question is related to whether an individual needs to change the level of different competencies as they climb the career ladder. According to a study by Dai, Tang, and Meuse (2010), changes in competency priorities and required skill levels are observable when considering different hierarchical levels in an organization. As the authors point out, communicating clear competency levels and skills required at each level of leadership is of crucial importance, and plays a clear role in succession management and leadership development efforts of organizations.

Many different models, some are specific to organizations

When considering what it means to have a competent leader, manager, or employee, many organizations tend to have Human Resources departments create their custom competency models (Sanghi, 2007). These models include names of competencies, competency descriptions, and observable behaviors. Some organizations even go so far as to develop levels of competency expected for different seniority levels.

In the 1980s, a Pipeline model of leadership development was created by Charan and associates (2000, as cited by Dai, Tang, & De Meuse, 2010) and involved six distinct requirements depending on the different organization levels. The model defined which new requirements, values, skills, and other characteristics were required at each point, from the initial role of managing self, up to managing an enterprise. In our work with different organizations, we also find that some have adopted this approach, having key competencies which apply to all layers of the organization but with the different levels of requirement (and observable behaviors) expected for specific seniority levels. This approach can help HR measure developmental needs and create tailor-made development plans, depending on a unique set of needs.

Is it possible to be high on competence but still underperform? There are differences between the top management and HR perspectives of what competencies are needed and the actual employee experience at work. Graham & Tarbell (2006) found that the 'credibility competency' of HR professionals' perception differs between layers of the organization, with top management favoring attaining results, management expertise and relationships, and employees emphasizing trust. It is important to understand that these discrepancies can cause issues if HR professionals are tasked with selecting the best candidate for the position which then may be perceived as less competent by the top management.

Measuring competencies (competency assessment methods and approaches)

The measurement of competencies can be carried out by multiple methods described so far: behavioral event interviews, observation of measurable behaviors, 360-degree evaluations, or complex assessment center methods. The last part of this chapter presents a case study based on a business case, showing how these methods can be combined to provide an insightful understanding of individual needs and subsequent development.

Leaders' developability: Can leaders get better at what we expect them to do?

Why does it make sense to invest in leadership development?

Few will doubt the importance of quality leadership for the successful functioning of organizations. This is mainly because leaders manage and coordinate the activities of a large number of employees, as a result of which they have a significantly greater influence on the overall results of the organization than individual contributors (Bertrand & Schoar, 2003; Crossland & Hambrick, 2011; Lieberson & O'Connor, 1972). Leadership is also one of the most important predictors of whether employees stay in an organization or start looking for work elsewhere (Rubenstein, et. al, 2018), making leaders key figures in the ongoing 'war for talent.' From this perspective, it makes sense for companies to pay increased attention to the effective development of their leaders.

Do the organizations believe that leaders can improve at what they do?

And the organizations are apparently well-aware of this importance. This is evidenced, for example, by the recurrence of leadership-related topics in the Global Human Capital Trends Reports from Deloitte mapping current trends in human capital management (Deloitte Insights, 2020).

Another piece of evidence comes from the Chief Learning Officer Business Intelligence Board whose data from 2017 shows that nearly 94 % of learning organizations either plan to increase or maintain their current investment in leadership development (Prokopeak, 2018). And the evidence is not limited to attitudes. The practical measures that are taken by organizations in this area also show that they attach great importance to the development of their leaders. For example, according to Training Industry (2021), approximately $360 billion was spent on leadership development globally in 2020. Thus, it seems that organizations put their money where their mouth is and believe that leaders can improve at what they do. But do we have any evidence that leaders are improving what they do by virtue of some development programs and interventions?

What can science tell us about the effectiveness of leadership development programs and interventions?

Fortunately, there are relatively a lot of scientific studies that provide quite solid evidence that leadership development programs have a positive effect on a leader's performance. For example, Collins and Holton (2004) in their meta-analysis of the effectiveness of managerial leadership development programs showed that these programs enhance performance, knowledge, and expertise at the individual, team or group, or organizational level. The size of the estimated effects was not at all negligible. The effect size for knowledge outcomes ranged from 0.96 to 1.37, expertise outcomes from 0.35 to 1.01, and system outcomes averaged 0.39. In more practical terms, this means that 83 %–92 %, 64 %–84 %, and 65 % of managers who have undergone a managerial leadership development program outperformed the average manager who had not participated in such programs in case of knowledge outcomes, expertise outcomes, and system outcomes, respectively. Similarly, Theeboom, Beersma, and van Vianen (2013) conducted a meta-analysis of the effectiveness of coaching, one of the most popular developmental intervention methods in business practice. In their analysis, they focused on the individual-level outcome categories of performance/skills, well-being, coping, work attitudes, and goal-directed self-regulation, and showed that coaching has significant positive effects on all outcomes with effect sizes ranging from 0.43 (coping) to 0.74 (goal-directed self-regulation). Such effect sizes correspond to a 62 % and 70 % probability of superiority, i.e., a chance that a person picked at random from the treatment group will have a higher score than a person picked at random from the control group. Another meta-analysis focused on the effectiveness of organizational training in general (Arthur et al., 2003) and revealed average training effectiveness of 0.60 standard deviations (SD) for reaction criteria, 0.63 SD for learning criteria, 0.62 SD for behavioral criteria, and 0.62 SD for results criteria.

What is the effectiveness of leadership development programs and interventions in the real world?

Such results should lead us all to the conclusion that, in general, leadership development programs and organizational training are effective, and therefore very useful for organizations. However, despite the abundance of scientific studies showing the contrary, it's not uncommon to hear in business practice complaints and doubts about the effectiveness of leadership training programs (Kaiser & Curphy, 2013). For example, in the CEB study from 2011 75 % of the nearly 1500 senior managers at 50 organizations were dissatisfied with their companies' learning and development function, and only 25 % of them reported that it was critical to achieving business outcomes (Beer, Finnström & Schrader, 2016). Thus, one may ask what could be behind such a gap between the academic world and business practice. There are several legitimate suspects.

One of them is a quite well-known and widespread phenomenon of the 'science-practice gap' that manifests in the discrepancy between the research evidence for interventions and assessment methods, on the one hand, and their routine use in practice, on the other (Lilienfeld et al., 2015). Some studies show that such a gap is quite common also among HR professionals (e.g., Rynes, Colbert & Brown, 2002). Due to this gap, HR professionals may use developmental methods that are not adequate for the intended purpose. The situation is exacerbated by the fact that the field of leadership development is full of charlatans, quacks, and suspect 'snake oil' practices that can thrive in a professional environment characterized by the aforementioned 'science-practice gap' (Sherman & Freas, 2004). Thus, when comparing the results of scientific studies that strive to meet high-quality standards of validity and reliability with common HR practice, it is only natural that scientific studies will show greater effects than HR practice which is littered with a variety of non-valid and unreliable methods. The positive news is that scientific studies at least show the potential that HR practice can aspire to as something realistically achievable.

Another relevant factor is the natural variability in the types of developmental interventions adopted and their effectiveness depending on the type of outcome targeted. As shown, for example, by Arthur and associates (2003) in their meta-analysis, the used training method and the skill or task characteristics trained are related to the effectiveness of training programs. A similar conclusion was also reached by Collins and Holton (2004) in their meta-analytic study: 'practitioners can attain substantial improvements in both knowledge and skills if sufficient front-end analysis is conducted to ensure that the right development is offered to the right leaders.' In another meta-analysis that was focused on the effectiveness of occupational stress management intervention programs, it was revealed that cognitive-behavioral programs consistently produced larger effects than relaxation, organizational, multimodal, or alternative interventions (Richardson & Rothstein, 2008). In other words, developmental intervention methods are not created equal, at least not in all circumstances, and if HR practitioners ignore this fact, they may negatively affect the value that their organization could gain by adopting an appropriate developmental intervention.

Besides that, there may be a bunch of other moderating variables that can influence the effectiveness of implemented developmental interventions. One good example of such moderation effect in the field of employee development is presented in the meta-analysis that studied the effects of feedback interventions on performance (Kluger & DeNisi, 1996). Even though the overall average effect size was positive (with improved performance by 0.41 of SD), there was a huge part of the analyzed effect sizes (a full one-third) that indicated decreased performance. The authors suggested and tested a theory that would help explain the heterogeneity of observed effect sizes. Their theory relied on the assumption that feedback interventions may differ in the locus of attention among three general and hierarchically organized levels of control: task learning, task motivation, and meta-tasks (including self-related) processes. The moderator analyses revealed that feedback intervention effectiveness decreases as the locus of attention moves up the hierarchy closer to the self and further from the task. Another example of a moderator variable influencing the effectiveness of developmental programs could be the characteristics of those who deliver these programs. For example, in the case of coaching, there is a study that suggests that when assessing determinants of the helpfulness of coaching, clients value more the qualities of and the relationship with the coach and make little distinction between specific coaching methods of that same coach (de Haan, Culpin & Curd, 2011).

What is preventing leaders from achieving significant change?

It is thus clear that several factors can get in the way of the implementation of successful development programs and prevent leaders from effectively developing and changing their behavior and improving their performance. However, in addition to these factors, which may be specific to formal development programs, there are also some more general psychological principles and regularities that can help us better calibrate our expectations about the realistic outcomes of implemented development programs and perhaps even design better development programs that will be more successful.

One of the things we need to consider when trying to change ourselves or someone else is that many human characteristics are largely biologically determined, which naturally limits the amount of change we can achieve through some developmental intervention. As the First Law of Behavioral Genetics states, all human behavioral traits are heritable (Turkheimer, 2000). This law applies to leadership as well. In their twin study, Arvey et al. (2006) have shown that 30 % of the variance in leadership role occupancy can be explained by genetic factors, while a non-shared environmental factor accounts for the remaining variance in leadership role occupancy. At first glance, this finding may seem like good news for developmental interventions, especially in the context of relatively higher heritability of other behavioral traits (e.g., intelligence, the heritability of which can vary between 60 % and 80 % during adulthood), however, one should be aware of the fact that the remaining 70 % of variability may be hard to influence by some systematic, non-random efforts, i.e., by some developmental intervention. Unfortunately, this less optimistic view is in line with the evidence suggesting that only a relatively small part of the variance in a person's job performance can be attributed to deliberate practice and training – 26 % for games, 21 % for music, 18 % for sports, 4 % for education, and less than 1 % for professions (Macnamara et al., 2014).

One of the reasons why it might be difficult for people to overcome the inertia of their natural behavioral tendencies is the phenomenon called *genetic amplification* (Plomin & Deary, 2014). This concept expresses the interdependence of nature (genotype) and nurture (environment), whereby initially small genetic differences are magnified as people select, modify, and create environments that match their genetic dispositions. For example, naturally extroverted people may tend to put themselves in situations where they will be the center of attention in large crowds, which may in turn reinforce their already heightened extraversion. Behavioral stability is apparent also in studies that show a relatively high rank-order correlation of traits across two, even very distant time points (Costa, McCrae, & Löckenhoff, 2019). Despite ongoing mean-level changes in the trait level, e.g., increase in measures of social dominance, conscientiousness, and emotional stability over people's lifetime (Roberts, Walton & Viechtbauer, 2006), people's trait values often changed by the same amount in the same direction, so their relative ordering is largely preserved (Roberts & DelVecchio, 2000). For example, for the Big-Five personality traits, reported test-retest rank-order correlations over several years range from 0.44 to 0.76 (Seifert et al., 2022). Such findings correspond well to our personal experiences when we meet an old acquaintance after a very long time, e.g., a former classmate from high school, and yet we have a strong feeling that she has not changed much and that we can predict her behaviors pretty well. Moreover, it seems that even more dramatic life events do not have a huge effect on longer-term changes in people's traits. For example, a well-known study by Brickman, Coates, and Janoff-Bulman (1978) on lottery winners showed that the effect of winning the lottery on their respective level of happiness was only short-lived and, after some time, was not distinguishable from the level of happiness of people from the control group. Other studies also support the hypothesis of a surprisingly high degree of stability in people's subjective well-being, which seems to depend more on their personality and/or genes than on situational circumstances, despite the apparent short-term influence of events and situations on people's emotions and feelings of well-being (e.g., Diener, Larsen & Emmons, 1984; Kozma, Stone & Stones, 2000; Magnus, Diener & Fujita 1993). It means that events can move people above or below their subjective well-being baseline, but sooner or later they will return to this stable set point again (so-called *dynamic equilibrium theory* of subjective well-being; Headey & Wearing, 1989).

Given such findings, it is understandable that people need a lot of perseverance and dedication to form and keep new behavioral habits that go against their natural behavioral proclivities. The irony is that the ability to change itself is largely genetically determined too. Developability requires one to be inquisitive to be open to new, alternative options and courses of action, humble to admit own mistakes, imperfections, and weaknesses, and empathetic to care about the opinions and feelings of others. All these characteristics show – as the First Law of Behavioral Genetics states – a high degree of heritability. It means that there are leaders who are naturally more receptive, or conversely resistant to systematic efforts to change their behaviors and improve their performance. An unfortunate consequence of this is that those leaders who usually self-select into leadership development programs (due to their naturally high developability) are often also those who need it least, and those who need it most (due to their naturally low developability) tend to ignore them or actively avoid them.

Another related roadblock to effective leaders' development is that leaders often do not have access to proper feedback on their performance, so they do not have an accurate picture of their strengths and weaknesses, an important prerequisite for development as demonstrated by the already mentioned meta-analysis of studies on the effects of feedback interventions on performance (Kluger & DeNisi, 1996). There may be several reasons why feedback does not reach leaders. One of them may be widespread overconfidence bias that makes people believe that they are more skilled than they are. For example, in Svenson's (1981) famous study, she asked students about their driving competence concerning a well-defined group of drivers and found that most considered themselves more skilled and less risky than the average driver in each group. This *better-than-average* effect was demonstrated also in many other domains, e.g., in personality assessment (Dunning, Meyerowitz & Holzberg, 1989), athleticism, leadership, and ability to get along with others (College Board, 1976–1977; as described in Alicke & Govorun, 2005) or teaching (Cross, 1977). And given that leader emergence is linked with higher levels of extraversion and more authoritarian personality (Ensari et al., 2011), i.e., with personality traits that are associated with higher confidence, we may reasonably suppose that in the population of leaders, this overconfidence bias can be even more exaggerated. This increased confidence can then cause leaders to focus primarily on their strengths and ignore the weaknesses they should be working to address. Behind the emphasis on strengths and ignoring, shortcomings may also be the assumption of leaders that admitting shortcomings could be perceived by those around them as a sign of weakness that could be exploited in office policy. Another reason why leaders have insufficient feedback may be the oft-cited 'loneliness' they experience in their high-level managerial position, from which it is often very difficult to see all the important details of reality and where information only reaches them vicariously through those who often tell leaders only what they think they want to hear.

Are there any tools that increase the likelihood of change for leaders?

It is not surprising, then, that in such a situation many companies are trying to put in place some formal mechanism to provide more valid, reliable, and regular feedback to their leaders. The tools often used for this purpose are personality assessments and 360-degree feedback surveys. While the former provides leaders with information about their leadership potential based on their long-term, relatively stable behavioral tendencies, the latter provides leaders with information about their current leadership performance based on multisource feedback provided by their direct reports, peers, supervisors, and external clients. Given that the results of personality assessments do not change too much over time (Gnambs, 2014), it is not very useful for measuring the effect of leadership development programs on leaders' behaviors. 360-degree feedback is much better suited for this purpose because it is more sensitive to the current manifestations of leadership behavior in the specific situations in which leaders are regularly encountered by those around them.

However, simply being exposed to feedback does not mean that a person will automatically change their behavior. Such change also requires a willingness and systematic effort to change, and a determination to overcome the obstacles to change that is always sure to appear. This was nicely demonstrated in a quasi-experimental study by Smither associates (2003) in which they compared two groups of senior managers. Managers from both groups received multisource feedback, but only one group of them worked with an executive coach to review their feedback and set goals. The authors of the study found that managers who worked with an executive coach were more likely than other managers to set specific (rather than vague) goals, ask for ideas for improvement from their supervisors, and improve their ratings on a multisource feedback survey the following year based on ratings from their direct reports and supervisors.

After reviewing the opportunities and limitations of developing leaders, it becomes clear that changing leader behavior and performance is possible, but not easy. Without providing leaders with a supportive environment (e.g., in the form of regular multisource feedback and a coach with compatible characteristics) that increases their self-awareness and commitment to change, and without their willingness to change and perseverance in the face of obstacles and setbacks, any significant change would be difficult, if not impossible. Without these prerequisites, they would likely behave in the way they usually do, following their nature and deeply ingrained habits. Now let us look at a case study that presents a successful leadership development program that got these prerequisites right.

An example of leadership development

Assessment Systems, an HR consulting company operating in the CEE region, was approached by a customer with a request to help them initiate and implement a major leadership culture change across the whole company. The company was an established, integrated electricity conglomerate with operations in several countries. Its principal businesses encompassed generation (Including renewables, coal-water- and nuclear-operated power plants), trading, and distribution of power and heat, as well as coal mining. It also controlled over 100 daughter companies with a total of tens of thousands of employees.

The trigger communicated by the customer to engage in this project were growing challenges and changing paradigms in the energy industry. Projects were increasing in size, complexity, risks, and costs. At the same time, society was transforming and demanding more from both business and government (World Economic Forum, n.d.).

In the first year, a round of development initiatives was introduced to the board-1 directors (direct subordinates of division directors) plus some more employees nominated by the division directors. The first step in this program was an assessment of the level of six key strategic managerial competencies using a combination of 360-degree feedback and the Hogan Personality Inventory (HPI) psychometrics tool. Each of these competencies was elaborated into three distinct behavioral descriptions. All 18 behavioral descriptions were integrated into 360-degree feedback. Each behavioral item was assessed on a quality-oriented 5-point scale (ranging from *does not meet expectations* to *exceptional performance – model example*), which was common for all the items (see Table 1 for an example).

Table 1. Example of behavioral anchoring of the 5-point scale

<table>
<tr><td colspan="2">Competency:</td><td>Leadership</td></tr>
<tr><td colspan="2">Behavioral item 1/3:</td><td>Inspires others and is able to motivate them</td></tr>
<tr><td colspan="3">Rating scale anchor points and interpretations:</td></tr>
<tr><td>1</td><td>Does not meet expectations</td><td>Demotivates his/her subordinates by his/her behavior. Enforces his/her opinions from a position of strength, does not use relevant arguments.</td></tr>
<tr><td>2</td><td>Meets some expectations</td><td>Does not find motivating his/her subordinates important Focuses on meeting the goals only, not on the team. Unnecessarily devotes time to things that should be handled by someone else.</td></tr>
<tr><td>3</td><td>Meets expectations</td><td>Listens actively, takes interest in individuals in his/her team. Chooses appropriate motivational instruments according to personalities of his/her team members.</td></tr>
<tr><td>4</td><td>Exceeds expectations – inspires</td><td>Constantly motivates, increases others' involvement. Inspires others to perform better (more efficiently).</td></tr>
<tr><td>5</td><td>Exceptional performance – a model example</td><td>Inspires others to reach excellent results through his/her behavior and attitudes. Often sought out as a couch or adviser.</td></tr>
</table>

All 18 behavioral items of the 360-degree feedback were elaborated similarly. To standardize the assessment across all divisions, but also to improve the quality and acceptance of the ratings, the standard scale was supported by behavioral anchoring of each point of the scale for each item. This approach, although not very common for 360-degree feedback, exists as a possibility (Rogelberg & Waclawski, 2001).

In parallel, each competency was also mapped to subscales of the Hogan Personality Inventory following guidelines published by Hogan, Hogan and Warrenfeltz (2009). This allowed us to present each participant with the following reports: a 360-degree report, an HPI report, and a personalized summary report including the HPI to competence mapping. To assure a distinctive comparison of the examined profiles, the results of the 360-degree feedback were transformed into percentiles.

In the first round of administration, 77 ratees were assessed by several hundred raters in the 360-degree feedback. The nomination of ratees was in two steps: ratees nominated their evaluators themselves, while in the next step the nominations needed to be approved by their direct supervisors and by the CEO. This was to assure that the evaluator's list was well-balanced and as objective as possible. Sources of rating included supervisors, subordinates, colleagues, and internal clients, as well as the self-assessment. Besides personalized reports, ratees had an opportunity for a one-hour individual coaching style feedback session on the results of both the 360 and HPI by professional business psychologists or coaches. The results were also interpreted to ratees direct superior. The direct superiors also received an aggregated report on the whole team with the company and division benchmarks for each competency and scale.

The next step in this initiative was a meeting between each ratee and her or his direct superior to discuss the feedback results and agree on the next development steps. For all items, both the ratee and the direct superior agreed upon the results, and those were written down in a structured 1-page/slide called a *personal card*. Following these steps, half-day competency development workshops (one per competency, in the duration of 3,5 hours) were offered to participants.

The subsequent part of the developmental program was the presentation of the personal cards during a Personnel Development Forum (PDF), a two-day session for all board members. The PDF, facilitated by the HR

Director, had a single agenda: to discuss the development possibilities for participants, including development suggestions, succession possibilities, and career possibilities. The purpose of the managerial growth program was not only to help develop individual skills and competencies but also identify strengths and potential areas of development for the whole organization and to reinforce the organization's desired core values that were embodied in the selected six competencies. It thus became a central tool for introducing changes in the corporate culture and reinforcing the leadership of the customer. The implementation of 360-degree feedback was considered so successful that it was later rolled down to two divisions at the Board-2 level. Even more, several months afterward the Board joined for a PDF again, extending the list of participants with additional 40 colleagues.

The program also continued in the following year during which all directors were rated after one year period again using 360-degree feedback. In the repeated evaluation of the same group, a rating of the degree of change for each competency was added to the 360-degree feedback as well. For similar approaches, see also Smither and Walker (2001). Such continuity of the program with the same target group using identical tools allowed for impact analysis of the applied developmental tools.

First, when comparing year-on-year (YoY) results of all individual results measured by aggregated competency scores in percentiles, it was observed that while most participants remained within the same cluster (stars remained stars and weakly rated participants tended to remain weak), some participants developed relatively faster in YoY ratings than others. See Graph 1 which outlines the change in competency assessment.

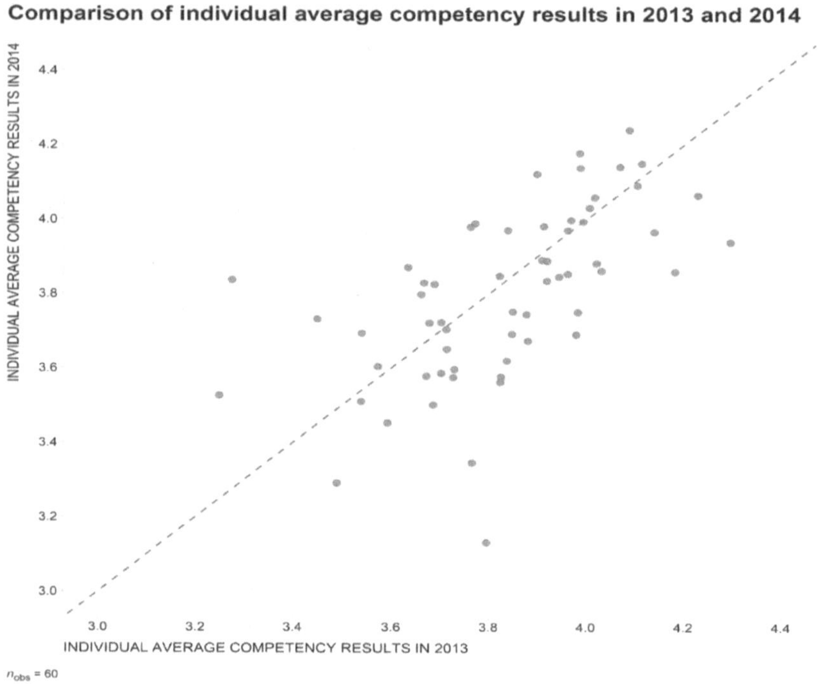

Graph 1. Comparison of individual average competency results in 2013 and 2014

When studying factors that were associated with different speeds of development, the impact of individual one-hour coaching feedback of the participant with a business coach was discovered (see Graph 2).

Also, the impact of participation in at least 2 half-day competency development workshops was observed, but not as large as in the case of coaching feedback to be detected as statistically significant (see Graph 3).

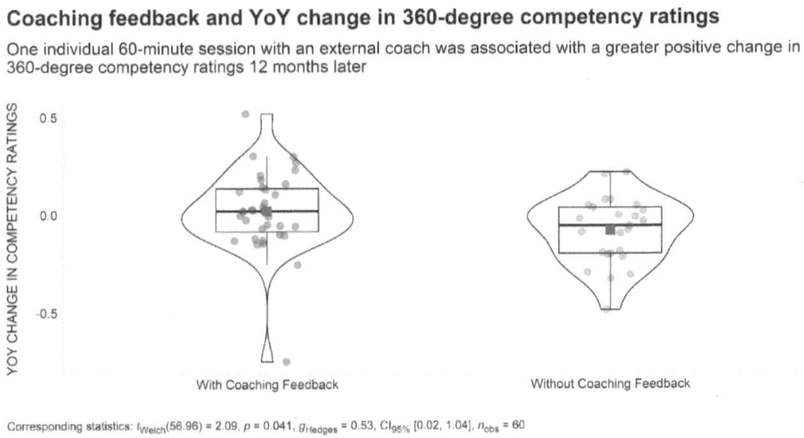

Graph 2. Comparison of the magnitude of change in average competency results between 2013 and 2014 among individuals who did and did not receive coaching feedback.

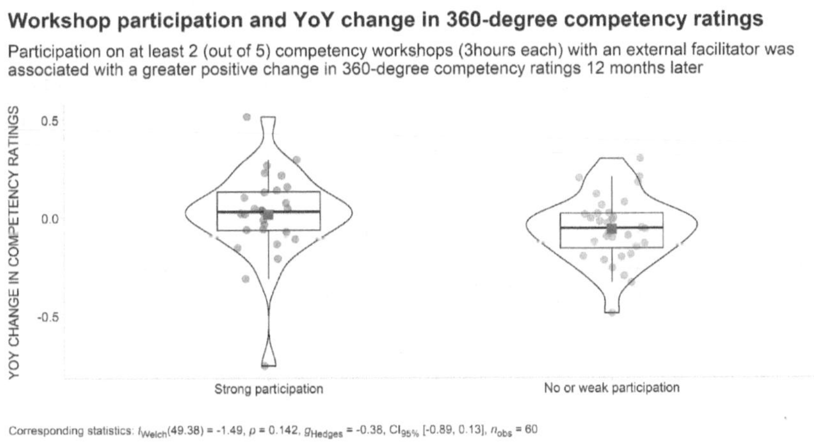

Graph 3. Comparison of the magnitude of change in average competency results between 2013 and 2014 among individuals with strong and no or weak participation in competency development workshops. Strong participation is defined as attending at least 2 of the 5 workshops.

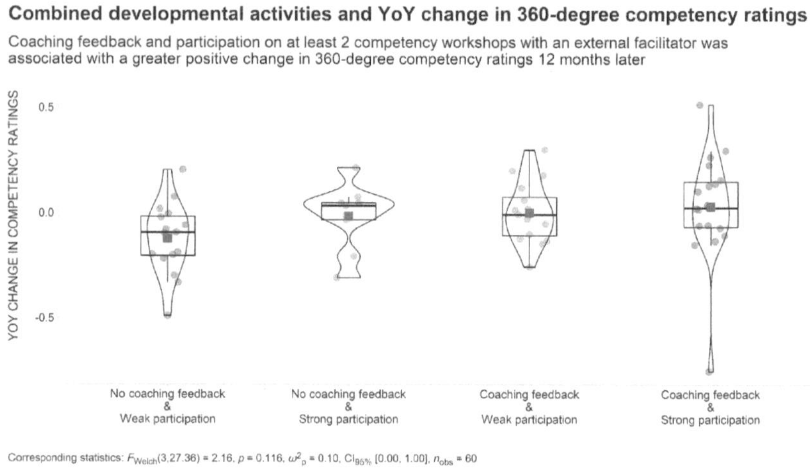

Graph 4. Comparison of the magnitude of change in average competency results between 2013 and 2014 among individuals with increasingly strong combination of developmental interventions (coaching feedback and participation in workshops) from left to right.

When combined, there are only slight and statistically non-significant differences between groups of individuals who participated in increasingly strong developmental interventions (from not receiving coaching feedback & weak participation in workshops to receiving coaching feedback & strong participation in workshops; see Graph 4).

Last but not least, the correlation between YoY development of the 360 ratings and the HPI scale 'Learning approach' was demonstrated (see Graph 5).

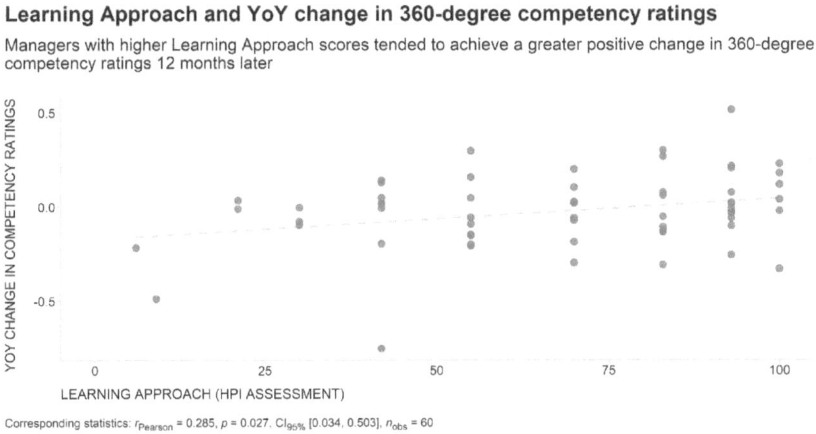

Graph 5. Correlation between the HPI scale 'Learning approach' and the magnitude of change in average competency results between 2013 and 2014.

Furthermore, a chart combining 360 results (interpreted as competency level rated by observers) and HPI personality results mapped to the same competencies (interpreted as personality-anchored potential for a specific competency) was created (see Graph 6).

For the following year, to utilize the assigned HR budget most efficiently, a stratified approach was suggested based on the quadrant in which they were plotted (i.e., differentiated HR approach and segmented interventions for different populations).

- Top-right quadrant – high competency high potential: 'PROMOTE' segment. This population was recommended to be treated as top talents and considered for promotion.
- Top-left quadrant – high competency low potential: 'RETAIN' segment. This population was recommended to be maintained and stabilized on their current positions.
- Bottom-left quadrant – low competency and low potential: 'REPLACE' segment. This population was recommended to be considered for possible replacement. Surprisingly, most of the participants who left the company voluntarily within the initial two years of the project were inhabiting this quadrant, so no active steps were needed to be taken.

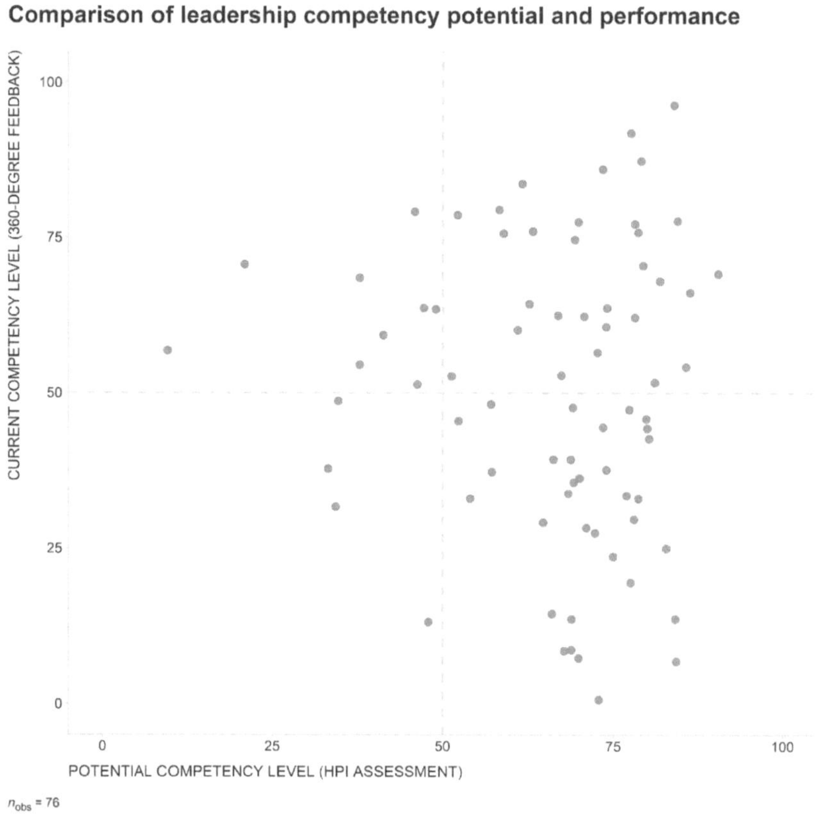

Graph 6. Comparison of leadership competency potential and performance as measured by HPI personality inventory and 360-degree feedback survey, respectively.

- Bottom-right quadrant – low competency and high potential: 'DEVELOP' segment. This population was recommended as the best-fitting target group for most of the future development and training activities, to capitalize on their potential and help grow their competencies further.

References

Alicke, M. D., & Govorun, O. (2005). The better-than-average effect. In M. D. Alicke, D. A. Dunning, J. I. Krueger, M. D. Alicke, D. A.

Dunning & J. I. Krueger (Eds.), *The self in social judgment* (pp. 85–106). New York, NY: Psychology Press.

Arthur, W., Jr., Bennett, W., Jr., Edens, P. S., & Bell, S. T. (2003). Effectiveness of training in organizations: A meta-analysis of design and evaluation features. *Journal of Applied Psychology, 88*(2), 234–245. DOI: https://doi.org/10.1037/0021-9010.88.2.234.

Arvey, R. D., Rotundo, M., Johnson, W., Zhang, Z., & McGue, M. (2006). The determinants of leadership role occupancy: Genetic and personality factors. *The Leadership Quarterly, 17*(1), 1–20. DOI: https://doi.org/10.1016/j.leaqua.2005.10.009.

Beer, M., Finnström, M., & Schrader, D. (2016, Oct). Why Leadership Training Fails—and What to Do About It. *Harvard Business Review*. https://hbr.org/2016/10/why-leadership-training-fails-and-what-to-do-about-it.

Bertrand, M., & Schoar, A. (2003). Managing With Style: The Effect Of Managers On Firm Policies. *The Quarterly Journal of Economics, 118*(4), 1169–1208. DOI: https://doi.org/10.2139/ssrn.376880.

Brickman, P., Coates, D., & Janoff-Bulman, R. (1978). Lottery winners and accident victims: Is happiness relative? *Journal of Personality and Social Psychology, 36*(8), 917–927. DOI: https://doi.org/10.1037/0022-3514.36.8.917.

Capaldo, G., Iandoli, L., & Zollo, G. (2006). A situationalist perspective to competency management. *Human Resource Management, 45*(3), 429–448. DOI:10.1002/hrm.20121.

College Board. (1976–1977). *Student descriptive questionnaire*. Princeton, NJ: Educational Testing Service.

Collins, D. B., & Holton, E. F. (2004). The Effectiveness of Managerial Leadership Development Programs: A Meta-Analysis of Studies from 1982 to 2001. *Human Resource Development Quarterly, 15*(2), 217–248. DOI: https://doi.org/10.1002/hrdq.1099.

Costa, P. T., McCrae, R. R., & Löckenhoff, C. E. (2019). Personality across the lifespan. *Annual Review of Psychology, 70*, 423–448. DOI: https://doi.org/10.1146/annurev-psych-010418-103244.

Cross, K. P. (1977). Not can, but will college teaching be improved? *New Directions for Higher Education, 17*, 1–15. DOI: http://dx.doi.org/10.1002/he.36919771703.

Crossland, C., & Hambrick, D. C. (2011). Differences in managerial discretion across countries: how nation-level institutions affect the degree to which CEOs matter. *Strategic Management Journal, 32*(8), 797–819. DOI: https://doi.org/10.1002/smj.913.

de Haan, E., Culpin, V., & Curd, J. (2011). Executive coaching in practice: what determines helpfulness for clients of coaching? *Personnel Review, 40*(1), 24–44. DOI: https://doi.org/10.1108/00483481111095500.

Deloitte Insights (2020). *2020 Global Human Capital Trends Report.* Deloitte. https://www2.deloitte.com/cn/en/pages/human-capital/articles/global-human-capital-trends-2020.html.

Diener, E., Larsen, R. J., & Emmons, R. A. (1984). Person X Situation interactions: Choice of situations and congruence response models. *Journal of Personality and Social Psychology, 47*(3), 580–592. DOI: https://doi.org/10.1037//0022-3514.47.3.580.

Dunning, D., Meyerowitz, J. A., & Holzberg, A. D. (1989). Ambiguity and self-evaluation: The role of idiosyncratic trait definitions in self-serving assessments of ability. *Journal of Personality and Social Psychology, 57*(6), 1082–1090. DOI: http://dx.doi.org/10.1037/0022-3514.57.6.1082.

Dzwigol, H., Dzwigol-Barosz, M., Miskiewicz, R., & Kwilinski, A. (2020). Manager competency assessment model in the conditions of Industry 4.0. *Entrepreneurship and Sustainability Issues, 7*(4), 2630–2644.

Ensari, N., Riggio, R. E., Christian, J., & Carslaw, G. (2011). Who emerges as a leader? Meta-analyses of individual differences as predictors of leadership emergence. *Personality and Individual Differences, 51*(4), 532–536. DOI: https://doi.org/10.1016/j.paid.2011.05.017.

Furnham, A. (2016). *The elephant in the boardroom: The causes of leadership derailment.* Springer.

Giles, S. (2016, March 15). The most important leadership competencies, according to leaders around the world. *Harvard Business Review.* https://hbr.org/2016/03/the-most-important-leadership-competencies-according-to-leaders-around-the-world.

Gnambs, T. (2014). A meta-analysis of dependability coefficients (test–retest reliabilities) for measures of the Big Five. *Journal of Research in Personality, 52*, 20–28. DOI: https://doi.org/10.1016/j.jrp.2014.06.003.

Hagan, C. M., Konopaske, R., Bernardin, H. J., & Tyler, C. L. (2006). Predicting Assessment Center Performance with 360-Degree, Top-Down, and Customer-Based Competency Assessments. *Human Resource Management, 45*(3), 357–390. DOI: https://doi.org/10.1002/hrm.20117.

Headey, B., & Wearing, A. (1989). Personality, life events, and subjective well-being: Toward a dynamic equilibrium model. *Journal of Personality and Social Psychology, 57*(4), 731–739. DOI: https://doi.org/10.1037/0022-3514.57.4.731.

Hill, L. A., Le Cam, A., Menon, S., & Tedards, E. (2022, February 14). *Curiosity, not coding: 6 skills leaders need in the digital age.* Harvard Business School Working Knowledge. https://hbswk.hbs.edu/item/six-unexpected-traits-leaders-need-in-the-digital-era.

Hogan, R., Hogan, J., & Warrenfeltz, R. (2009). *The Hogan guide: Interpretation and use of Hogan Inventories.* Tulsa, OK: Hogan Assessment Systems, Inc.

Jokinen, T. (2005). Global leadership competencies: a review and discussion. *Journal of European Industrial Training, 29*(3), 199–216. DOI:10.1108/03090590510591085.

Kaiser, R. B., & Curphy, G. (2013). Leadership development: The failure of an industry and the opportunity for consulting psychologists. *Consulting Psychology Journal: Practice and Research, 65*(4), 294–302. DOI: https://doi.org/10.1037/a0035460.

Kasianiuk, K., Szklarski, B., & Żylicz, P. O. (Eds.). (2021). *Failed Leadership (Management in Digital Times).* Peter Lang GmbH.

Kim, P. S. (2020). New development: Competency assessment system and practice in government—the South Korean experience. *Public Money & Management*, 1–4. DOI: doi:10.1080/09540962.2020.1802891.

Kluger, A. N., & DeNisi, A. (1996). The effects of feedback interventions on performance: A historical review, a meta-analysis, and a preliminary feedback intervention theory. *Psychological Bulletin, 119*(2), 254–284. DOI: https://doi.org/10.1037/0033-2909.119.2.254.

Kozma, A., Stone, S., & Stones, M.J. (2000). Stability in components and predictors of subjective well-being (SWB): implications for SWB structure. In Diener, E., Rahtz, D.R. (eds) *Advances in Quality of Life Theory and Research. Social Indicators Research Series*, vol 4. Springer, Dordrecht. DOI: https://doi.org/10.1007/978-94-011-4291-5_2.

Leary, T. G., Green, R., Denson, K., Schoenfeld, G., Henley, T., & Langford, H. (2013). The Relationship Among Dysfunctional Leadership Dispositions, Employee Engagement, Job Satisfaction, and Burnout. *The Psychologist-Manager Journal, 16*(2). DOI: 10.1037/h0094961.

Lieberson, S., & O'Connor, J. F. (1972). Leadership and organizational performance: A study of large corporations. *American Sociological Review, 37*(2), 117–130. DOI: https://doi.org/10.2307/2094020.

Lilienfeld, S. O., Ritschel, L. A., Lynn, S. J., Cautin, R. L., & Latzman, R. D. (2015). Science-Practice Gap. In *The Encyclopedia of Clinical Psychology* (pp. 1–7). John Wiley & Sons, Inc. DOI: https://doi.org/10.1002/9781118625392.wbecp566.

Macnamara, B. N., Hambrick, D. Z., & Oswald, F. L. (2014). Deliberate Practice and Performance in Music, Games, Sports, Education, and Professions: A Meta-Analysis. *Psychological Science, 25*(8), 1608–1618. DOI: https://doi.org/10.1177/0956797614535810.

Magnus, K., Diener, E., Fujita, F., & Pavot, W. (1993). Extraversion and neuroticism as predictors of objective life events: A longitudinal analysis. *Journal of Personality and Social Psychology, 65*(5), 1046–1053. DOI: https://doi.org/10.1037//0022-3514.65.5.1046.

McClelland, D. C. (1998). Identifying Competencies with Behavioral-Event Interviews. *Psychological Science, 9*(5), 331–339. DOI:10.1111/1467-9280.00065.

Patterson, V. L. (2016). Leadership Failures. In Farazmand A. (Eds.) *Global Encyclopedia of Public Administration, Public Policy, and Governance.* Springer, Cham. DOI: https://doi.org/10.1007/978-3-319-31816-5_1891-1.

Plomin, R., & Deary, I. J. (2014). Genetics and intelligence differences: five special findings. *Molecular Psychiatry, 20*(1), 98–108. DOI: https://doi.org/10.1038/mp.2014.105.

Prokopeak, M. (2018, March 21). *Follow the Leader(ship) Spending.* Chief Learning Officer. https://www.chieflearningofficer.com/2018/03/21/follow-the-leadership-spending/.

Ready, D. A., Cohen, C., Kiron, D., & Pring, B. (January 2020). *The New Leadership Playbook for the Digital Age. Reimagining What It Takes to Lead.* MIT Sloan Management Review.

Richardson, K. M., & Rothstein, H. R. (2008). Effects of occupational stress management intervention programs: A meta-analysis. *Journal of Occupational Health Psychology, 13*(1), 69–93. DOI: https://doi.org/10.1037/1076-8998.13.1.69.

Roberts, B. W., & DelVecchio, W. F. (2000). The rank-order consistency of personality traits from childhood to old age: A quantitative review of longitudinal studies. *Psychological Bulletin, 126*(1), 3–25. DOI: https://doi.org/10.1037/0033-2909.126.1.3.

Roberts, B. W., Walton, K. E., & Viechtbauer, W. (2006). Patterns of mean-level change in personality traits across the life course: A meta-analysis of longitudinal studies. *Psychological Bulletin, 132*(1), 1–25. DOI: https://doi.org/10.1037/0033-2909.132.1.1.

Rogelberg, S. G., & Waclawski, J. (2001). Instrumentation Design. In D. W., Bracken, Timmreck, C. W., & A. W. Church (Eds.), *The Handbook of Multisource Feedback* (pp. 79–95). San Francisco: Josey-Bass.

Rubenstein, A. L., Eberly, M. B., Lee, T. W., & Mitchell, T. R. (2018). Surveying the forest: A meta-analysis, moderator investigation, and future-oriented discussion of the antecedents of voluntary employee turnover. *Personnel Psychology, 71*(1), 23–65.DOI: https://doi.org/10.1111/peps.12226.

Rynes, S. L., Colbert, A. E. & Brown, K. G. (2002). HR professionals' beliefs about effective human resource practices: Correspondence between research and practice. *Human Resource Management, 41*(2), 149–174. DOI: https://doi.org/10.1002/hrm.10029.

Seifert, I. S., Rohrer, J. M., Egloff, B. & Schmukle, S. C. (2022). The development of the rank-order stability of the Big Five across the life-span. *Journal of Personality and Social Psychology, 122*(5), 920–941. DOI: https://doi.org/10.1037/pspp0000398.

Sherman, S., & Freas, A. (2004, Nov). *The Wild West of Executive Coaching*. Harvard Business Review. https://hbr.org/2004/11/the-wild-west-of-executive-coaching.

Smither, J. W. & Walker, A. G. (2001). Measuring the Impact of Multisource Feedback. In D. W. Bracken, C.W. Timmreck A. & A. W., Church (Eds.), *The Handbook of Multisource Feedback* (pp. 256–271). San Francisco: Josey-Bass.

Smither, J. W., London, M., Flautt, R., Vargas, Y. & Kucine, I. (2003). Can working with an executive coach improve multisource feedback ratings over time? A quasi-experimental field study. *Personnel Psychology, 56*(1), 23–44. DOI: https://doi.org/10.1111/j.1744-6570.2003.tb00142.x.

Spencer, L. M. & Spencer, S. M. (1993). *Competence at work: Models for superior performance*. John Wiley & Sons.

Svenson, O. (1981). Are we all less risky and more skillful than our fellow drivers? *Acta Psychologica, 47*(2), 143–148. DOI: https://doi.org/10.1016/0001-6918(81)90005-6.

Theeboom, T., Beersma, B., & van Vianen, A. E. M. (2013). Does coaching work? A meta-analysis on the effects of coaching on individual level outcomes in an organizational context. *The Journal of Positive Psychology, 9*(1), 1–18. DOI: https://doi.org/10.1080/17439760.2013.837499.

Training Industry (2021, March 29). *Size of the Training Industry*. Training Industry. https://trainingindustry.com/wiki/outsourcing/size-of-training-industry/.

Turkheimer, E. (2000). Three Laws of Behavior Genetics and What They Mean. *Current Directions in Psychological Science, 9*(5), 160–164. DOI: https://doi.org/10.1111/1467-8721.00084.

World Economic Forum (n.d.). Retrieved from http://www.weforum.org/issues/energy.

Yarbrough Landry, A., Stowe, M., & Haefner, J. (2012). Competency assessment and development among health-care leaders: results of a cross-sectional survey. *Health Services Management Research, 25*(2), 78–86. DOI: 10.1258/hsmr.2012.012012.

John Wilson (Donghua University, China)

Lionel Huntley Henderson (Sino-British College, University of Shanghai for Science and Technology, China)

Wance Tacconelli (Department of Educational Research, Lancaster University, UK)

Grażyna Rembielak (WUT BS, Warsaw, Poland)

MBA education – Pandemic to Paradigm and 4th Generation Management Development?

Abstract: This chapter considers the ongoing and potential long-term impact of the Covid-19 pandemic and underlying work-related megatrends on management development programmes, viz. part-time (PT) Master of Business Administration (MBA) programmes offered by business schools that are signatories to the United Nations-related initiative of Principles for Responsible Management Education (PRME). In doing so, it considers whether a new paradigm and/or a new generation of management development may emerge from and be shaped by the experience of the pandemic. The research is based on semi-structured interviews with senior business school academic managers in seven countries and each of whom had current or previous responsibility for PT MBA provision. The research findings in respect of the impact of the pandemic and the significance of involvement in PRME on the nature of MBAs in general and PT MBAs in particular present a mixed picture.

Keywords: MBA, management development, PRME

Introduction

The COVID-19 pandemic has had a global impact on organisations in all sectors, including universities. Kandri (2020) believes it has moved higher education along the road to a new paradigm and that, once the pandemic has passed, a new model will emerge. Particularly in the case of Master of Business Administration (MBA) programmes, any changes in higher education provision and the models adopted may reflect changes in the workplace, including those relating to what Microsoft (2021) has called the 'next great disruption' i.e. hybrid working (see also McKinsey report, De Smet et al., 2021).

In the case of MBA programmes, Mintzberg (2004), argued that first and second generations of management development were, respectively, based on learning from the experience of others followed by creating experiences for learning. He argued (Mintzberg, 2004, p28) for a 'third generation' of management development: 'What managers need now, above all else, is to slow down, step back, and reflect thoughtfully on their everyday life experience…The motto for third-generation management development is, "Use work, don't make work."' Given the experiences of COVID-19, it might be argued that a fourth generation is needed.

This chapter reports on research that explores the consequences for MBA programmes of these developments, specifically part-time (PT) MBAs as they represent a niche pathway that is under-researched in the literature. The findings are based on interviews with business school Deans and/or current or recent Directors of PT MBAs in schools that are signatories to the United Nations initiative Principles for Responsible Management Education (PRME, 2020, see also www.unprme.org) and drawn from across seven countries i.e. Austria, Canada, China, New Zealand, Poland, United Kingdom (UK) and the United States (US). The interviews were intended to gain a greater understanding of their response to and likely impact of the pandemic, work-related megatrends and PRME (see also Henderson & Wilson, 2023).

The research explores whether there is evidence for Kandri's (2020) assertion and the extent to which lessons might be learned for the fourth generation of management development. In doing so, it addresses the questions: how has the experience of the pandemic influenced the mode of delivery of the PT MBA and what might be its longer-term impact; in what ways is the relevance of the PT MBA quality assured; in responding to these issues, what has been the influence of PRME involvement?

The changing nature of work

In the period before the pandemic, a number of significant changes in work patterns were identified. The UK professional body the Chartered Institute of Personnel and Development (CIPD) identified certain 'megatrends'

(CIPD, 2013) over the previous 30 years, and though their focus was on the UK 'most (but not all) of the trends....have been present in most advanced industrialised economies' (p3). The report identifies seven trends, i.e. deindustrialisation and the rise of knowledge-based services; technological change and globalisation; demographic change – an ageing population and migration; increased female labour market participation; increased educational participation; decline of collective workplace institutions viz. trades unions; greater diversity in employment relationships and how we work.

The presence and pace of these trends will vary with the economy, but their emergence (or, in the case of globalisation, re-emergence) is part of the broad neo-liberalism that has characterised many economies from the mid-to-late-1970s to the present day, essentially involving: a rejection of Keynesian social democracy; a public choice critique of state activity; a belief in the efficacy of markets and the 'hollowing out' of the state (Rhodes, 1994); privatisation, deregulation, and encouragement of market forces. Such trends in the economic environment have had a profound influence on the labour market, including the rise of the precariat (Standing, 2014), and been reflected *within* organisations, including the decline of workplace institutions identified by CIPD (2013).

In the period between its 2013 report and the emergence of COVID-19, CIPD (2020) identified other megatrends, including those relating to: the opportunities afforded by extending people's working lives; flexible working (including remote working); the opportunity afforded by an older workforce; incidence of self-employment; overall workloads; trust in the workplace.

Alongside these trends have been developments in artificial intelligence and the emergence of what Deloitte (Volini et al., 2019) describes as 'superjobs' and which, it is said, change the landscape about how organisations think about work. Superjobs are said to be 'Roles that combine work and responsibilities from multiple traditional jobs, using technology to both augment and broaden the scope of the work performed and involve a more complex set of domain, technical, and human skills' (p32).

A Deloitte report (Volini et al., 2019) suggests there has been an evolution from standard jobs (roles requiring a specified and narrow skillset) to hybrid jobs (roles requiring a combination of technical and soft skills which, historically, have not been combined in the same job) to superjobs.

As such, superjobs are said to be significantly different from traditional roles that had fixed job descriptions and stable tasks. Superjobs involve work that remains after parts of jobs have been automated and require a mix of skills e.g., problem-solving, data interpretation, communications and listening, customer service and empathy, teamwork and collaboration.

These developments are now taking place within a broader macroeconomic context given the disruption caused by the pandemic and which prompted, in many countries, a dramatic return to Keynesian government intervention (see Economist, 2020) but whether this will prove to be a long-term reversion to a Keynesian social democratic consensus or, for a number of major economies, a short-term suspension of neo-liberalism remains to be seen. There has been much debate on the appropriate level and nature of state intervention and regulation and, in the case of China, how and when fully to re-open the economy.

Narrowing it down to the organisational context, living in a world of rapid changes, especially during the pandemic, leads to debates regarding leaders' responsibilities as organisations face new challenges. Harvard Business Publishing Corporate Learning (HBPCL) (2018) in their Research Report stress the importance of leadership development and the role learning and development (L&D) and innovative leadership development programmes play in supporting organisational transformation, especially in the case of millennials and who constitute a large proportion of the workforce globally. The HBPCL (2018) research results show that if an organisation wants to be successful in their transformation in a rapidly changing environment, L&D should become their critical activity and innovative methods of development should be incorporated, such as access to the content that is relevant for the learner and easy access from anywhere "just in time, just for me" (p13).

The significance of leadership was also stressed in the Development Dimensions International /DDI/ CEO Leadership Report (2021). In times of rapid change, even more accelerated by the pandemic, confidence in the capability of leaders is the factor that will most influence organisational success. The results shown in the Report indicate that it is imperative for CEOs to develop future talent but, to do that, CEOs and executives also need development and support from their organisation and its employees (p1).

Despite the fundamental nature of the changes in the workplace and the economic environment in which they are now taking place, before the pandemic, Volini et al. (2019) stated their " research shows that while organizations **expect** new leadership capabilities, they are still largely promoting traditional models and mindsets – when they should be developing skills and measuring leadership in ways that help leaders effectively navigate greater ambiguity, take charge of rapid change, and engage with external and internal stakeholders" (p37) [emphasis in original]. When asked: 'what do you believe are the unique requirements for 21st century leaders?', the results were as follows. See Table 1.

Despite the challenges of the 21st century, only 30 % said their organisations were effectively developing leaders. To this can be added serious concerns over transparency and trust (reflecting the research of CIPD, 2013, see also Nelson, 2020) and the need to put in place different performance measures for leaders e.g. rather than focus exclusively on

Table 1. Leadership for the 21st Century

What do you believe are the unique requirements for 21st century leaders?	%
Ability to lead through more complexity and ambiguity	81
Ability to lead through influence	65
Ability to manage on a remote basis	50
Ability to manage a workforce with a combination of humans and machines	47
Ability to lead more quickly	44
Why do you believe there are unique requirements for 21st century leaders?	
New technologies	75
Pace of change	66
Changing demographics and employee expectations	57
Changing customer expectations	

Source: Deloitte report (Volini et al., 2019, Figure 1 p38). **Note:**
- The survey was based on 9,453 respondents from around the world
- 80 % of respondents believed that 21st century leadership has unique and new requirements and only they answered the above questions
- Respondents were invited to select all that apply rather than identify their own requirements/reasons

driving strategy, achieving good financial results and managing operations well, emphasis could be placed on success in establishing a culture that promotes employee engagement feedback, leadership capability assessments and the ways in which leaders align themselves with the organisation's leadership principles.

If such points were valid before the pandemic, then it seems reasonable to suggest that they will apply *a fortiori* post-pandemic, in part reflected in the 2021 Work Trend Index of Microsoft (2021). Microsoft states unequivocally (p2) that 'The year 2020 changed work forever' and anticipates an irreversible transition from pandemic-induced remote working to a post-pandemic model of hybrid working – a blended model of homeworking and office-based working. It identifies '7 urgent trends every business leader needs to know in 2021' and actions in response to them. See Table 2. This is also consistent with reports published by CIPD during and since 2020 e.g. its reports on hybrid working (CIPD, 2021).

Perhaps, however, many of these reports underestimate the impact on organisations themselves, including hierarchies. Sinofsky (2021) points out that organisations that have survived the pandemic through using technology have not yet realised that the *fact* of their survival by means of technology itself demonstrates the need to rethink everything they were doing prior to the pandemic: 'The post-pandemic world will provide the impetus and tools to rethink the Corporation, and more broadly innovation, and how work is structured and how individuals contribute to that work. Yet, we continue to operate as we always have. In fact, many companies are looking to the post-pandemic world through the lens of how quickly we can return to *normal*....The answer is not to change a little but to change a lot.' [Emphasis in original].

In doing so, however, perhaps even more attention needs to be paid to the human cost of current models of working. Research by NatCen Social Research (2021) has revealed a 'significant relationship between working from home and increased mental distress during the pandemic' and 'workers, employers and institutions need to better understand the long-term implications on wellbeing of working from home when designing new ways of working.' This can be illustrated by the report of NBER (2020), based on data from 3.15m users across the US, Europe and the Middle East, and found 'significant and durable increases in length of the

Table 2. Organisations: Global Trends and Responses

Trend
1. Flexible working is here to stay – 73 % of respondents wanted flexible remote work options
2. Business leaders are out of touch with employees and need a wake-up call – there was a 23 % difference between those with and those without decision-making authority who said they were 'thriving' (61 % to 38 %)
3. High productivity is masking an exhausted workforce – nearly 1 in 5 believe their employer does not care about their work-life balance, 54 % feel overworked and 39 % feel exhausted, in part through digital overload caused by excessive emails, times spent in virtual meetings etc
4. Gen Z (those aged 18–25) are most at risk and need to be re-energised. This overlooked demographic is struggling far more than baby-boomers (born before 1964), Gen X (born 1964–80), or millennials (1981–95)
5. Shrinking networks are endangering innovation – engagement and virtual interactions with broader networks greatly reduced as a result of lockdown and this will adversely affect productivity and innovation
6. Authenticity will spur productivity and wellbeing – a tough year made work more human, including getting to know more about colleagues' home life and pets and also crying with a colleague
7. Talent is everywhere in a hybrid work world – 46 % of those surveyed are planning to change jobs, and remote opportunities are more attractive to diverse talents
Response
1. Create a plan to empower people for extreme flexibility e.g. 66 % of business decision makers are considering redesigning work spaces
2. Invest in space and technology to bridge the physical and digital worlds
3. Combat digital exhaustion from the top
4. Prioritise rebuilding social capital and culture
5. Rethink employee experience to compete for the best and most diverse talent

Source: Microsoft (2021). Note:
• The report is in part based on a study of 31,092 full-time employed or self-employed workers conducted between 12th to 25th January 2021.
• In the responses there were variations across countries and sectors as well as age groups
• A series of related reports is available at: www.microsoft.com/en-us/worklab

average workday' (Abstract) and although 'It is unclear if this increase in average workday span represents a benefit or drawback to employee well-being…..the change in work schedule may be a consequence of a blurred distinction between work and personal life, in which it becomes easy to overwork due to the lack of clear delineation between the office and home' (p8). See also Microsoft (2021) and Table 2 above.

Such research findings reinforce the actions taken in some countries (see, for example, TaylorWessing, 2021; Hunt, 2021) to give a legal right to disconnect and/or ban out-of-hours emails. The increased workload many employees have experienced, whether imposed or self-imposed, and dubious practices (Muir, 2021) including 'fire and re-hire' ('dismissal and re-engagement') (e.g. House of Commons Library, 2021), perhaps indicate that some businesses are not only absolutely failing to rise to the ethical challenges posed by the pandemic (Nelson, 2020) but, in failing to do so, are perhaps increasing the likelihood of experiencing the Icarus paradox (Miller, 1992) and will fail in a post-pandemic environment.

PRME and PT MBAs

The current context - including megatrends, the organisational and work-related human impact of the pandemic, increased concerns relating to the conduct of some organisational leaders and managers, particularly the conduct that contributed to the economic crash of 2007–08 and exhibited by some during the pandemic – can be combined with the ever-more urgent need to address sustainability issues, not least those related to climate change and a post-pandemic world. The extent to which higher education institutions (HEIs), and particularly business schools, are rising to these challenges is unclear.

In response to the 2007 global economic crash, the academic stakeholders of the United Nations Global Compact recommended the development of a principle-based global engagement platform for academic institutions. In turn, this led to PRME, intended to embed sustainability within the management education curriculum. It defines its vision and mission as follows: 'PRME's vision is to create a global movement and drive thought leadership on responsible management education. PRME's mission is to transform management education and develop the responsible decision-makers of tomorrow to advance sustainable development' (PRME, 2021a). As at the end of 2021, there were over 800 PRME-signatory institutions worldwide, the overwhelming majority of which were business schools.

The PRME model has six Principles (PRME, 2021b), see Table 3, intended to develop responsible leadership and, in particular, to ensure that business and management schools 'provide future leaders with the skills needed to balance economic and sustainability goals, while drawing attention to the Sustainable Development Goals (SDGs) and aligning academic institutions with the work of the UN Global Compact' (PRME, 2021a). The 17 SDGs are intended to be achieved by 2030 (UN, 2021).

Although it is most closely associated with management education, PRME is of relevance to all disciplines as many students will go on to become practising managers irrespective of their technical background. In doing so, consideration of the meaning of *responsible* management, including ethics and the significance of the UN SDGs should, perhaps, be a prominent feature across all university programmes and not just those in business schools. This is of particular relevance to postgraduate (PG) programmes and not least the MBA given its nature as a generic graduate business and management award and, specifically, PT MBAs as they are

Table 3. Principles for Responsible Management Education

Purpose	We will develop the capabilities of students to be future generators of sustainable value for business and society at large and to work for an inclusive and sustainable global economy.
Values	We will incorporate into our academic activities, curricula, and organisational practices the values of global social responsibility as portrayed in international initiatives such as the United Nations Global Compact.
Method	We will create educational frameworks, materials, processes and environments that enable effective learning experiences for responsible leadership.
Research	We will engage in conceptual and empirical research that advances our understanding about the role, dynamics, and impact of corporations in the creation of sustainable social, environmental and economic value.
Partnership	We will interact with managers of business corporations to extend our knowledge of their challenges in meeting social and environmental responsibilities and to explore jointly effective approaches to meeting these challenges.
Dialogue	We will facilitate and support dialog and debate among educators, students, business, government, consumers, media, civil society organisations and other interested groups and stakeholders on critical issues related to global social responsibility and sustainability.

Source: PRME (2021b)

normally targeted at practising professionals with a minimum of two- or three-years' experience at an appropriate level within an organisation.

To explore the above issues, specifically the consequences for PT MBA programmes of the pandemic, work-related megatrends and PRME, a series of interviews was conducted with key business school personnel.

Methodology

A qualitative research approach was adopted, involving semi-structured interviews with selected PRME-signatory business school Deans and current or recent Directors of PT MBA programmes. The interviews were intended to gain a greater understanding of their response to and likely impact of the pandemic and work-related megatrends. The research is based on nine interviews involving ten interviewees from seven countries as listed above. See also Tables 4 and 5. All interviewees received the questions in advance and all except one, where written responses were supplied, were conducted by Zoom in the period May-July 2021 and lasted approximately one hour in length and recorded. All the respondents were informed their responses would be anonymous. The questions are shown in Appendix 1.

Table 4. Profile of Interviewees

Interview	Role	Country
A	Director Executive MBA	UK/China
B	Associate Dean	UK
C	Director Executive MBA and Country Director	US/China
D	Associate Dean of Professional Programmes	New Zealand
E	Director of Executive MBA	UK
F and G	Associate Dean (F); Director of Executive MBA (G)	UK
H	Dean of Business School	Poland
I	Director of Executive MBA	Austria
J	Director of Executive MBA	Canada

Table 5. Profile of PT MBAs under investigation

MBA of Interviewee:	A	B	C	D	E	F & G	H	I	J
Established	2020[1]	2018	1996	Late 1970's		2016	1998	2020[1]	1967
Annual Intake[2]	80	75	150	60		300	90		100
Accredited[3]	CMI	CMI	-	AMBA	CMI ILM	ILM	EPAS	-	-
Mode of Delivery Pre-Pandemic	Offline Block release	Online plus 8 contact days	Offline Weekends	Offline Block release	Various	Various		Online	

Notes:
1. In the case of A, the specific joint MBA was established in 2020 but builds on a long-established MBA programme and a mode offered in another major city; in respect of I, the date reflects a re-launch but since 2015 the MBA has been offered in blended learning mode
2. Annual intake is the total across a number of cohorts, on average 3 cohorts. The figure is an estimate as various MBAs of different durations are offered.
3. This refers to programme- and not School-level accreditation: Chartered Management Institute (CMI); Association of MBAs (AMBA); Institute for Leadership and Management (ILM); E[uropean Foundation for Management Development] Programme Accreditation System (EPAS)

Research Findings and Discussion

The interviewees were drawn from a wide-range of institutions reflecting an equally wide range of PT MBAs in respect of location of delivery, types of accreditation (if any), entry criteria, student profile (local to international, different levels of seniority), primary markets served, international franchises, composition of modules, breakdown of credits, variety of assessment and duration. Irrespective of this diversity, however, all institutions of course have had to respond to the pandemic.

Impact of the pandemic on the mode of delivery

With regards to delivery, Interviewee A distinguished between responses from different markets. For instance, the experience of their own institution was that there was a very clear preference for offline delivery for students in the Middle East. In the case of China, the institution had been instructed to offer the course offline or postpone any further cohorts, necessitating finding staff locally given the travel restrictions. When asked if colleagues wished to return to the world *ante*-pandemic or were adjusting with equanimity to a new world, Interviewee A stressed the unique nature of PT MBA cohorts and the enormous experience they collectively have, with the role of the faculty being that of facilitator tasked with '*unlocking the potential in the room*' and commented that faculty:

> '*desperately need engagement and interaction and in the online world it has dropped off a cliff so there is a strong desire from the faculty to return to predominantly face-to-face delivery*'

and the evidence, it was said, is that the students have the same view. Interviewee H stated that their business school had already established plans in respect of online provision and the pandemic simply acted as a catalyst, albeit a dramatic one:

> *....[online plans] accelerated enormously, it was a tectonic change, we moved from one to a hundred at the speed of light*

though it was also said that, in the case of the students, they wished to return to some proportion of face-to-face teaching. Interviewee H said the pandemic did not represent much of a threat as the underlying point is that the popularity of MBAs is linked more to general economic conditions rather than the pandemic *per se* but recognised the relationship between the two e.g. any downturn in the economy might lead to unemployment or underemployment but, in turn, could provide more time and perhaps more incentive to study for an MBA. The reduced opportunity cost of studying such a programme during a recession was also mentioned by Interviewee I.

Interviewee G saw the pandemic as both an opportunity and a threat. It had forced changes in teaching styles and, in the case of PT MBA, which, it was said, is facilitator-led, offering it online required considerable planning and infrastructure. However, it was also acknowledged that if every institution can offer a programme online, each one needs to be clear on their point of differentiation. In the case of Interviewees F and G, much support had initially been offered by their university to encourage students to travel to the campus but, as the pandemic unfolded, travel proved impossible and many more students than anticipated are studying online. Various enrichment activities have been built-in, e.g., masterclasses and 'no detriment' policies adopted, and this seemed to have had a positive impact in terms of student retention. The point was similar to that made by Interviewee A but the outcomes appeared to be more positive than experienced by Interviewee E, who commented on a much-increased incidence of suspension of studies and withdrawals. Interviewee J commented on the inadequacy of the data in respect of retention.

Interviewee B saw opportunities and stated that the pandemic had '*proven you can actually recruit well…and deliver the MBA only online and [this] provides flexibility for learners and opens up a wider pool*'. This was consistent with evidence from regional employer surveys undertaken by Interviewee B's business school in September 2017, two-and-a-half years before the pandemic, and which revealed that employers preferred not to see weekly contact or block or weekend delivery. This necessitated a hybrid/blended model incorporating a minimum of eight days of class contact. This model was put in place prior to the pandemic and therefore did not require Interviewee B's business school to make any material changes to what had already been established based on employer feedback and, further, this model might be extended to other courses as the university had already established a subsidiary company to develop online provision.

It is, of course, the case that a number of universities around the world have been offering MBAs online for some time, including that of Interviewee J, whose business school had been offering such a mode since

1996, its longevity illustrating its success and a concomitant level of experience amongst a significant proportion of the faculty.

It is important to note that, in the case of Interviewees B and E, their university, as with others in the UK, had taken advantage of UK Government apprenticeship funding and coupled their PT MBA with the Senior Leader Degree Apprenticeship programme such that students could emerge not only with an MBA but also a professional qualification i.e. Chartered Manager (member of the Chartered Management Institute) or Member of the Institute of Leadership & Management. However, a lower funding threshold had been announced in January 2021 and this may lead to the apprenticeship being decoupled from the MBA by those business schools that previously benefited. Despite Interviewee B's optimism, therefore, there was a recognition that changes in UK Government funding could have a serious and adverse impact on recruitment and there is a need to '*build and establish the MBA…get more alumni, more ambassadors… and [continue to build] a good reputation with employers [such as the National Health Service]*'. The point was also made as to the benefits of collaborating with a local further education college as a means of securing funding and establishing the best possible arrangements for all parties.

In adopting a fully online model, Interviewee C said that the process had been well-managed but:

> '*I cannot say it was good for the programme but the programme was flexible enough to stay with it and also encouraged the students to stay in…the online classes…..but they really wanted to go back into the class, and some students wanted to stop and start again after the pandemic, but we got through it.*'

When asked why the students were so keen to get back into the classroom, the response was simply '*I think they like each other very much*' and there was a belief that the Chinese students enjoy being together in teams and meeting and working with people from other companies: '*it is a very social kind of experience*'. This point was also made by Interviewee J, who stated:

> *MBA is always about the social too, it's a social and academic process, so I think if you don't engage in the social process, you're missing probably 50% of what an MBA is all about.*

An additional opportunity arising from the new model was illustrated by Interviewee A who said that students around the world can now benefit from virtual networking and having access to events such as guest speakers, including leading Chief Executives. Although this was of course possible prior to the pandemic, it actually never happened and such events were confined to Interviewee A's students in the UK. There is now a real opportunity, it was said, to add value in a way that was not happening prior to the pandemic, a point reinforced by Interviewee J.

Interviewee D commented on the impact on the mode of delivery and said to some extent the initial approach had been one of '*suck it and see*' but now '*the genie is out of the bottle….and the mixed mode of delivery is here to stay*'. This view was also shared by Interviewee E who on balance tended to see it as an opportunity: '*We will go back to normal to some degree……but we will never go wholly back to the old ways of doing things*' and that a hybrid approach will continue to be adopted, involving students onsite, live streamed for those who cannot attend physically and recorded for those who cannot make the session. This type of approach, it was said, will become a key element of future provision: '*We are effectively trying to fuse what happened before the pandemic with what happened as a result of the pandemic in terms of how we deliver….*' but '*I do believe most of our learners will want to attend on campus….*'

It is perhaps worth saying that this view from Interviewee E, based in the UK and whose students are largely recruited locally, was the same as that of Interviewee C in respect of Chinese students in China and Interviewee J in Canada i.e. they want to be back on campus. As Interviewee J stated: '*80 % of students and close to 100 % of faculty, they want face-to-face*' though there was also recognition of the potential gains of an asynchronous provision in terms of scalability and efficiency.

However, in some cases, the experience on campus may be very different post-pandemic, as illustrated by Interviewee F who stated: '*whether we will ever go back to those large lecture theatres, I'm not sure*'. This was further illustrated, subsequent to all except one of the interviews, by the University of Manchester's decision, July 2021, to retain online all lectures that do not have an interactive element, however defined, even after the pandemic is over and without any reduction in tuition fees (see Hall, 2021).

The staff development needs were commented on by Interviewees E and G but, in the case of Interviewee E, it was said that perhaps the rapid switch to online was actually made easier by the simple fact the pandemic forced it to happen but this also placed greater emphasis on parts of the existing staff support mechanisms e.g. mentoring.

Interviewee C commented on the workload impact, especially for those faculty who still wish to teach live, albeit online, as they also needed to produce videos to ensure online options are available but faculty had considerable discretion in determining their own approach. Despite this, the view was that mixed mode of delivery will become even more expansive, not least because online provision offers huge potential in respect of international markets. In part contrast to this, however, Interviewee D suggested that their MBA programme is too conservative in some respects, reflecting disagreements amongst colleagues e.g. in relation to assessments that Interviewee D believed were far too traditional (viz. high number of time-constrained examinations) but which had not been challenged by the accrediting body. The pandemic, however, had transformed the assessment in a positive way as at the time of the interview there were no formal time-constrained examinations and '*it would be interesting to see what happens when the world normalises in the future*'.

There was no doubt on the part of Interviewee D that the pandemic had accelerated changes that, otherwise, '*would never have happened in the foreseeable future*'. For example:

> '*in the three years I was involved....not one person came to me with a serious suggestion of mixed methods delivery...it was just something you would speak about rarely and informally...*'

This positive aspect of the experience of the pandemic, it was suggested, may have been enhanced but for the fact that universities are '*slow-moving organisations*' and, in the case of Interviewee D's business school, it is one in which each department has '*a complete lack of understanding of what other departments...do*'. It was stated that an attempt to reach out to other departments to develop a new programme had failed and one cost of the pandemic had been '*stagnation*', rather than acceleration, in respect of curriculum developments.

With regards to universities being '*slow-moving*', this observation was shared by Interviewee A but, by way of contrast, Interviewee H stated that decisions had been taken very quickly at the beginning of the pandemic to shift to online, to support faculty members and to invest in equipment:

> *....[we] offered all our faculty members training, support, manuals and it was very much appreciated; students were happy and members of the staff were very happy...There was not much opposition from faculty members...or criticism... or negative reaction.*

Similarly, Interviewee F commented that a Global MBA had been rapidly developed as a direct result of the pandemic and also gave examples of how the pandemic had forced changes in decision-making arrangements, making them much speedier, and there was an expectation that the new arrangements would remain in place post-pandemic. Similarly, Interviewee B stated:

> *One thing the pandemic must have taught anyone or any organisation across the world is that you have got to be more agile and more innovative.......to be more pro-active and strategic....*

Relevance and quality assurance

Interviewee A stated that the pressures and urgency to respond to the pandemic had been the priority rather than conducting in-depth discussions on changes in the world of work and how these might influence the curriculum. Such changes are more likely to be accommodated over time, for instance through periodic reviews, the natural development of electives and use of guest speakers.

This was also the case with Interviewee I who suggested that nothing fundamentally has changed as a result of the pandemic, in part reflecting the fact that in the previous five years a blended learning model had been adopted. Rather, the pandemic had simply accelerated changes already taking place and, from a teaching perspective, it simultaneously provided an opportunity:

> *The experience of the pandemic did not explicitly result in any curriculum or syllabus changes. However, courses on Global Macroeconomics, Entrepreneurship & New Venture Creation, and Innovation & Digital Transformation discuss the pandemic as an external shock, opportunity and threat for entrepreneurial ventures, and as an accelerator for digitalization initiatives within and among companies.*

It was also stated that the MBA of Interviewee I had been relaunched:

> *....in autumn 2020 after an extensive market analysis. The state-of-the art curriculum focusing on entrepreneurship, leadership and digitalization reflects current*

and future topics in management. The structure and contents of the curriculum are the results of various workshops, including internal and external expertise.

Given the fact that the above discussions and relaunch took place mid-pandemic, and not to downplay the nature of any adjustments to the curriculum, it is particularly interesting to note that it would appear no material change resulted from the circumstances in which the review took place. The key themes identified by Interviewee I were somewhat similar to those identified by Interviewee H, who said that one of the school's PT MBAs focused on three themes: technology and finance; digital transformation; industry 4.0. However, the experience of Interviewee I was perhaps slightly at odds with that of Interviewee B who stated:

....so there is an opportunity further to develop leaders....maybe framed around the lessons learned from the pandemic......maybe it is an opportunity for business schools to rethink their MBA curriculum......I also think the whole society and sustainability piece has gained more traction.

The sustainability and ethical issues linked to entrepreneurship, leadership and digitalisation may be covered but they are not identified as key themes by Interviewee I, though comments of relevance to PRME were made (see *PRME* below). Similarly, Interviewee H commented on key sustainability- and energy-related issues that are discussed within the theme of technology and finance. In the case of Interviewee J, great emphasis was placed on equality, diversity and inclusion (EDI) but this was the case prior to the pandemic and perhaps reflected increased emphasis on the needs and aspirations of Canada's Indigenous and Black communities.

The emphasis on '*society and sustainability*' by Interviewee B was also seen as a mark of differentiation because '*I don't see our local competition really hammer home that society and sustainability agenda like we do*'. Interviewee J highlighted the particular geographic location of the university and which naturally leads the development of particular programmes relating to oceans and ocean-based businesses, climate technology and the environment, all combined with an emphasis on EDI.

With regards to curriculum relevance, Interviewee C stated that '*we are constantly scanning the economic and business environment*' and gave examples of current China-related developments that are now included in the curriculum, e.g. Belt and Road Initiative, RCEP (Regional

Comprehensive Economic Partnership) which is a free trade agreement (FTA) between the ten member states of ASEAN (Association of South East Asian Nations) and six FTA partners. These are supplemented by other modules, core or elective, on issues of global relevance e.g. antitrust and regulation, internet of things, some of which are determined in large part by the Chinese partner and others by the US partner. Interviewee C also commented on the seniority and organisational breadth of the students and what can be learned by asking them what they would like to experience on study tours and this can help inform future developments.

Interviewee C as Director attended all classes online and was greatly reassured by what was happening and this level of reassurance, it was said, was subsequently confirmed by student feedback. The origin of Interviewee C's university was also commented on as it began as an online university and so, in a way, the pandemic took it back to its origins and placed it in a very favourable position given the expertise and resources that had been built up over many years, though this was not necessarily an advantage in China given the clear preference of the students to be together in a classroom.

More generally in relation to quality assurance, particularly in the case of UK-based interviewees, much emphasis was placed on the frameworks in place, internally and externally. In the case of the latter, for instance, there is the Quality Assurance Agency (QAA) and the Office for Students, supplemented by the Competition and Markets Authority whose role is to promote competition for the benefits of consumers (i.e. students in this instance).

An inevitable adverse impact of the pandemic was on international study visits. Though not all interviewee MBAs included this option, it was mentioned by Interviewee D who stated that students had been denied the opportunity to experience a different culture and that this of course could not be simulated.

PRME

Although all respondents recognised the importance for their school of being a signatory to PRME, their responses regarding the influence of PRME on the nature of their MBA programmes varied. While some respondents argued that the impact of PRME involvement was marginal, for others it was significant with the remainder being in-between.

Interviewee A stated that PRME was merely a box-ticking exercise that was of benefit in the early-stage application process for the accreditation it was seeking. In fact, in comparing PRME to some business school accreditation bodies, Interviewee A argued that AACSB (Association to Advance Collegiate Schools of Business) and EQUIS (European Foundation for Management Development [EFMD] Quality Improvement System) had a more profound influence on the school's MBA programme:

> *AASCB have just adjusted their standards at the end of 2020 and now they have a specific one about social engagement and entrepreneurship... EQUIS as well, the themes of diversity and ethics are integrated into literally every single chapter. Those two accreditations hold considerably more weight than PRME.*

Similarly, Interviewee C recognised that PRME involvement was rather irrelevant in the design of the MBA curriculum even though the collaborative partner was a PRME signatory:

> *PRME hasn't really come up at any time. And quite honestly, I didn't know anything about it until recently. With regard to the UN, I don't think we even think about the UN very much. We think about the IMF, we look at the World Bank and we're definitely interested in the Federal Reserve. Remember, we're a business school and we're interested in those kinds of things.*

However, there were also a few cases where the influence of PRME was acknowledged. For example, Interviewee B stated that PRME involvement was perceived as being central not only to the design of the courses but also to the organisation's mission and it was the foundation for its priorities, strategies and plans:

> *When I moved here PRME was not in place. So, I got to work and made sure that it was at the heart of the MBA. At the end of last year, our Associate Dean worked with key stakeholders to understand what is the business school about and what do we stand for. In developing a brand strategy, sustainability and a societal focus became one of our core values. So PRME is now central and will be even more central to the School activities as we move forward. My role is to raise awareness and to embed PRME in everything that we do.*

Similarly, Interviewee F stated that the business school is '*completely committed to PRME as part of our strategy.....PRME is embedded in our programmes*'.

For other interviewees, however, it was suggested that the influence of PRME on their MBA programmes was much more moderate i.e. its impact was neither significant nor insignificant. This point was illustrated by Interviewee D:

> *PRME is certainly an influencing factor, but it is quite discrete. We have our occupational standards, which are very overt and we know that we have to meet them, and we have to do it that way. PRME is more of a strategic focus. It's something we're embedding as a school. It's becoming part of our mindset rather than necessarily thinking about a set of principles that we have to do. It's almost in the background.*

Similarly, Interviewee I stated:

> *we have developed an exclusive training program for faculty to anchor and embed responsibility, ethics, and sustainability as fundamental values in management education as well as in research at higher education institutions and drive them forward. The program designers critically discuss the implications of the pandemic on responsible management and are sharing these learnings and insights correspondingly.*

Overall, based on the evidence collected from the interviews, the influence of PRME involvement on the various MBA programmes differed, ranging from marginal to significant. This variation could be explained by a variety of factors, including the school's strategic positioning, the number of years it has been a signatory to PRME and the availability of resources.

Summary

Several key themes emerged from the discussions.

In general, rather than leading to a completely different model that would not have existed without the pandemic, the interviewees believed the pandemic accelerated changes that were already happening or being planned, though the extent to which this might be supported by evidence, for instance from university strategic plans, is something that would require further research. There is clear evidence that the institutions running MBA programmes responded very quickly, albeit out of necessity, to the pandemic, not least the immediate switch to online learning and, in one case (Interviewee F), it led to the development of a Global MBA. However, the likelihood that this speed of action will be sustained was not obvious. There was some evidence from three of the interviewees that the external shock of the pandemic may make universities more agile in the future and that some of the arrangements that had been put in place in response to the pandemic, intended to speed-up decision-making (e.g. allowing certain decisions to be taken at a lower level in the organisation), may remain, but seven out of ten interviewees did not make this observation and some expressed the view that universities fundamentally remain slow-moving and that, actually, the pandemic slowed-down rather than accelerated developments, particularly in relation to curriculum development.

On balance, interviewees believed the pandemic to be both an opportunity and a threat for PT MBAs and universities generally, though one interviewee stated it was exclusively an opportunity. However, it was inferred from the interviews that higher education post-pandemic may not be as different as some may expect or wish it to be but there was a general view that a complete return to the *status quo ante* pandemic will not happen.

With regards to delivery mode and future-proofing the curriculum, there are varying practices relating to employer surveys to inform decisions but a common theme was an emphasis on external input, either independently of or, where relevant, driven by accreditation viz. professional bodies and employers.

Irrespective of any trends towards accreditation, there were different views as to the actual significance of accreditation in relation to recruitment – with one interviewee suggesting that the recruitment benefits of accreditation are assumed and unquestioned rather than ever demonstrated - but it is significant with regards to curriculum and, for some interviewees, it also encouraged engagement with alumni.

There appears to be greater emphasis in some MBAs on sustainability issues, linked to future-proofing, though this might have been expected to be even greater given: the fact the interviews took place as a result and in the midst of a pandemic; the potential zoonotic cause of the pandemic; the imminence of COP 26; the ever-present and -increasing global evidence of climate change.

The apparent lack of emphasis on sustainability and the SDGs in some of the MBAs was reflected in the mixed evidence in respect of the influence of PRME and it would have been interesting to know how many of the interviewees would have mentioned PRME had it not been included in the questions.

There were varying emphases across the interviewees' PT MBAs on the balance between the acquisition of technical knowledge and the development of leadership behaviours and varying arrangements in respect of (pre-pandemic) international visits and the benefits of being exposed *in situ* to different international cultures.

There was no evidence that the assessment arrangements had been, or would be, materially affected by the pandemic.

The interviews demonstrated varying levels of guidance/prescription to faculty in relation to online delivery and, similarly, varying levels of staff development.

There was evidence of increased internal competition i.e. courses competing with each other for students, between different MBA courses and between MBA and non-MBA courses and, without exception, the interviewees observed a trend to students' self-financing, though there was a general belief that employers value candidates with MBAs.

Limitations

The interviewees were chosen in part on the basis of their seniority, the fact they would be able to give informed responses to the questions asked and because in total they reflected a wide variety of countries and PT MBAs. However, there was no triangulation to corroborate comments being made, for example by use of secondary data such as university or school strategic plans and minutes of meetings. Similarly, the views of other faculty were not obtained and, importantly, no discussions were held with students or employers. All these areas would be extremely useful ones for further research, as would a quantitative survey within and across countries to generate more evidence as to the medium- to long-term impact of the pandemic.

Conclusion

The impact of the worst pandemic in over a hundred years has been tragic for so many people around the world. The scale of the tragedy is ongoing and its longer-term impact on a whole range of issues remains unknown. These issues include people's health (from 'long-Covid' to non-Covid illnesses and postponed operations), post-pandemic politico-economic consensus and the ethical and practical issues of inequitable availability of vaccines and healthcare around the world. These issues are unfolding alongside, and contributing to and influenced by, global challenges including climate change and the SDGs.

Organisations, including HEIs, must respond, and help shape the response, to these unprecedented challenges. In this context, management development, including PT MBAs, must be proportionate to the challenge.

It is clear that business schools, and HEIs generally, have, through necessity, responded rapidly and creatively in offering online versions of their awards and, to this extent, Kandri (2020) was perhaps correct to say a new model has emerged and there will be no return to the *status quo ante* pandemic. In developing a new model, some HEIs, inevitably, were better prepared than others, and were able to build upon a tradition of online learning. However, despite the rapid changes in mode of delivery, it is perhaps debatable as to whether the changes relating to curricula reflect the magnitude of the challenges now faced, including those highlighted by CIPD (2021, 2013), Microsoft (2021) and Deloitte report (Volini et al., 2019). This might be further illustrated by the interviewee responses relating to PRME which, on the whole, and despite some exceptions, indicated a weak to moderate impact of PRME in business school deliberations. It is also unknown how many interviewees would actually have mentioned PRME had they not been prompted.

Given the nature of the challenges now faced, and building on the work of Mintzberg (2004), perhaps a fourth-generation management development is needed. If the motto for third-generation management development was *Use work, don't make work* perhaps a motto for a fourth-generation might be *Make work sustainable, for individuals and society* and the contribution of PT MBAs in this regard could be considerable given the nature of them and the practitioners they attract.

Appendix 1 Semi-structured interview questions

General

1. Please supply some information about your PT MBA (or equivalent) – e.g. when established; numbers of students and trends over time; any

key changes in the programme curriculum over time; any key distinguishing characteristics such as overall philosophy or accreditation.

2. Are your students *mainly* self-financed or financed by their employers and have you seen any changes in the balance between the two?
3. Do you regard the pandemic as a threat or an opportunity in the provision of PT MBA programmes for (a) universities and business schools in general and (b) your School/programme?

Mode of delivery

4. How has the experience of the pandemic influenced the mode of delivery of the PT MBA and how were any changes quality-assured?
5. What will be the impact of the pandemic on the mode of delivery of your PT MBA in the medium- to long-term?

Relevance, satisfaction and future proof

6. In what ways is the relevance and 'future proof' nature of the PT MBA quality-assured? For example, does the programme have an external advisory board; are there key strategic objectives in relation to faculty selection for the programme and their development?
7. Has the experience of the pandemic led to:
   - *irreversible* changes in relation to the MBA content and teaching *directly attributable* to the pandemic and/or
   - *acceleration* of changes that were happening or were planned to happen *independently* of the pandemic?
8. Are there any specific features in the external environment that have influenced the curriculum or which you anticipate will do so?

PRME

9. In responding to these issues, what has been the influence of PRME involvement?

References

CIPD (2021, April). *Flexible Working: Lessons from the Pandemic.* www.cipd.co.uk/Images/flexible-working-lessons-from-pandemic-report_tcm18-92644.pdf

CIPD (2020). *Megatrends reports.* https://www.cipd.co.uk/knowledge/work/trends/megatrends#gref

CIPD (2013). *Megatrends: The trends shaping work and working lives.* www.cipd.co.uk/knowledge/work/trends/megatrends/trends-shaping-working-lives

DDI. (2021). *CEO Leadership Report.* Global Leadership Forecast Series. Retrieved November 12, 2021, from https://www.ddiworld.com/research/ceo-leadership-report

De Smet, A., Dowling, B., Mysore, M., & Reich, A. (2021). It's time for leaders to get real about hybrid. The McKinsey Quarterly. https://www.mckinsey.com/~/media/mckinsey/business%20functions/organization/our%20insights/its%20time%20for%20leaders%20to%20get%20real%20about%20hybrid/its-time-for-leaders-to-get-real-about-hybrid.pdf

Economist (2020, July 25). Starting over again: The covid-19 pandemic is forcing a re-think in macroeconomics. Retrieved November 12, 2021, from https://www.economist.com/briefing/2020/07/25/the-covid-19-pandemic-is-forcing-a-rethink-in-macroeconomics

Hall, R. (2021, July 5). Manchester University sparks backlash with plan to keep lectures online. The Guardian. https://www.theguardian.com/education/2021/jul/05/manchester-university-sparks-backlash-with-plan-to-keep-lectures-online

Harvard Business Publishing Corporate Learning (2018). *The 2018 State of Leadership Development. Meeting the Transformation Imperative.* Research Report. Retrieved November 12, 2021, from https://www.harvardbusiness.org/insight/the-state-of-leadership-development-report

Henderson, L.H. & Wilson, J. (2023). 'MBA futures: Images from Principles for Responsible Management Education (PRME) signatories during the COVID-19 pandemic' *Futures* 145 (2023) 103047

House of Commons Library (2021, April 26). *Fire and re-hire tactics.* Retrieved November 12, 2021, from https://researchbriefings.files.parliament.uk/documents/CDP-2021-0066/CDP-2021-0066.pdf

Hunt, E. (2021, June 29). It just doesn't stop!' Do we need a new law to ban out-of-hours emails?. The Guardian. https://www.theguardian.com/money/2021/jun/29/it-just-doesnt-stop-do-we-need-a-new-law-to-ban-out-of-hours-emails

Kandri, S. E. (2020, May). How COVID-19 is driving a long-overdue revolution in education. In World Economic Forum (Vol. 12). Retrieved June 19, 2020, from https://www.weforum.org/agenda/2020/05/how-covid-19-is-sparking-a-revolution-in-higher-education/

Microsoft (2021). Work Trend Index: Annual Report: The Next Great Disruption Is Hybrid Work–Are We Ready. https://ms-worklab.azureedge.net/files/reports/hybridWork/pdf/2021_Microsoft_WTI_Report_March.pdf

Miller, D. (1992). The Icarus paradox: How exceptional companies bring about their own downfall. Business Horizons, 35(1), 24-35.

Muir, I. (2021, February 24). Don't be a fake: the pandemic has found-out low integrity leadership. CMI. www.managers.org.uk/knowledge-and-insights/article/dont-be-a-fake-the-pandemic-has-found-out-low-integrity-leadership/

NatCen Social Research (2021). *Stay home: affecting lives*. Retrieved November 12, 2021, from https://www.natcen.ac.uk/media/2075969/Stay-home_affecting-lives.pdf

National Bureau of Economic Research (NBER) (2020). *Collaborating During Coronavirus: The Impact of COVID-19 on the Nature of Work*. Retrieved July 5, 2021, from https://www.nber.org/system/files/working_papers/w27612/w27612.pdf

Nelson, J. S. (2020, June 3). 5 Ethical Challenges During Covid-19 That Businesses Need To Meet. Ethical Systems. www.ethicalsystems.org/5-ethical-challenges-during-covid-19-that-businesses-need-to-meet/

PRME (2021a). PRME's Vision and Mission. Retrieved April 27, 2021, from www.unprme.org/about

PRME (2021b). Six Principles. Retrieved April 26, 2021, from www.unprme.org/what-we-do

PRME (2020). How Business Schools are responding to COVID-19 – examples from the PRME community. Retrieved April 26, 2021, from https://primetime.unprme.org/2020/03/26/how-business-schools-are-responding-to-covid-19-examples-from-the-prme-community-updated-regularly/

Rhodes, R. A. (1994). The hollowing out of the state: The changing nature of the public service in Britain. The Political Quarterly, 65(2), 138–151.

Sinofsky, S. (2021, June 18). Creating the Future of Work: From Trauma to Opportunity. Learning by Shipping, Medium. Retrieved July 5, 2021, from https://medium.learningbyshipping.com/creating-the-future-of-work-449c66707e35

Standing, G. (2014). The precariat. Contexts, 13(4), 10–12.

TaylorWessing (2021, February 23). Latest changes in employment law in Slovakia: Home Office. Retrieved July 5, 2021, from https://www.taylorwessing.com/en/insights-and-events/insights/2021/02/latest-changes-in-employment-law-in-slovakia

United Nations (UN) (2021). The 17 Goals. Retrieved April 27, 2021, from https://sdgs.un.org/goals.

Andrzej Wodecki, Warsaw University of Technology, Poland

Artificial Intelligence in Managerial Development

Abstract: Generally, the use of artificial intelligence is not particularly advanced. Intelligent solutions are often triggers for critical organizational changes. AI can be of significant help to organizations, including in managerial development to unprecedented levels. At the same time, it generates many new challenges. Managers should know its potential, be able to implement it, and then use it effectively in daily practice. This article aims to introduce the most important AI capabilities in the context of managerial development, present the potential impact of intelligent technologies on training systems, present possible opportunities, and threats, and point out the most exciting trends in the future.

Keywords: Artificial intelligence, Development, Managers

Artificial intelligence as a catalyst for change

Artificial intelligence (AI) is as popular a concept as it is underdefined. There are many definitions of it in the literature, focusing on aspects of training methods, technology, or applications. Despite this, most managers agree that AI has a very high potential to generate value for their organizations.

According to a McKinsey report (Chui, 2021), the level of adoption of AI solutions is steadily increasing (from 50 % in 2020 to 56 % in 2021, according to 1,843 managers surveyed). In contrast, research from PricewaterhouseCoopers (PricewaterhouseCoopers, 2021) indicates that for 86 % of 1,032 respondents (managers of U.S. companies), AI will be a mainstream technology. Leaders of these organizations increasingly understand the potential of AI and advanced analytics in their business, expecting these technologies to support day-to-day operations and better understand customer behavior, increase the flexibility of supply chains and distribution networks, or be able to design new data-driven business models. Interestingly, there is much evidence that the COVID-19 pandemic has dramatically accelerated the adoption of AI (McKendrick, 2021). For instance, the AI perspective has been shown to significantly enrich organizations' human resources management in times of COVID (Tuffaha, Perello-Marin & Suarez-Ruz, 2022).

AI is primarily used in service operations (service-operations optimization, contact-center automation), product and/or service development (AI-based product enhancement, product-feature optimization), marketing and sales (customer-service analytics, customer segmentation), and risk management (risk modeling and analytics, fraud detection) (Chui, 2021). Intelligent solutions help companies first and foremost to reduce the cost of operations and, secondarily, to increase revenue. In addition, the rate of growth of return on investment in AI supports cautious optimism about the impact of these technologies on the economy's productivity (Brynjolfsson & Petropoulos, 2022; Wodecki, 2019).

Intelligent systems are also seen as a source of new products or services and as an opportunity for start-ups to work more closely with mature companies. This is because young companies can implement advanced technologies faster, while mature organizations have a broader customer and product base and thus better data and experimental field for AI. Additionally, more and more managers point to AI as a catalyst for rethinking organizations' value systems and ethical attitudes (see McLean et al., 2021; Volkmar, Fischer & Reinecke, 2022).

What distinguishes companies that are spectacularly successful in AI implementations from those with only moderate results in this area? According to the above-mentioned McKinsey report, high-performers:

1. Are more likely to apply sophisticated best practices in the full lifecycle management of AI models.
2. They better forecast and control the budgets of such projects.
3. Are more professional in identifying and mitigating key risk factors of such initiatives.

Innovative approaches to strategic planning are also critical: according to experts from PricewaterhouseCoopers (PricewaterhouseCoopers, 2021), it is beneficial to design, in the context of AI implementation, so-called 'strategic flywheels' (Subramanian & Rao, 2019) to identify potential positive feedback loops triggering exponential value creation once a certain critical mass is exceeded.

It turns out that more and more managers are pointing to the great potential of AI in addressing talent and employee shortages at different levels of the organization (the COVID-19 pandemic has significantly affected the scale of these problems). AI can be successfully applied in designing career paths, supporting employees in performing their current jobs (automation of repetitive tasks, support for data analysis or decision-making processes), etc. Unfortunately, the development of such solutions, in turn, requires AI competencies that are severely lacking in the labor market, managers including. No wonder there are more and more attempts to use AI to solve the lack of talent in this area.

Intelligent solutions are becoming a catalyst for change in many organizations, industries, and even markets, generating many unprecedented challenges. To be able to fully exploit their potential, it is necessary to have access to talent: not only people developing AI solutions but also managers at various levels of management. The role of the leader should be not only to determine the direction of development or support such initiatives but also to prepare the organization to be able to function in an agile way in a new, fast-changing reality.

Intelligent systems in managerial work and education

Education is a very particular area of application for artificial intelligence. For years, Learning Management Systems (LMS) have been generating large amounts of data that are later used to, for example, identify learning profiles, personalize learning, predict learning progress, or formulate training objectives. Good practices in this area, developed mainly in university environments (Aldosari, 2020), can also be successfully applied in management education.

To effectively exploit the potential of big data and AI systems, organizations should thoughtfully modify their medium- and long-term strategies (AI-driven policies), which in turn requires adequate preparation. As a result, a kind of feedback loop can be observed: artificial intelligence systems have the potential to support the development of managers effectively, but the effective implementation of intelligent technologies requires knowledge about the fundamentals of their operation and the potential of applications. In short: AI can significantly help organizations, especially in managerial development, but managers should know its potential, be able to implement it, and then use it effectively in daily practice.

The directions of managers' development are conditioned by changes in the broadly understood business environment. One of the possible ways of identifying them is to analyze the employees' competencies most desired by employers. Thus, consequently, the competencies that are currently most sought after may serve as a valuable indication for managers in their development and, indirectly, indicate the development trends of their industries shortly.

For instance, *LinkedIn-Learning*, the educational initiative of the popular social networking system aimed at employees and employers, based on a survey of 1,260 training professionals and 814 learners, identifies resilience and adaptability, technology/digital fluency, communication across remote and distributed teams, emotional intelligence, and cross-functional collaboration as the TOP5 skills currently (the year 2021). The following five are: leading through change, change management, dealing with stress, time management, and creativity (LinkedIn Learning's Workplace Learning Report 2021, n.d.). The business skills with the fastest-growing interest include customer experience, digital marketing, financial statements, forecasting, and analytical skills. The analysis of competencies with the fastest-growing interest was based on the LinkedIn Learning portal statistics, which take into account the behavior of more than 722 million users from over 200 countries and data on interest in 16,700 courses developing about 36,000 skills. As can be seen, soft skills are still considered the most important, but there is growing interest in analytical skills that can improve the management of key functional areas such as sales and finance.

Workplace Learning Predictions can be a source of equally important inspiration. For example, Udemy, one of the leading providers of online training, indicates the following trends in corporate training: focused capability academies (in-depth training initiatives to develop and sustain skill capabilities that support specific business strategies and function areas), Communities of Practices as a place to update knowledge and skills quickly, creation of talent exchanges within the organization, and generation Z as a particularly intensive learner, primarily based on social learning (Udemy, 2020).

All our considerations are worth complementing with an analysis of HR managers' expectations of advanced technologies. Maity and Souvik summarize these future needs within the SIP model: Seamless, Intuitive, and Personalized (Maity, 2019). Companies are changing faster, growing, and entering new markets, which requires increasingly mature methods of managing knowledge, both tacit and explicit. This knowledge should be easy and accessible to employees at a specific time, place, and context, all included in the term 'Seamless.' Further, training and development practices are gradually moving from classrooms to screens, increasingly mobile devices. The lack of access to a live trainer makes the intuitive nature of KM? and training applications (Intuitive) particularly important. Finally, the increasing specialization of professions combined with the vast number of potential sources of knowledge requires increasingly better personalization methods, not only in terms of the content itself but also in learner characteristics such as learning styles (Personalization).

Artificial intelligence systems have many capabilities that can contribute to a greater or lesser extent to improving managerial development processes. For example, the Natural Language Processing (NLP) and understanding (NLU) systems described later help in knowledge extraction and content generation, learning analytics systems enable precise behavioral profiling, and recommendation systems enable advanced personalization not only of the content itself but also of the learning objectives or trainers. However, many questions arise about how this can be applied in the practice of managerial development?

First, it might be interesting to know how AI can help discover, codify, and redistribute the knowledge accumulated in an organization? How can it be used to identify critical skills for our organization or ourselves? Furthermore, how can artificial intelligence help develop the most desirable 'soft' and 'hard' skills? In the area of learning methods, it may be interesting to ask about the potential of AI in personalizing learning processes, particularly the selection of content and the methods of its delivery? Or how can AI improve the intuitiveness not only of training applications but also of the entire Learning Journey? The growing role of learning communities, in turn, stimulates the question of how AI can help create them or, more broadly, support social learning? Finally, how can AI help construct focused-capabilities academies? How can it help identify these key capabilities?

Furthermore, what competencies should managers develop concerning the above? In what direction to change organizations to best leverage the potential of AI in these areas? Moreover, what can be expected in the future?

This article aims to introduce the most important AI capabilities in the context of managerial development, present the potential impact of intelligent technologies on training systems, present possible opportunities, and threats, and point out the most exciting trends in the future. And, at least partially, answer the questions formulated above.

AI methods and techniques in education

Artificial intelligence is most often referred to as a collection of methods and techniques that replace and/or complement human cognitive activities (cf., e.g., (Russell & Norvig, 2020)). For this paper, we will narrow this definition to systems that can learn from data to identify patterns, recognize objects, and predict future states using supervised, unsupervised, and reinforcement learning methods.

Intelligent systems in education have been used for many years (X. Chen et al., 2020). One of their primary applications is Educational Data Mining (EDM), using statistical methods, machine learning, and so-called Deep Learning to analyze educational data. This makes it possible to identify, in particular, individual learning methods and preferences, as well as situations in which learners achieve above-average results. The results of these analyses are used, for example, to predict the risk of dropping out of the training process so that appropriate preventive measures can be taken in good time. EDM is sometimes considered as part of a broader group of analytical processes referred to as Learning Analytics (LA) (Baepler & Murdoch, 2010), which involves analyzing data about learners' behavior and context to understand and optimize learning processes and the environments/ situations in which they are implemented.

The results of EDM and LA can further be used to optimize Computer-Based Education (CBE) training processes, increasingly referred to as e-learning. This optimization most often boils down to personalization of content, processes, and delivery methods to learners and continuous improvement through analysis of user feedback and learning outcomes. The whole process is most often realized using many advanced IT systems, ranging from Learning Management Systems, through systems for creating interactive content, final applications (web and mobile) for their distribution and aggregation of behavioral data, to AI systems generating appropriate forecasts and recommendations.

Natural language processing (NLP) and understanding (NLU) methods are an exciting group of AI methods that complement this landscape qualitatively new. They operate at several different levels, while their potential is increasingly recognized in knowledge management (Liebowitz, 2021). At the lowest (word and sentence) level, they enable recognition of the meaning of individual words in a given context (Named Entity Recognition: NER). At the paragraph level, they provide the ability to recognize sentiment and paraphrase the text. At the document level, it becomes more interesting: NLP/NLU systems can autonomously group documents (identifying appropriate clusters), classify them (assigning appropriate labels), and further automatically summarize, formulate document-based questions (true/false, multiple-choice, fill-in-the-gap), and paraphrase such formulated questions. This makes it possible to create systems that formulate questions and verify the reliability of the content of the documents under study by comparing their message with trusted sources (truth/false verification). Natural language generation systems make it possible to create interpretations of information contained in natural language data (so-called Data-to-Text systems), while Text-2-Data systems make it possible to query databases by asking questions in natural language. Organizations with large repositories of electronic documents (i.e., virtually all of them) can also use NLP systems to extract knowledge from such databases using, e.g., document segmentation and knowledge graphs (H. Chen & Luo, 2019), which in turn can not only help identify the most important (or fastest-growing) topic areas but also become the basis for automated question generation systems (e.g., in the form of chatbots).

A separate category of AI-based systems that can, in some sense, be used in managerial development is the so-called Digital Twin of Organization

(Riss et al., 2020). Allowing for the modeling of organizations, they enable, in particular, the testing of various decision-making scenarios. As a result, they can serve to forecast and identify optimal scenarios and provide a very interesting environment for the development of managerial skills, being a tailored version of a managerial game for a given organization.

As can be seen, intelligent systems can not only help to effectively distribute the best possible educational content to a company's employees (including, of course, managers), but they can also increasingly effectively assist in identifying key knowledge areas, codifying knowledge (e.g., through summaries), and generating relevant training content (including questions and tests). But how can this impact staff management and manager development?

The possible impact of AI on workforce management and manager development

Management development is a particular example of broader workforce management practices. We will begin our consideration of the application of AI in this area.

AI is particularly applicable to performance analysis. AI-based programs enable managers and employees to monitor performance from a holistic perspective: from the goal formulation phase to the job performance evaluation. AI also helps in planning career paths and succession, understanding employee retention and attrition (Sivathanu & Pillai, 2018), and managing employee emotions (Henkel et al., 2020), which may help in preventing job burnout (Kong et al., 2021). As mentioned above, AI is also increasingly used in improving knowledge management processes: from identification to creation to distribution, enabling managers to process large amounts of information and use it to make decisions and formulate better action strategies.

AI systems play a unique role in optimizing training processes (Maity, 2019). As already mentioned, they allow identifying the current level of knowledge, preferred learning methods and styles, and emotions, although presently (to the author's knowledge) they do not allow a full assessment of characteristics such as capabilities, personality traits, motivational constructs, values and interests, attitudes, and perceptions (Bell et al.,

2017). Similar analyses can also be performed to generate desirable trainer characteristics (Maity, 2019), which can further be used to personalize the training process. The integration of training management systems, Human Resources Management systems, and advanced analytics, in turn, makes it possible to identify competency gaps and create personalized development plans.

The area where the potential of AI manifests itself most strongly is training personalization. Based on behavioral profiles of employees, trainers, and characteristics of training content, AI helps select training that best meets the current needs of learners, taking into consideration not only the content but also the channel and form of delivery, location, time, training and development objectives, and even the psychological profile of the trainer. On the other hand, they help trainers choose the best methods for the trainee, including the scope, duration, frequency, and channels of access to the course, and even the interface of the application they use. Lastly, they help remove human bias from the process of recruiting employees for training.

AI can be used to personalize not only specific training sessions but also entire training programs. Intelligent systems can dynamically adjust the pace of training to the learner's current progress based on regular measurements of training effectiveness. They also enable incremental changes to training programs based on trainee engagement analyses.

Predictive systems make it possible to predict the risk of an employee dropping out of training and their future training needs. In combination with a system for measuring learning progress, competence profiles, and work efficiency analyses, this can be a basis for planning further development activities.

As a result, AI systems not only enable automation of repetitive and time-consuming activities in the area of workforce management (interpreting needs assessment surveys, scheduling training programs, mapping trainers to trainees, scheduling training programs, etc.) but also offer completely new qualities (e.g., widely understood personalization, dynamic adaptation to users' needs and capabilities, or development of managerial skills through the use of organizational simulators). The possibilities are many: the key question is, however, to what extent can they be used in a given organization? And, if it is limited, what can be done to unlock this potential?

Challenges and recommendations

Artificial intelligence offers many possibilities. Unfortunately, their actual availability is often very limited. As a result, companies struggle to implement inherently risky custom implementations and seemingly simple-to-implement, ready-made 'off-the-shelf' solutions. Why is this happening? And what can be done to exploit the potential of AI in management education fully?

The success of an organization largely depends on how effectively it can combine people, processes, and technology to generate new value while optimizing costs. Thus, the mere availability of technology is not enough: it is also necessary to transform processes (and, more generally, ways of working) and convince and prepare people. This applies to virtually all innovations, of which intelligent solutions are one in particular.

The use of artificial intelligence is still at an early stage of development. Focusing on the human factor, Chang, Abdalla, and Lasyoud (2021) identified three categories of reasons for this situation: the job-replacement approach (Huang & Rust, 2018), psychological contract approach (Farndale et al., 2020; Rousseau, 1989), and demands-resources approach (Bakker & Demerouti, 2007). In the first case, workers fear that technologies (in our case: AI) will replace them (or, more precisely, allow them to replace simple, repetitive tasks first, then: more complex ones, to eliminate some jobs over time finally). The second concept relies on the assumption that employees are interested in 'negotiating': a given technology can be accepted if it offers a particular value. It simplifies certain tasks, creates more space for creative work or leisure, reduces risk or responsibility, or improves profits that will later be redistributed within the company. On the other hand, the demands-resources approach hinges upon the assumption that there are demands that should be delivered with resources in every job. An imbalance between these sides causes stress: most often when the demands are greater than the available resources. AI solutions paradoxically, at least initially, can appear on the demands side: once they are implemented, companies may expect users to use solutions that are unfamiliar and alien to them, increasing demands rather than contributing to improved efficiency.

The above analyses, necessarily presented here in a simplified manner, result in the following recommendations for managers interested in AI implementation in their organization, especially in the area of their own and other employees' development:

1. When presenting the project idea, it should be clearly emphasized that the purpose is not to replace employees but to support them in their daily work and increase their capabilities (which is sometimes referred to as 'human augmentation').
2. Indicate the benefits that the implementation of AI will bring. In the case of training, they are simple and understandable: development activities will be better tailored to individual needs and work conditions/context, delivered through the user's preferred channel, and simply more interesting (e.g., simulators or augmented reality).
3. Design solutions so that they are as easy and intuitive to use as possible, properly prepare employees to use the solutions (training), provide a continuous system of ad hoc support (helpdesk). So as to reduce the effort of implementation and as soon as possible make intelligent solutions not a 'demand,' but a 'resource.'

Naturally, this requires managers to be prepared appropriately. They should learn the basics of AI operation, participate in the implementation of AI themselves and use them actively. In many cases, it may also be necessary to manage (or at least mentor) the implementation of such a system. In addition, while learning the specifics of AI, they should pay special attention to the ethical aspects of such projects and the psychological aspects of human-machine relations to anticipate the possible negative side-effects of implementation and prepare their organization accordingly. After the implementation, they should actively use the new solutions.

However, in the practice of many companies it may turn out that implementation of AI with its resources (based on its own data, content, systems, and employees) is simply impossible (lack of resources), economically ineffective, or very risky. In such situations, it is worth analyzing the offer of training providers (e.g., e-learning) or Learning Management Platforms in terms of the solutions described above. It turns out that more and more providers implement advanced learning analytics and AI solutions in practice (using the services of companies specializing in this field). Thus, it may turn out that intelligent solutions will become more and more within our reach, both in terms of technology and price.

Future trends

The use of AI in education is the subject of intense research (cf. e.g., Hwang et al., 2020). There are many reasons for this. On the one hand, modern industries are developing very dynamically, generating more and more new solutions, more and more data, and knowledge, which requires increasingly better-prepared employees willing and able to learn new things quickly and effectively. On the other hand, information overload, especially for young people, increases the risk of decreasing cognitive skills, particularly concentration impairment, which may negatively affect the learning abilities that are necessary nowadays. On the other hand, the dynamic development of cognitive psychology, genetics, and other fields supporting the study of learning, coupled with the growing capabilities of analytical systems, may support these problems and point to new and interesting research areas. It is not surprising, then, that new concepts such as Research Machines, Thinking Infrastructures, and AILSci (Ai and Learning Sciences) (Williamson, 2020) are emerging on the frontlines of research to explore the potential of interdisciplinary research such as educational genomics (Plomin, 2018).

What can a manager expect from this research? We live in a time of information overload. Indeed, we are bombarded with a vast amount of information coming from more and more sources. This can have a negative impact not only on our concentration but also on our ability to analyze incoming content in-depth and even on our general well-being and health. Training processes are also primarily based on information transfer and thus exacerbate this negative phenomenon.

Artificial intelligence can help solve these problems. In particular, the development of information technologies is accompanied by diagnostic methods and cognitive skills development. Using the latest (neuro)cognitive science findings, providers of various IT systems, especially cell phone manufacturers, are introducing new functionalities oriented towards reducing cognitive overload and improving concentration. It is worth paying particular attention to this trend and treating the ability to manage one's attention (especially the ability to oscillate between modes of concentration and de-concentration, while adjusting tasks with specific cognitive requirements to the current state) as one of the elements of managerial competence development, in which AI can play a special role.

Final reflections

The author of this study advocates the view that we are shaped by the situation in which we find ourselves to a large extent. As a result, if we want to develop in a particular direction, we should carefully 'design' the situation so that it helps us to achieve the planned developmental goal.

Artificial intelligence systems are slowly becoming an integral part of our environment, even if we are not fully aware of their presence. This does not only refer to the solutions described in this publication: here, we treat AI as a generally understood solution that can significantly support human cognitive functions. Being a part of managers' operating environment, they become more or less an essential 'component' of the situations in which they find themselves.

As a result, AI can influence managers' development significantly more than described in this paper. Aware of this, managers can start using intelligent systems to improve their operations (e.g., by using advanced business intelligence systems) and by interacting with them to improve their competencies, develop new skills, or broaden their horizons. For example, they can learn their business by interacting with simulators of their organizations (the so-called digital twins), testing the effects of various scenarios. Or maybe they can prepare themselves for new roles, such as 'AI translator,' 'AI trainer' or 'business value architect.' The possibilities appear virtually endless.

References

Aldosari, S. A. M. (2020). The Future of Higher Education in the Light of Artificial Intelligence Transformations. *International Journal of Higher Education*, 9(3), 145–151.

Baepler, P., & Murdoch, C. J. (2010). Academic analytics and data mining in higher education. *International Journal for the Scholarship of Teaching and Learning*, *4*(2), 1–9. Scopus.

Bakker, A. B., & Demerouti, E. (2007). The Job Demands-Resources model: State of the art. *Journal of Managerial Psychology*, *22*(3), 309–328. DOI: https://doi.org/10.1108/02683940710733115.

Bell, B. S., Tannenbaum, S. I., Ford, J. K., Noe, R. A., & Kraiger, K. (2017). 100 years of training and development research: What we know and where we should go. *Journal of Applied Psychology*, *102*(3), 305–323. DOI: https://doi.org/10.1037/apl0000142.

Chang, K. (2020). Artificial intelligence in personnel management: The development of APM model. *The Bottom Line*, *33*(4), 377–388. DOI: https://doi.org/10.1108/BL-08-2020-0055.

Brynjolfsson, E., & Petropoulos, G. (n.d.). The coming productivity boom. *MIT Technology Review*. Retrieved March 22, 2022, from https://www.technologyreview.com/2021/06/10/1026008/the-coming-productivity-boom/.

Chang, K., Abdalla, Y. A., & Lasyoud, A. A. (2021). Artificial Intelligence in Personnel Management: Opportunities and Challenges to the Higher Education Sector (HES). In A. M. A. Musleh Al-Sartawi, A. Razzaque, & M. M. Kamal (Eds.), *Artificial Intelligence Systems and the Internet of Things in the Digital Era* (pp. 278–289). Springer International Publishing. DOI: https://doi.org/10.1007/978-3-030-77246-8_27.

Chen, H., & Luo, X. (2019). An automatic literature knowledge graph and reasoning network modeling framework based on ontology and natural language processing. *Advanced Engineering Informatics*, 42, 100959. DOI: https://doi.org/10.1016/j.aei.2019.100959.

Chen, X., Xie, H., Zou, D., & Hwang, G.-J. (2020). Application and theory gaps during the rise of Artificial Intelligence in Education. *Computers and Education: Artificial Intelligence*, *1*, 100002. DOI: https://doi.org/10.1016/j.caeai.2020.100002.

Chui, M. (2021). *Global survey: The state of AI in 2021*. McKinsey Analytics. https://www.mckinsey.com/business-functions/mckinsey-analytics/our-insights/global-survey-the-state-of-ai-in-2021.

Farndale, E., McDonnell, A., Scholarios, D., & Wilkinson, A. (2020). Human Resource Management Journal: A look to the past, present, and future of the journal and HRM scholarship. *Human Resource Management Journal*, *30*(1), 1–12. DOI: https://doi.org/10.1111/1748-8583.12275.

Grace, K., Salvatier, J., Dafoe, A., Zhang, B., & Evans, O. (2018). Viewpoint: When Will AI Exceed Human Performance? Evidence from AI Experts. *Journal of Artificial Intelligence Research*, *62*, 729–754. DOI: https://doi.org/10.1613/jair.1.11222.

Henkel, A. P., Bromuri, S., Iren, D., & Urovi, V. (2020). Half human, half machine–augmenting service employees with AI for interpersonal emotion regulation. *Journal of Service Management*, *31*(2), 247–265. DOI: https://doi.org/10.1108/JOSM-05-2019-0160.

Huang, M.-H., & Rust, R. T. (2018). Artificial Intelligence in Service. *Journal of Service Research, 21*(2), 155–172. DOI: https://doi.org/10.1177/1094670517752459.

Hwang, G.-J., Xie, H., Wah, B. W., & Gašević, D. (2020). Vision, challenges, roles and research issues of Artificial Intelligence in Education. *Computers and Education: Artificial Intelligence, 1*, 100001. DOI: https://doi.org/10.1016/j.caeai.2020.100001.

Keding, C. (2021). Understanding the interplay of artificial intelligence and strategic management: Four decades of research in review. *Management Review Quarterly*, *71(*1), 91–134. Scopus. DOI: https://doi.org/10.1007/s11301-020-00181-x.

Kong, H., Yuan, Y., Baruch, Y., Bu, N., Jiang, X., & Wang, K. (2021). Influences of artificial intelligence (AI) awareness on career competency and job burnout. *International Journal of Contemporary Hospitality Management, 33*(2), 717–734. DOI: https://doi.org/10.1108/IJCHM-072020-0789.

Liebowitz, J. (Ed.). (2021). A Research Agenda for Knowledge Management and Analytics. Edward Elgar Publishing.

LinkedIn Learning's Workplace Learning Report 2021 (n.d.). https://learning.linkedin.com/content/dam/me/business/en-us/amp/learning-solutions/images/wlr21/pdf/LinkedIn-Learning_Workplace-Learning-Report-2021-EN-1.pdf.

Maity, S. (2019). Identifying opportunities for artificial intelligence in the evolution of training and development practices. *Journal of Management Development,* 38(8), 651–663. DOI: https://doi.org/10.1108/JMD-03-2019-0069.

Malik, A., Budhwar, P., Patel, C., & Srikanth, N. R. (2022). May the bots be with you! Delivering HR cost-effectiveness and individualised employee experiences in an MNE. *The International Journal of Human Resource Management*, *33*(6), 1148–1178. DOI: https://doi.org/10.1080/09585192.2020.1859582.

McKendrick, J. (2021, September 27). AI Adoption Skyrocketed Over the Last 18 Months. *Harvard Business Review*. https://hbr.org/2021/09/ai-adoption-skyrocketed-over-the-last-18-months.

McLean, S., Read, G. J. M., Thompson, J., Baber, C., Stanton, N. A., & Salmon, P. M. (2021). The risks associated with Artificial General Intelligence: A systematic review. *Journal of Experimental & Theoretical Artificial Intelligence*, 1–15. DOI: https://doi.org/10.1080/0952813x.2021.1964003.

Plomin, R. (2018). *Blueprint: How DNA Makes Us Who We Are*. The MIT Press.

PricewaterhouseCoopers (2021). *AI Predictions 2021*. PwC. Retrieved March 22, 2022, from https://www.pwc.com/us/en/tech-effect/ai-analytics/ai-predictions.html.

Riss, U. V., Maus, H., Javaid, S., & Jilek, C. (2020). Digital Twins of an Organization for Enterprise Modeling. In J. Grabis & D. Bork (Eds.), *The Practice of Enterprise Modeling* (pp. 25–40). Springer International Publishing. DOI: https://doi.org/10.1007/978-3-030-63479-7_3.

Rousseau, D. M. (1989). Psychological and implied contracts in organizations. *Employee Responsibilities and Rights Journal*, *2*(2), 121–139. DOI: https://doi.org/10.1007/BF01384942.

Russell, S., & Norvig, P. (2020). Artificial Intelligence: A Modern Approach (4th edition). Pearson.

Sivathanu, B., & Pillai, R. (2018). Smart HR 4.0 – how industry 4.0 is disrupting HR. *Human Resource Management International Digest*, *26*(4), 7–11. DOI: https://doi.org/10.1108/HRMID-042018-0059.

Subramanian, R., & Rao, A. (2019, June 24). How to build disruptive strategic flywheels. *Strategy+ Business*, *19*.

Tuffaha, M., Perello-Marin, M. R., & Suarez-Ruz, E. (2022). Key elements in transferring knowledge of the AI implementation process for HRM in COVID-19 times: AI consultants' perspective. *International Journal of Business Science & Applied Management*, *17*(1), 81–97

Volkmar, G., Fischer, P. M., & Reinecke, S. (2022). Artificial Intelligence and Machine Learning: Exploring drivers, barriers, and future developments in marketing management. *Journal of Business Research*, *149*, 599–614. DOI: https://doi.org/10.1016/j.jbusres.2022.04.007.

Udemy (2020). Workplace Learning Trends Report: the Skills of the Future. Retrieved September 24, 2021, from https://business.udemy.com/resources/5-workplacelearning-trends-2020/.

Williamson, B. (2020). New digital laboratories of experimental knowledge production: Artificial intelligence and education research. London Review of Education. DOI: https://doi.org/10.14324/LRE.18.2.05.

Wodecki, A. (2019). Influence of artificial intelligence on activities and competitiveness of an organization. In *Artificial Intelligence in Value Creation* (pp. 133–246). Palgrave Macmillan, Cham.

Sunita Malhotra, People Insights, Belgium

Rebecca Griffiths, GriffithsHuntPR, UK

Workplace Coaching and Mentoring

Abstract: Coaching and Mentoring have been considered integral to business for the last 30 years. As of 2019, it was estimated that 71 % of Fortune 500 companies were running mentoring schemes (Association for Talent Development, 2019) and that there were 71,000 professional coach practitioners worldwide (International Coach Federation, 2020). Despite this, it is important to re-examine what mentoring and coaching are and how they can be carried out for maximum impact, in the light of the monumental hurdles managers at all levels face in the twenty-first century. Research by the CEMS Global Alliance in Management Education (CEMS, 2021) found that the COVID-19 crisis and the subsequent acceleration of digital capability globally reshaped markets, rapidly accelerated the rate of technological progress, broke supply chains, dismantled business models and affected a global sea-change in the way that we do business, communicate, work and in our attitudes to the work that we do. Combined with shifts already in motion, including the widening diversity of the workforce, globalisation, environmental challenges, increased hunger for learning and changing expectations of the millennials, it seems as though successful modern-day managers must be akin to superheroes. In this chapter we examine the key elements of successful coaching and mentoring, suggesting how companies can remove restrictive twentieth-century shackles, to meet the multifaceted challenges facing modern day managers.

Keywords: Coaching, Mentoring, Management, Leadership, Post-COVID, Definition of Twenty-First-Century Coaching and Mentoring

The Changing Face of Coaching and Mentoring

Mentoring has roots in Ancient Greece, when Odysseus, the King of Ithaca, entrusted the education of his son to his friend Mentor while he fought in the Trojan war. Although references to mentoring have been found in print in English since 1750 (Boswell, 2016), the concept became a core part of business language by the mid-1980s and has continued to be integrated in professional literature into the twenty-first century. However, the twentieth-century model of mentoring, broadly speaking, involved an older, experienced mentor advising a younger mentee.

Coaching came into its own in the 1960s and 70s; in particular contemporary coaching was underpinned by the theories of Abraham Maslow (Maslow, 1968), who believed that people had an urge to achieve their full potential, and of Carl Rogers, the psychologist behind modern-day client-based therapy (Rogers, 1978). Timothy Gallwey later proposed the concept of the 'inner game' in his *Inner Series* books – originally applied to sports such as Tennis and Skiing, but later adopted by the global business community – in which he suggested that the 'inner game' of a player, or psychological attitude, was as important as the 'external game' or physical skill (Gallwey, 2001). Following the publication of John Whitmore's book Coaching for Performance (Whitmore, 1992), executive coaching started to burgeon in the UK toward the end of the twentieth century. Corporates adopted Whitmore's GROW Model widely – an acronym for Goal, Reality, Options, and Will – and the concept of business coaching has steadily gained momentum since then.

Distinctions between Mentoring and Coaching

As David Clutterbuck's model depicts (Clutterbuck, 2011), while coaching and mentoring share many similarities, it is also essential to distinguish between the two disciplines to ensure success. Confusion often arises when language is used loosely in companies to describe the two concepts in relation to professional development. Fundamentally, both mentoring and coaching help individuals to implement long-lasting changes, through commitment to action, both at work and in life. Proficient questioning techniques, observation skills and listening skills are essential to ensure success. However, there are crucial distinctions that must be made in order that an individual does not lose out on the benefits of coaching and/or mentoring. For example, Boston University researchers discovered that mentoring can be a strong antidote to stress from trauma – extremely valuable for moving deep into emotional and personal issues which might be impacting work and life (Kram & Hall, 1989). A coaching setting may be completely inappropriate for tackling this kind of personal issue.

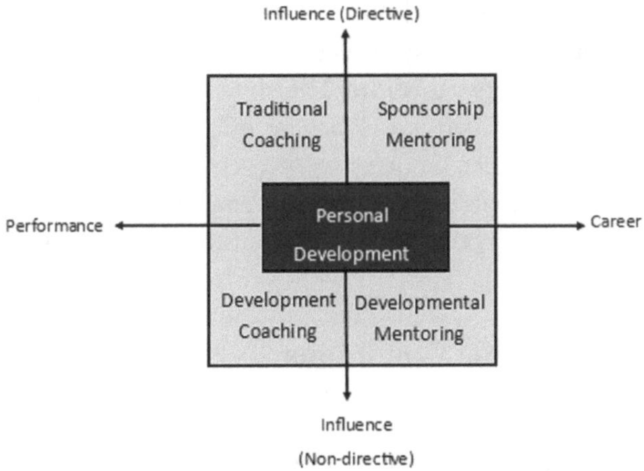

Figure 1. Comparison of Mentoring and Coaching according to David Clutterbuck

Mentoring is all about focusing on the individual. It is a sounding board – a long-term two-way exchange about learning, development, and life, with no agenda. Coaching on the other hand is performance-focused, often driven by a specific agenda – typically about job or task competence, behaviours, and skills. Coaching can either be one-off or long-term: typically formal, as opposed to the informal two-way exchange of mentoring. In the next section, we expand more on these two concepts.

Mentoring

According to David Clutterbuck and David Megginson, mentoring is 'off-line help by one person to another in making significant transitions in knowledge, work or thinking' (Clutterbuck & Megginson, 1999).

Mentoring is a long-term, flexible, informal, two-way exchange of real learning, for development and building networks. American politician John C Crosby was quoted saying that 'mentoring is a brain to pick, an ear to listen, and a push in the right direction' (Crosby, n.d.), while a quote from motivational speaker and author Zig Ziglar summarizes mentoring outcomes brilliantly: 'A lot of people have gone further than they thought they could because someone else thought they could' (Ziglar, n.d.).

Mentoring in its traditional sense enables an individual to follow in the path of an older and more experienced colleague who can pass on knowledge or secure career progression. The shift to collective leadership and ecosystems-thinking which we elaborate on later in this chapter means mentoring can no longer be one way. Reverse mentoring is also an efficient tool for sharing knowledge, creating engagement, developing leadership and, building intergenerational relations based on mutual acceptance (Gadomska-Lila, 2020).

Successful Mentoring Conditions

Meticulous Matching

Mentor-mentee matching must be executed meticulously by companies. Choosing a mentor or being matched have both been proven to be effective strategies depending on the nuances of the situation. Analysis by the University of Sydney of an academic mentoring programme pointed to the importance of two factors in the pairing process: personal connections and facilitation (Bell, 2011). Successful mentors are willing and able to commit time and energy. They are knowledgeable and experienced individuals with good listening skills who can act as a sounding board while being non-judgmental and sensitive to the needs of others. At the same time, they are honest and candid – able to give positive, constructive feedback to help others develop their career and create networks. Importantly they are self-aware, with an innate ability to navigate in an organisation's culture and operate with high levels of integrity (Zachary & Fischler, 2009).

In turn, mentees are able to take initiative; willing to commit as much time and energy as their mentor, and able to set clear goals and follow through on them. They are good listeners and communicators, open to receiving and giving feedback, and eager to learn and share. Self-awareness of strengths and weaknesses is crucial for the mentor and the mentee alike. Mentees need to be risk-takers, willing to step out of their comfort zone, and build relationships through disclosing (People Insights, 2021).

Confidentiality

Confidentiality is key to creating successful conditions for mentoring. According to David Clutterbuck, successful mentoring 'is about confidence – trust in the other person's discretion and judgement. The greater the level of co-confidence, the higher the level of honesty and personal disclosure within the mentoring conversations' (Clutterbuck, 2013).

Adequate Training

Without training for mentors and mentees, the process can become an informal 'chat,' rather than a two-way exchange of real learning which leads to growth and development.

Regular Check-ins

Without regular pulse surveys and opportunities to take the temperature of a relationship, the relationship will fall flat, and growth will be stunted.

Evaluation

Mentoring is directed at learning, whilst coaching at outcomes. Without continuously assessing what is working well and what is not, it is not possible to draw valuable learnings from the mentoring experience.

Mentoring myths

1. **The mentor must always be more senior to the mentee.** Jordan and Sorrell document how reverse mentoring (which pairs younger employees with executives to mentor them around cultural and strategic issues) can be extremely effective in the retention of the millennials, sharing digital skills, driving company culture, and promoting diversity (Jordan & Sorrell, 2019).
2. **The mentoring relationship must be mentor-driven.** Mentoring is a two-way street, so it is possible for a mentee to drive the relationship if that is appropriate for the given situation.
3. **Mentoring leads to immediate results or to a job.** Mentoring is focused on long-term outcomes.
4. **Mentoring is 'chatting.'** Sharing experience via conversation is not mentoring. Structured learning is essential in addition to maintaining momentum.

5. **Mentoring is easy and does not take time.** On the contrary, becoming a mentor or mentee takes large amounts of time investment and commitment.

Coaching

According to experienced international executive coach-mentor Eric Parsloe, successful coaching results in learning and development as well as improvement of performance. To be effective a coach requires understanding of process as well as styles, skills, and techniques appropriate to the context in which the coaching takes place (Parsloe, 1999).

In their book Coaching in Organizations, authors Madeleine Homan Blanchard and Linda Miller of The Ken Blanchard Companies say: 'coaching is a deliberate process using focused conversations to create an environment that results in accelerated performance and development' (Miller & Blanchard, 2017).

Coaching focuses on accelerated performance in both the immediate and longer-term, with a specific business, organisation or people agenda. It is a formal relationship usually initiated by a company, which can involve a one-off event or ongoing continuous development around a specific task or competence.

In a business environment, where agility and self-leadership are key, the traditional directive approach – explaining and demonstrating a new approach or skill for your coachee to copy and implement – is no longer so relevant. Just as quality guru Joseph Juran coined the phrase 'the vital few and the trivial many' to describe the Pareto principle (Juran, n.d.), which states that 80 percent of desired results are driven by a vital 20 % of actions, so a coach should only look to direct 20 % of the time, letting the coachee guide the majority of learning.

Often coaches feel that they can fix a specific issue, when in fact they cannot. Guided Coaching (a model which we explain later in the chapter) is an approach that allows coachees to discover the answers for themselves, eventually becoming 'self-coaches' and – ironically – making the original coach redundant (Malhotra, 2021).

Coaching models

A wealth of literature exists on key coaching models and systems. According to The Center for Creative Leadership Handbook of Coaching in Organisations, the components of an integrated coaching system are Executive Coaching, Mentoring, Peer Coaching, HR Coaching, Manager as Coach, Digital Goal Tracking & Reminder Systems and Team & Group Coaching. These elements help learners ensure that learning does not stay in the classroom, but is effectively applied in the workplace, sustaining increased performance and lasting change (Riddle, 2015).

In addition, five of the top major coaching models are:

1. GROW – created by Sir John Whitmore in the 1980s, the GROW model provides a basic understanding of how to structure training sessions (Whitmore, 1992).
2. FUEL – another useful coaching model which involves the use of open-ended questions instead of leading questions in four steps (Peak Performance Center, n.d.).
3. OSKAR – based on a solution-focused approach (Insoo Kim Berg, 2004).
4. CLEAR – developed by Peter Hawkins the CLEAR model helps clients with transformational change (Hawkins, 2007).
5. STEPPPA – this model is based on the fact that behaviour is a result of our emotions (Austerity Health, 2020).

Successful Coaching Conditions

A study by Jack Zenger and Joseph Folkman asked 3761 leaders to rate their coaching skills. When this was compared with the rating of team members, the leaders who had rated their coaching skills highly were seen as ineffective by team members (Zenger & Folkman, 2016). This example demonstrates the common disconnect between perceived and actual coaching skills, which leads to the failure of coaching. As such, coaching conditions for both parties involved are vital. The process for successful coaching is depicted in our diagram below.

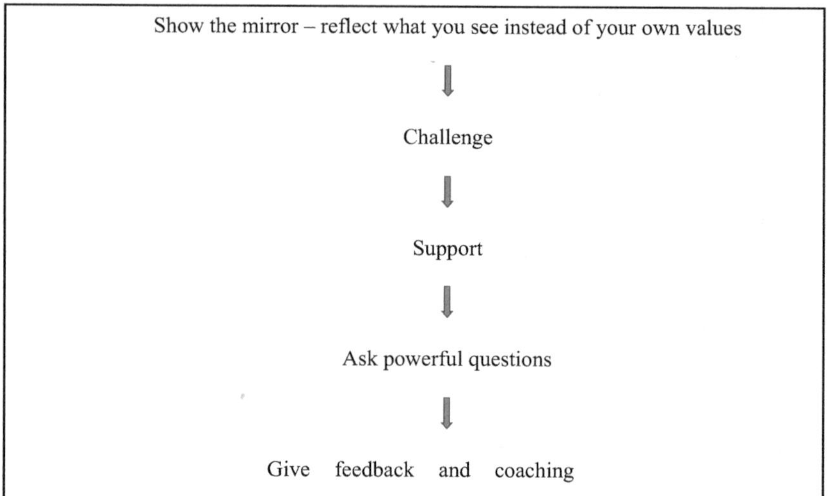

Source: (Malhotra & Griffiths, 2021).

Figure 2. The process for successful coaching

Feedback is an integral part of coaching. Unless you coach someone on how to fix an issue then feedback is pointless as more often than not people know what the problem is, but not how to fix it.

The following ingredients provide the optimum conditions for successful coaching:

Motivation

Individuals must have the innate desire to be coached and are both self-motivated and self-aware around specific areas for development. A key question to ask at the beginning of a coaching experience is whether or not a coachee would pay for development out of their own pocket (People Insights, 2021). In his motivator-hygiene theory Frederick Herzberg describes growth factors (or *motivators*) as 'achievement, recognition for achievement, the work itself, responsibility, and growth or advancement' (Herzberg, Mausner, & Snyderman, 1959). If a coachee feels coerced into coaching by senior management without taking personal responsibility – a typical workplace phenomenon – the coaching experience is set to fail.

Concrete desired outcomes must be framed in positive language from the outset to make the coaching experience sustainable in the long term. Questions could be: What feedback will you be getting from others when you have achieved your development goal? What will team members be saying about you that they are not saying today? What will you be feeling if you achieve your aims? The measures must be so real that coachees can visualize and sense successful outcomes (People Insights, 2021).

Focus on One Thing

Less is more when it comes to coaching, so it is crucial to start with one area for development and then move forward. The research found that people who tried to achieve multiple goals were less likely to succeed than those who focused on a single goal (Dalton & Spiller, 2012), suggesting that if you wish to master a particular habit you must focus on one thing at a time.

Development of Strengths not Weaknesses

Remedial coaching does not work. When managers have several balls to juggle at once, it is too easy to settle for developing weaknesses or 'problem areas.' However, this is a draining experience for both parties involved. Instead of developing talent by developing weaknesses, coaching must unleash the full potential of individuals and harness strengths, as defined by Marcus Buckingham, originator of the strengths movement, who challenges and inspires people to find and apply their strengths for success both in work and life (Buckingham, 2007).

Openness to Other People's Map of Reality

Polish-American scientist and philosopher Alfred Korzybski first remarked that 'the map is not the territory' describing the relationship between reality and the representation of reality (Korzybski, 1933). This has since been translated into a concept central to Neuro-Linguistic Programming (NLP), explaining that the map of the world we may have in our minds is just a reflection of our beliefs and that others may hold alternate views (Schneider, 2011). If the coach believes the world is wonderful, whilst the coachee is pessimistic, it is not the coach's job to pour optimism onto the fire of negativity; rather to interrogate compassionately to find out why the coachee sees the world that way and try to understand it.

Effective Stakeholder Management

Ensuring that stakeholders – including the most senior leaders – are aligned on what coaching success looks like from the outset is crucial, for companies to harness the power of neurodiversity. A survey in 2014 of executive and business coaches, organisations and clients found considerable agreement among participants on the benefit of multi-stakeholder contracting, where stakeholders other than the coach and coachee have a say in setting outcomes. (Turner & Hawkins, 2016)

A common example in leadership coaching is that desired outcome for stakeholders is 'gravitas' or 'leadership presence.' In this sense gravitas equals extrovert. Fundamentally, if a person being coached is introverted, they will not change, however, they can have gravitas in a more understated manner, so it is important to be clear on what the term gravitas means in both coachee and senior leaders' minds. Although coaching can change behaviour, it cannot transform someone into a different person (People Insights, 2021).

Definition of Clear Milestones

Setting well-defined checkpoints at every step of the coaching journey, in order to involve key stakeholders in the process, is the difference between a good, average and poor coach. Humans are hardwired to resist change (Pennington, 2018). Often when participant behaviour changes as a result of coaching, colleagues lament that the person is different and effectively mourn for the person they once were, which is an enormous setback for the coachee. It is essential that outcomes are laid out clearly, checkpoints defined, and measures of success are abundantly clear as part of pre-coaching.

Coaching myths

1. **Coaching is only for those with performance issues** – Days of remedial coaching are gone. Coaching is now about enhancing strengths.

2. **Anyone can coach – it is just asking questions.** Coaching has the capacity to destroy if carried out incorrectly, so effective coaching is an ethical responsibility. Just as a study of athletes proved that poor coaches engendered self-doubt, demotivated, and divided the team, the same can be applied to the workplace context. (Gearity & Murray, 2011).
3. **Coaching takes a long time.** In fact, so long as it is targeted, coaching can be brief. Many companies embrace corridor coaching, check-ins and coaching via Slack – the messaging and communication tool for business – around bite-sized insights.
4. **You need to be a 'rock star' to coach one.** It is possible to coach someone without the same experience. The key is the ability to ask the right questions.
5. **You can coach someone even if they are not willing.** If someone does not want to change their behaviour, there is nothing you can do to help them.

Coaching and Mentoring to Meet Modern Challenges

CEMS research examining the future of leadership in a post-COVID-19 world, outlines how there has been an accelerated shift from the rigid structure and systems that have long characterized organisations and models of leadership to something more flexible, open, and agile – new models of collective leadership and management that are predicated on inclusivity, empathy, tolerance of failure, growth mindset and openness in communication (CEMS, 2021).

What is certain in this climate is that coaching and mentoring are more important than ever before. A University of Amsterdam study published in the Journal of Positive Psychology found that 'coaching has significant positive effects on performance and skills, well-being, coping, work attitudes and goal directed self-regulation' and that 'coaching is an effective tool for improving the functioning of individuals in organisations.' (Theeboom, 2013, p. 12).

Rebecca Jones and her associates (Jones, Woods, & Guillaume, 2016) carried out a **meta-analysis** (a statistical analysis that combines the results of multiple scientific studies) to synthesise the to-date research on the **effectiveness** of workplace **coaching.** They considered solely workplace **coaching** provided by internal or external coaches. The **analyses** showed that **coaching** had positive effects on organisational outcomes and foremost on work attitudes and motivation (incl. self-efficacy, well-being, satisfaction) and development of skills (e.g., leadership skills, technical skills, or competencies). The findings indicated that **coaching** was more effective when conducted by internal coaches and when multisource feedback was excluded. Moreover, workplace **coaching** was effective whether conducted face-to-face or using blended techniques (i.e., blending face-to-face with e-**coaching**).

In turn, research by McInerney (McInerney, Giga, & Morris, 2021) revealed that enduring outcomes of executive coaching (the one for top management) are systematically identifiable in two distinctive domains: **'psychological resourcing'** (Coach as teacher, Building confidence, Metabolising the learning) and **'leader identity development'** (Intrinsic motivation, Work identity, and Mental reframing of relationship to subordinates), Reid and colleagues (2020) found that combining teaching and coaching (vs usage of either one or the other) in executive education provides a more holistic individualised learning experience thanks to incorporation of insights and methods from the other approach. Underhill (2006, pp. 292–307) made a systematic review of studies on the impact of **mentoring** for the mentee and the organisation. This quantitative meta-analytic review revealed overall effect of mentoring was significant and positive, **especially** on career outcomes for individuals. Individual career outcomes were analysed and reported. At the same time, the findings suggested informal **mentoring** produced a more significant impact on career outcomes than formal **mentoring**.

Just as the business world is transforming, coaching and mentoring must adapt to these significant global trends.

A Shift to Digital and Hybrid Working

Although the transition to digital working has been accelerating for a number of years, the 2020 pandemic acted as a catalyst, which according to McKinsey, has accelerated the digitization of their companies' customer and supply-chain interactions and of their internal operations by three to four years (McKinsey, 2020). In its Future of Jobs Report 2020, the World

Economic Forum estimates that 85 million jobs may be displaced while 97 million new roles may emerge across 26 countries by 2025 (World Economic Forum, 2020). Many companies, including Facebook, have stated they will permanently embrace virtual working, post-pandemic and it is unlikely that many organisations will go back to the traditional, 5-day a week office environment. Just as Microsoft announced in June 2020 that it would upskill 25 million people in digital skills by the end of that year in response to the challenges posed by COVID-19 (Microsoft, 2020), in the same way coaching and mentoring must upskill leaders at all levels for this unknown reality – skills including empathy, growth mindset and hunger for learning.

A Shift to Collective Leadership

'Unboss,' the term coined by Lars Kolind and Jacob Bøtter, combines age-old philosophies of servant leadership with innovative new ideas for the twenty-first-century leadership (Kolind & Bøtter, 2012). The principle of Unboss centres around letting go of twentieth-century hierarchies, relinquishing control and trusting others – give people passion and purpose in their work and they will thrive. Teams must work together, drawing on the strengths of all members to solve problems more complex than they have ever encountered. Such a shift to a collective leadership model builds on people's unique expertise and shares the burden of managing critical situations (Reiche et al., 2021). This shift means that coaching and mentoring should not only be from senior to junior but is also happening successfully in reverse because in progressive organisations everyone may be – at least temporarily – a leader. Experience is not as important as it was in the past when leaders were expected to have years of hard graft behind them, combined with an encyclopaedia of knowledge. Successful leaders no longer must have all the answers, but they do need to know how to ask the right questions. This means that coaching and mentoring can be collective – carried out by ALL members of the organisation (Malhotra, 2019).

Connected Learners within Ecosystems

Gallup (2019) research revealed that 21 % of the millennials changed jobs in 2018 and that six in ten were open to new job opportunities. Connected learning means understanding the skills that the market is demanding and demonstrating the benefit of acquiring these for both the present and future. Even though your talented people may not stay forever, the more skills you accompany them in acquiring via coaching, the more you will enable your ecosystem to flourish. Gartner uncovered that building connected learners makes employees vastly more engaged and boosts high performance (Gartner, 2019).

A Shift in Soft Skills Needed to Lead

Vulnerability and the ability to be more caring, and empathetic are critical post-pandemic leadership qualities (CEMS, 2021). This involves a deep understanding of how people function, their cultures, and their perspectives. A new generation of leaders will need to learn this in order to open their minds to new approaches. Within this emerging reality, coaching and mentoring must play an even more important role in enabling self-motivated next generation decision-makers to build the competencies, qualities, and resilience to weather current storms while preparing for the next inevitable crises.

Increased Hunger for Learning

LinkedIn Learning's report *Leading with Learning* found a 130 % increase in learning in 2020 with a 159 % increase **in CEO championship of Learning and Development**, whilst nearly 60 % agreed that learning made them more adaptable (LinkedIn Learning, 2020). In this climate, coaching and mentoring become even more important in satisfying the appetite for desired learning opportunities. Leaders equally must start learning for themselves before they can coach and mentor in a virtual, hybrid workplace.

The Need for Psychological Safety

Amy Edmondson spoke of the importance of psychological safety – an absence of interpersonal fear – during an interview with McKinsey (Edmondson, 2020). Crucially, organisations that can create an environment of psychological safety for employees will thrive in post-pandemic.

As such coaches and mentors must ensure that individuals at all levels also have space to experiment. The more psychologically safe the environment, the less fearful people will be of failure (Malhotra, 2021). Through her research, Edmondson has also discovered that where high levels of psychological safety and accountability intersect, learning and growth happen, creating a 'Learning Zone' (Edmondson, 1999). This safe environment enables people to give more open and honest feedback without fear of recrimination, which leads to openness to coaching and mentoring and a safe environment to experiment and take risks.

Greater Emphasis on Purpose, Values and Beliefs

Coachees or mentees must draw more deeply on purpose – strengths, weaknesses and what motivates them – to develop the agility and resilience to thrive in a digital, hybrid workplace (People Insights, 2021). This means that modern day coaches and mentors must go deeper on purpose, values, and beliefs – even in formal workplace coaching. NLP pioneer Robert Dilts' Logical Levels of Change Model – which explores the idea that 'any system of activity is a subsystem embedded inside of another system which is embedded inside of another system, and so on,' – is a powerful tool to help leaders identify what enables or limits the effectiveness and can be used to move below the surface of a coaching or mentoring relationship (Dilts, 2014).

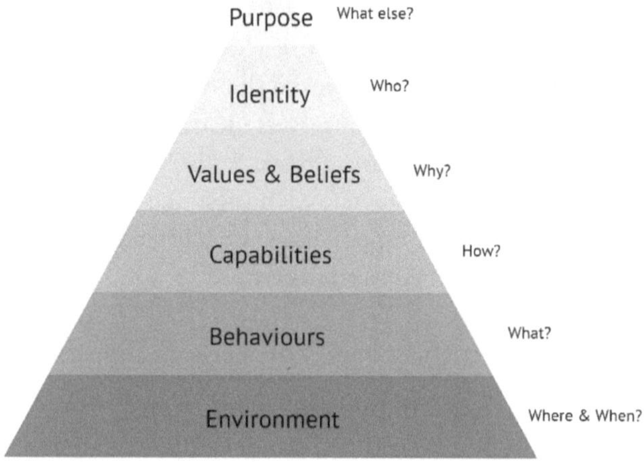

Figure 3. Dilts' Logical Levels of Change
Source: (Dilts, 2014).

Importance of Growth Mindset

The belief that if you work hard and persevere you can grow, initiated by Carol Dweck, has risen in prominence within the workplace over the past few years. According to Dweck, it is not just abilities that count, but whether we approach them with a fixed or growth mindset (Dweck, 2007). Growth mindset implies innate curiosity: that you can grow when things do not work out and always know there is more to achieve.

Growth mindset employees tend to be high performers because even though the work environment keeps changing, they are driven by an inner motivation to keep learning and growing. Conditions for modern-day coaching and mentoring must support employees in developing a growth mindset, by expanding belief boundaries and deepening their understanding of how beliefs and values are influencing their emotions. A coaching or mentoring culture that supports growth mindset is crucial to keeping performance levels high and expanding employee belief boundaries (Integrity Solutions, 2017).

Globalization

The rapid increase of globalization over the past few years has meant that managers interact with significantly different cultures on a daily basis: via international assignments or as part of remote global teams. An increasingly virtual world presents the challenges that cultural elements at play might not be obvious or easy to recognise. Hofstede's cultural dimensions theory provides a useful model in this respect, to show the effects of a society's culture on the values of its members, and how these values relate to behaviour (Hofstede, 1984).

For successful coaching and mentoring, coaches must take into consideration the cultural model. Leveraging cultural differences may mean recognition of different cultures; adaptation (not adoption); integration to evaluate situations from cultural perspectives yet stay focused on reality; leveraging differences for synergy (Law, 2013).

The Coaching and Mentoring Response

Below we suggest a 5Cs Approach for modern coaching and mentoring, which builds on lessons and models from the past to create a flexible, all-encompassing twenty-first-century method.

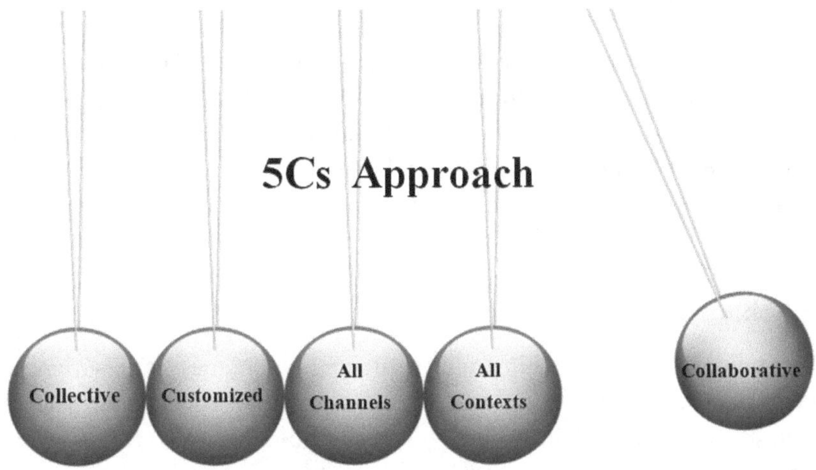

Figure 4. 5Cs Approach
Source: (Malhotra & Griffiths, 2021).

Collective

To satisfy increased hunger for learning and meet the need for a collective leadership environment, coaching and mentoring must also become collective – more fluid, carried out at all levels, inter-generationally, amongst ALL functions. Leaders must be also highly inclusive and learn from others with less leadership experience: coined 'humble heroes' and 'tech-savvy humanists' (Leinwand, Mani, & Sheppard, 2021). This inclusivity can aid the development of the soft skills modern-day managers need, including empathy and vulnerability.

Customized

In a hybrid, globalised environment, when purpose, values and beliefs are integral, individual customization becomes more important, because companies need to look at individual work rhythm to figure out how people work according to their preferences. In an insightful article for Harvard Business Review *How to do Hybrid Right,* Lynda Gratton (2021) discusses how Equinor, the Norwegian energy company, has put together 9 composite personas based on interviews with employees; this can help to adapt coaching and mentoring to personality types. Brit Insurance has created a Brit Playbook, to identify new ways of working using diagnostic tools and hackathons to enable employees globally to share their working preferences. Ericsson has engaged employees in 'jams' which were conducted virtually during a 72-hour period to help design hybrid working arrangements. (Gratton, 2021). Each individual has their own Map of Reality (values, purpose and beliefs, and cultural filter) which is based on their experiences and culture. Hence, coaching/mentoring content should be adapted to the individual in question.

All Channels

The ability to adapt coaching and mentoring techniques both within and outside of the virtual space will become even more key (Schreyögg & Schmidt-Lellek, 2017) in an era when psychological safety and growth mindset are integral to success. Coaches are already starting to use virtual tools and ecosystems such as Coach Master, The Coach Space, The LearnScape and Avatar Coaching to enhance learner experiences.

All Contexts

Coaching in particular can be carried out everywhere, all the time. It can be practical and quick, or long and deep, going into root causes. It can be simple and embedded within everyday processes. It can encompass 2-minute coaching, 'nudge' coaching as well as 6–12 months programmes, both face-to-face and virtual. This strongly depends on individual preference. The more psychologically safe the environment, the more you can determine the appropriate context, through discovering where coachees feel most comfortable (People Insights, 2021). Netflix has been training managers to ask simple questions about what people need and what they are struggling with as part of everyday life, rather than creating a separate process. Staff give one another frank feedback and then use that within coaching to improve constantly as a matter of routine, using coaching tools and skills (Greenwood, 2021).

Collaborative

Quite simply, when all the above exist it creates a climate of collaboration within the organisation: between coach and coachee; mentor and mentee; within teams; at all levels of the organisation. The more connected learning we have, the more engaged employees can be and that will lead to a collaborative environment, which boosts high performance (Gartner, 2019).

Guided Coaching

Coaching can be directive or Guided. As discussed earlier in the chapter, in the light of modern leadership challenges, 80 % should be Guided. Through Guided Coaching individuals find answers, take responsibility for unearthing solutions, and apply that learning to new situations, developing the agility needed within a Volatile Uncertain Complex, and Ambiguous (VUCA) world. The coaching role is to guide the learning process and help the individual to self-learn through clever questioning, including a balance of clear and specific feedback based on behavioural observations and concrete coaching.

Guided Coaching Approach in 7 Steps (People Insights, 2021):

Feedback:

1. Set the Contract – ensure that both parties are ready and willing
2. Ask Individual to Self-assess
3. Provide Feedback from Observations

Coaching:

4. Ask Individual for their Own Ideas – how can they continue to improve on strengths?
5. Request Self-assessment, moving deeper into pros and cons of ideas
6. Leader can step in and offer extra ideas to add to step 5 from own experience
7. Decide on the Future Course of Action – mutual agreement

Case Studies[1]

Within this example, coaching takes place between a manager and their direct report, within a global organisation. The manager gives feedback and coaching using the seven steps of the Guided Coaching model.

Case Study 1 – Guided Coaching in Practice:

Florence and Joshua work in a large global firm. Joshua reports to Florence. He presented to the Executive Committee last week and it did not go well. Florence has called a meeting for feedback and coaching.

Step 1 – Set the Contract

Florence: Is this a good time to give you some feedback and coaching? Joshua: Yes, that would be excellent.

Step 2- Ask Individual to Self-Assess

1 All case studies are based on real People Insights coaching and mentoring cases.

Florence: How did you think you did in the presentation last week? What went well? What do you think you could have done differently?

Joshua: I thought I was concise and to the point. However, I don't feel that I answered the questions well.

Step 3 – Provide Feedback from Observations

Florence: I agree, I feel you effectively delivered the key points in a concise manner. Based on my observations (concrete example stated), I feel that you could answer the questions in a more concise manner. I feel you shared a lot of information per question.

Step 4 – Ask Individual for their Own Ideas

Florence: How do you feel you could be more effective in providing the information? What else might you consider answering questions even more effectively?

Joshua: I could keep details to a minimum and provide more only if asked for specific information. I could also restate my understanding of their question to be sure I fully got it before jumping to answer.

Step 5 – Request Self-assessment Moving into Pros and Cons

Florence: How might that help you to answer questions well? How might you encourage participation?

Joshua: I could make it more interactive by getting them to add to my understanding of the question. To encourage more participation, I could also break them into smaller groups to prepare questions and additional thoughts.

Florence: What are the pros and cons of breaking the audience into smaller groups? Joshua: A pro would be more engagement. A con would be that I would need more time, as smaller group exercises take time.

Step 6 – Leader Steps in to Offer Extra Ideas

Florence: Have you thought about having other members of the group co-present with you in future meetings? Would that help?

Joshua: That would make it more engaging as there would be more diversity.

Step 7 – Decide the Future Course of Action

Florence: How will you approach a similar situation in the future? What are the next steps given what we just discussed?

Joshua: I have another presentation next week and will change it to include a small group exercise and ask a colleague if they want to co-present.

Florence: That sounds like a plan. How can I support you further?

Joshua: I would like to meet again after the presentation for more feedback and coaching.

Florence: Ok done! All the best for your next meeting. Joshua: Thank you so much for today!

The coaching relationship is particularly effective within this case study as it aligns with the 5Cs: in particular it is Customized and Collaborative. The coach (manager) pays close attention the coachee's individual work rhythm, delivering helpful feedback and coaching and enabling him to determine a future course of action.

Case Study 2 – Coaching for Sustainable Results:

In the second example a very senior executive in a global organisation brings in an external coach to work on her customized content – her desired objective. The structured programme lasts 9–12 months and is carried out through a combination of virtual and face-to face sessions (5Cs model – Contexts, Channels, Customized).

Samantha recently started working with a coach to make her work and life even happier and more fulfilling.

The critical thing Samantha and her coach did in the first few meetings was help Samantha clearly articulate her Desired Outcome and define what success looked like in 'real life' in very practical terms. She focused on one thing and described it in vivid detail so she could almost touch and feel her desired outcome. In positive language this was:

'I have achieved a proper balance in my work and life which allows me to be happy and relaxed, and at the same time, feel fulfilled with my work accomplishments.'

A few of her measures were as follows:

- My husband and children will concretely see me more often, e.g., 3 times per week (vs once).

- People at work will see me smiling more (vs frowning).
- What I will not be doing = running between meetings.
- I will not be feeling my stomach churn as I drive home.
- My friends will say 'wow you have changed something in your life for the better.'

At the beginning of the coaching process the aim was to go deeper into Samantha's Values and Beliefs to find root causes of what was driving her mindset/behaviours today and why she was not able to find the proper balance. They did this over a period of 9–12 months using many different techniques and tools with the aim to make Samantha self-aware, find the root causes and then help her make the necessary changes for this to be sustainable, whilst remaining true to herself (i.e., not changing who she was as a person).

One of the main techniques was to go deeper into her Values and Beliefs through using Dilts' Logical Levels of Change Model. From this, she realised that one of her strong beliefs formed in her childhood was: 'I have to be Number One at everything I do; that means I have high standards and thus I am successful.'

In fact, this belief was making her stressed in everything she did, as she wanted to do things quicker and better than others to be Number One and feel successful. On reflection, all she wanted was a proper balance that allowed her to be happy and relaxed, and at the same time, feel fulfilled in her accomplishments. Her belief was limiting her from doing this.

The coach discussed with Samantha whether she would like to work on changing this belief at its root. The key thing was to check if she wanted to do that, to ensure that she would not lose anything good that came from that belief. Changing beliefs is deep and should not be taken lightly!

Samantha was excited to do so. Some of the key questions asked through a deeper process of changing beliefs were:

1 Have you always believed this?
2 Where did this belief come from?
3 Is it still valid?
4 What evidence do I have to support the belief?
5 Who do I know who holds the opposite belief?
6 What evidence suggests that this belief is untrue?
7 In what way is this belief absurd or ridiculous?

Through this process Samantha actually managed to change the belief that was stopping her, to a new one:

'I do the Best I can and be the Best I can; that means I have high standards and thus I am successful.'

Compared to her belief of being Number One, this was about doing the BEST she could. This fundamentally shifted her way of doing things, whilst still staying 'true' to herself, i.e., she worked and lived to the BEST of her ability.

Samantha was happy, relaxed, and felt fulfilled with her accomplishments. She worked for a few months on integrating this new Belief into every aspect of her life. She succeeded and has achieved her Desired Outcome. The change is sustainable and has become part of her everyday life.

The above case study demonstrates the 5Cs model working effectively alongside the Dilts model. The coach works with the coachee to move deeper into her values and beliefs to eventually achieve her Desired Outcome, making sure this is viable in the long term.

Mentoring Approach

The mentoring relationship is deeply individual and personal (People Insights, 2021).

Three key stages of mentoring contribute to the overall success (Zachary & Fischler, 2009). These three stages tie seamlessly into the 5Cs approach, as modern-day mentoring must always be Collective, Customized, through all Channels, in all Contexts and Collaborative.

1) **Getting Started – Preparing and Negotiating**

This involves the mentor reflecting on their own personal journey, who has guided them along the way and why they became a mentor in the first place. Only through this can a mentor support and guide the mentee in reflecting on their personal life journey and vision for future, in order to define what success looks like for the future and set SMART goals.

In the first few meetings the mentor and mentee must take time to get to know one other and talk about what mentoring means for both. They must determine relationship needs and expectations, agree on ground rules and discuss how to deal with confidential information & what topics/issues are outside scope of relationship (boundaries). Conversation also needs to touch briefly on how and when to close/end the relationship. A Mentoring

Agreement can be created as a result of the above. This demonstrates the 5Cs approach through Collaborative preparation by mentor and mentee.

2) **Maintaining Momentum – Enabling**

This involves creating a learning environment through reflecting on 'possible learning opportunities' for mentees that fit with their vision/goals and identifying together specific and concrete suggestions of actual learning opportunities. This stage should build & maintain relationship of trust through SMART communication:

- **Shared Meaning:** Clarify and confirm understanding on important issues, e.g., what success looks like on goals
- **Authenticity:** Speak your mind, disclose personal information, e.g., personal mistakes, confidentiality
- **Respect:** Mutual respect
- **Trust:** Be 'real' and honest, respect confidentiality

Managing barriers effectively may also be necessary by sharing failures and mistakes openly, keeping the focus on overall learning and how to get the most from the relationship, to ensure the relationship grows and barriers are addressed through effective listening and 2-way feedback. This demonstrates the 5Cs approach through Customized learning opportunities, Collective, Contexts and Channels.

3) **Coming to Closure**

The last stage of the mentoring relationship should examine whether there are additional things to talk about, making sure to prioritize and address them before end of the programme. Evaluation of the mentoring relationship is also important. What worked? What could have been better? Apply and integrate key learnings. Finally, celebration of the relationship is key, as well as time spent to determine the scope of the relationship after the programme (this creates a climate of Collaboration between the mentor and mentee in the long-term).

Case Study 3 – A Mentoring Story:

A medium sized company with offices around the world committed to building a mentoring programme, so brought in an external consultant to help them achieve this. The end result of this was 1000 mentoring pairs set up globally. The example below is based around the 'three key stages' mentoring approach, which by its Collaborative, Customized and Collective nature, ties seamlessly in with the 5cs.

Felix and Isabel were in a mentoring relationship. Felix was the mentor and Isabel the mentee. When they started, they had no idea what the difference was between coaching and mentoring. Luckily for them, their organisation had trained them both in mentoring.

Step 1 – Getting Started – Preparing and Negotiating

Felix and Isabel both prepared before they met the first time as they wanted to get a lot out of the relationship. Upfront questions were:

- What are the goals of our mentoring relationship and what will success look like?
- What do we expect from each other, i.e., ground rules, roles, attitudes?
- What could be possible barriers and solutions to overcome them?
- What are the 3–5 key actions we need to take to structure our interactions, in order to be on the right track?
- What are the possible areas/topics we could discuss?

Then they met for the first time, where they discussed their own preparation together and came up with a Mentoring Agreement, as a framework outlining answers to the above questions.

In the first few meetings they got to know each other, their personal styles and limitations and also very clearly discussed confidentiality and how to handle delicate matters as they were from the same organisation (i.e., if the mentee told the mentor they wished to leave the organisation, how would this be handled?).

Step 2 – Maintaining Momentum – Enabling

Felix and Isabel met regularly (once every three weeks as per their agreement) and used SMART communication.

Along the way they hit a few cultural and time barriers. Felix was very busy as he was travelling a lot for work and had other mentees, so Isabel took initiative to give feedback to Felix on this. This helped Felix to reprioritize and adjust how much time he was giving to Isabel.

Cultural issues also cropped up as Isabel, having lived in the Netherlands for quite a while, was used to sharing all her personal issues quite openly, whereas Felix was more guarded based on his own personal and cultural profile. They both decided to try to understand each others' cultures better through a cross-cultural questionnaire and discussion and resolved issues through being authentic, giving and asking for feedback.

Another way of maintaining momentum was ad hoc check-ins and recapping their learnings in a 'Learning Journal' outlining – what did I learn today? How will I apply what I have learned?

The check-ins entailed the following:

Relationship:

- Words to describe quality of our interaction
- What went well for us
- What we need to work hard at improving

Meeting:

- When our meeting was held
- What learning objectives we worked on
- Conditions that promoted learning

Learnings:

- One thing I learned about myself
- One thing I learned about my partner
- Personal Insights

They were in a mentoring relationship for a year before Isabel secured a role at another organisation, so they had a meeting to decide what to do in the future.

Step 3 – Coming to Closure

Felix and Isabel evaluated the mentoring relationship and talked about how they had applied and integrated new learnings. Because they really appreciated one another they decided that they would stay in touch with one another. Thus they 'closed' the mentoring relationship, but remained friends, even when Isabel had left the company.

5Cs within Coaching and Mentoring

As demonstrated by the case studies above, it is important to bear the 5Cs approach in mind when considering which model to follow as no single one is perfect, so any approach will require individual customization. Where an individual thrives on structure, a classic model may be necessary. If another requires greater flexibility a coach and mentor may need to mix and match elements of various models.

Conclusion

The Volatile, Uncertain, Complex and Ambiguous (VUCA) workplace climate of the 2020s is worlds apart from that of the hierarchical, structured, analogue twentieth century. Even the past five years have seen a monumental shift to hybrid collaboration between teams on a global scale; accelerated at high-speed by the COVID-19 pandemic, which vigorously forced everyone into the digital space in just a few weeks.

These days, although not every employee is a 'manager' by title, everyone must develop leadership skills within their own respective role if they hope to progress and thrive. As employees seek to develop essential skills, there is an increased hunger for continuous learning, at all levels of the organisation. Consequently, there is rising demand for relevant, frequent, bite-sized learning opportunities, which suit individual work/life patterns.

As we move forward apace into this uncharted territory, mentoring and coaching will be critical to the lifeblood of organisations; enabling managers to draw on their strengths, purpose, beliefs, and values, to navigate a changing landscape and develop an essential growth mindset.

For that reason, we must change the way in which we coach and mentor managers, as traditional *practices in coaching and mentoring do not meet the complex requirements of this new reality*. We must cast aside the rigid, directive, top-down, structured remnants of the twentieth century, moving to a flexible, guided, collaborative, personalised approach, which suits the needs and patterns of the modern-day professional. The alternative is losing talented managers to unscrupulous competitors, who can coach and mentor far more effectively.

This is where the 5Cs approach comes in. We have refrained from labelling it a model, because it is impossible to be fully prescriptive: every single mentoring and coaching relationship has to be taken on it own merit, according to individual needs and learning styles. Nevertheless, the 5Cs sets out guidelines for the successful modern-day coaching and mentoring relationship. Mentoring and coaching must be Collective, across all levels and generations; Customized to the individual; delivered through All Channels; in All Contexts. Importantly it must be Collaborative – a true two-way partnership between the two respective parties. The case studies at the end of the chapter illustrate three different scenarios in which the 5Cs have been deployed alongside other techniques, for the benefit of the individual as well as the organisation.

Building the right conditions for mentoring and coaching relationships using the 5Cs as a guide, drawing on successful aspects of the past and knowledge of new skills required, will build strong foundations for organisations and their managers within this new and challenging reality.

References

Association for Talent Development. (n.d). Retrieved from https://www.td.org/.

Austerity Health. (2020, June 1). *Top 5 Major Coaching Models Every Coach Should Know*. Retrieved from Austerity Health: https://austerityhealth.org/top-5-major-coaching-models/.

Bell, A. (2011). Looking for Professor Right: Mentee selection of mentors in a formal mentoring program. *Higher Education 61*(5), 545–561.

Boswell, B. J. (2016, April 19). Historical Print Context of the Term, 'Mentoring'. *Mentoring & Tutoring: Partnership in Learning, 24(1)*, 1–7.

Buckingham, M. (2007). *Go Put Your Strengths to Work: Six Powerful Steps to Achieve Outstanding Performance*. Simon & Schuster. Retrieved from Marcus Buckingham: https://www.marcusbuckingham.com/.

CEMS. (2021). *A Guide to Leadership in a Post-Pandemic World*. Paris: CEMS.

Clutterbuck, D., & Megginson, D. (1999). *Mentoring Executives & Directors*. Butterworth-Heinemann Ltd.

Clutterbuck, D. (2011). *Challenges for coaches: those you see and those you don't*. Retrieved from https://slideplayer.com/slide/7450994/.

Clutterbuck, D. (2013). *What do we mean by confidentiality in mentoring?* Retrieved from Clutterbuck Partnership: https://davidclutterbuck partnership.com/what-do-we-mean-by-confidentiality-in-mentoring/.

Crosby, J. C. (n.d.). Coaching and mentoring partnership. https://www.coachingandmentoringpartnership.co.uk/public/documents/more_inf ormatio n_mentoring.pdf

Dalton, A. N., & Spiller, S. A. (2012). Too Much of a Good Thing: The Benefits of Implementation Intentions Depend on the Number of Goals. *Journal of Consumer Research*.

Dilts, R. B. (2014). *A Brief History of Logical Levels*. Retrieved from NLPU: http://www.nlpu.com/Articles/LevelsSummary.htm

Dweck, C. (2007). *Mindset: the New Psychology of Success (Reprint Edition)*. Ballantine Books.

Edmondson, A. (1999, June). Psychological Safety and Learning Behavior in Work Teams. *Administrative Science Quarterly, 44*(2), 350–383.

Edmondson, D. A. (2020, July 2). Psychological safety, emotional intelligence, and leadership in a time of flux. https://www.mckinsey.com/featured-insights/leadership/psychological-safety-emotional-intellige nce-and-leadership-in-a-time-of-flux

Gadomska-Lila, K. (2020). Effectiveness of reverse mentoring in creating intergenerational relationships. *Journal of Organizational Change Management, 33*(7), 1313–1328.

Gallup. (2019). *Millenials: The Job-Hopping Generation*. Gallup.

Gallwey, W. T. (2001). *The Inner Game of Work: Focus, Learning, Pleasure, and Mobility in the Workplace*. Random House.

Gartner. (2019). *Connected Learners: A Better Approach to Bridging the Skills Gap*. Gartner.

Gearity, B. T., & Murray, M. A. (2011, June). Athletes' experiences of the psychological effects of poor coaching. *Psychology of Sport and Exercise, 12*(2), 213–221.

Gratton, L. (2021, May-June). *How to do Hybrid Right*. Retrieved from Harvard Business Review: https://hbr.org/2021/05/how-to-do-hyb rid-righ.

Greenwood, A. (2021, February 10). *The 4 Netflix HR Practices That Took Us from Average to Awesome*. Retrieved from Process.St: https://www.process.st/hr-practices/

Hawkins, P. (2007). *Coaching, Mentoring and Organizational Consultancy: Supervision and Development*. Open University Press.

Herzberg, F., Mausner, B., & Snyderman, B. B. (1959). *The Motivation to Work*. New York: John Wiley & Sons.

Hofstede, G. (1984). *Culture's Consequences: International Differences in Work-Related Values (2nd ed.)*. Beverley Hills CA: SAGE publications.

Homer. (n.d.). *The Odyssey*.

Insoo Kim Berg. (2004). *What is the Solutions Focused Approach?* Retrieved from The Solutions Centre: https://www.solutions-centre.org/what-is-the-solution-focused-approach/

Integrity Solutions. (2017, January 25). *How a Growth Mindset Culture Keeps Performance Levels High*. Retrieved from Integrity Solutions. https://www.integritysolutions.com/insights/blog/growth-mindset-coaching-culture-keeps-performance-levels-high.

International Coach Federation. (2020). *2020 ICF Global Coaching Study*. ICF.

Jordan, J., & Sorrell, M. (2019, October 03). *Why Reverse Mentoring Works and How to Do it Right. Harvard Business Review*. https://hbr.org/2019/10/why-reverse- mentoring-works-and-how-to-do-it-right.

Jones, R. J., Woods, S. A., & Guillaume, Y. R. (2016). The effectiveness of workplace coaching: A meta-analysis of learning and performance outcomes from coaching. *Journal of occupational and organizational psychology*, *89*(2), 249–277.

Juran, J. M. (n.d.). Retrieved from Juran: https://www.juran.com/.

Kolind, L., & Bøtter, J. (2012). *Unboss*. Jyllands-Postens Forlag.

Korzybski, A. (1933). *Science and Sanity. An Introduction to Non-Aristotelian Systems and General Semantics*. Institute of GS.

Kram, K., & Hall, D. T. (1989). Mentoring as an antidote to stress during corporate trauma. *Human Resources Management, 28*(4), 493–510.

Law, H. (2013). *The Psychology of Coaching, Mentoring and Learning, 2nd Edition*. John Wiley & Sons.

Leinwand, P., Mani, M. M., & Sheppard, B. (2021, April 23). *6 Leadership Paradoxes for the Post-Pandemic Era*. Retrieved from *Harvard Business Review*. https://hbr.org/2021/04/6-leadership-paradoxes-for-the-post-pandemic-era.

LinkedIn Learning. (2020). *Leading with Learning: Insights and Advice About the New State of L&D*. LinkedIn Learning.

Malhotra, S. (2019, September 12). *The New Leadership Ethos for the 21st Century*. Retrieved from HRD Connect: https://www.hrdconnect.com/2019/09/12/the-new-leadership-ethos- for-the-21st-century/.

Malhotra, S. (2021, February 9). *How Leaders can Reframe Failure in a Post-Pandemic World*. Retrieved from Chief Learning Officer: https://www.chieflearningofficer.com/2021/02/09/how-leaders-can-reframe-failure-in-a-post-pandemic-world/.

Malhotra, S., & Griffiths, R. (2021). 5Cs Approach for Coaching and Mentoring. Unpublished manuscript.

Maslow, A. (1968). *Toward a Psychology of Being, 2nd Ed.* New York: D. Van Nostrund.

McInerney, E., Giga, S., & Morris, A. S. (2021). Does it last? A systematic review of the enduring effects on managers from executive coaching. *International Coaching Psychology Review*, *16*(2), 22–50.

McKinsey. (2020). *How COVID-19 has pushed companies over the technology tipping point—and transformed business forever*. McKinsey.

Microsoft. (2020, June 30). *Microsoft launches initiative to help 25 million people worldwide acquire the digital skills needed in a COVID-19 economy*. Retrieved from Microsoft: https://blogs.microsoft.com/blog/2020/06/30/microsoft-launches-initiative-to-help-25-million-people-worldwide-acquire-the-digital-skills-needed-in-a-covid-19-economy/.

Miller, L., & Homan, M. (2017). *Coaching in Organizations*. CreateSpace Independent Publishing Platform.

Parsloe, E. (1999). *The Manager as Coach and Mentor*. McGraw-Hill Education.

Peak Performance Center. (n.d.). *Fuel Coaching Model*. Retrieved from Peak Performance Center: https://thepeakperformancecenter.com/development-series/skill-builder/interpersonal/coaching-for-performance/coaching-model/fuel-coaching-model/.

Pennington, C. (2018, April 03). *We are Hardwired to Resist Change*. Retrieved from Emerson HC: https://www.emersonhc.com/change-management/people-hard-wired-resist-change

People Insights. (2021). Retrieved from People Insights: https://peopleinsights.eu/home.html.

Reiche, B. S., Mendenhall, M. E., Szkudlarek, B., & Osland, J. S. (2021). At the Heart and Beyond: What Can Global Leadership Researchers Learn from Perspectives on the COVID-19 Pandemic? *Advances in Global Leadership*. Emerald Publishing Limited.

Reid, A., Cook, J., Viedge, C., & Scheepers, C. B. (2020). Developing management effectiveness: The nexus between teaching and coaching. *The International Journal of Management Education*, *18*(1), 100334.

Riddle, D. (2015). Creating an Integrated Coaching System. In D. Riddle, E. Hoole, & E. Gullette, *The Center for Creative Leadership Handbook of Coaching in Organizations* (pp. 49–81). Wiley.

Rogers, C. (1978). *On Personal Power: Inner Strength and Its Revolutionary Impact*. Robinson. Schneider, N. (2011, August 18). *The Map is not the Territory*. Retrieved from Global NLP Training: https://www.globalnlptraining.com/blog/the-map-is-not-the-territory/

Schreyögg, A., & Schmidt-Lellek, C. (2017). *The Professionalization of Coaching*. Springer.

Theeboom, T. (2013). Does coaching work? A meta-analysis on the effects of coaching on individual level outcomes in an organizational context. *The Journal of Positive Psychology*, 9(1), 1–18.

Turner, E., & Hawkins, P. (2016). Multi-stakeholder contracting in executive/business coaching: An analysis of practice and recommendations for gaining maximum value. *International Journal of Evidence Based Coaching and Mentoring*, *14*(2), 48–65.

Underhill, C. M. (2006). The Effectiveness of Mentoring Programs in Corporate Settings: A Meta-Analytical Review of the Literature. *Journal of Vocational Behavior*, *68*(2), 292–307.

Whitmore, S. J. (1992). *Coaching for Performance: The Principles and Practice of Coaching and Leadership*. Nicholas Brealey Publishing.

World Economic Forum. (2020). *Future of Jobs Report 2020*. World Economic Forum.

World Health Organisation. (2016). Scaling-up treatment of depression and anxiety: a global return on investment analysis. *Lancet Psychiatry*. Retrieved from https://www.who.int/news/item/13-04-2016-investing-in-treatment-for-depression-and- anxiety-leads-to-fourfold-return.

Zachary, L. J., & Fischler, L. A. (2009). *The Mentee's Guide: Making Mentoring Work for You*.

Zenger, J., & Folkman, J. (2016, June 23). People Who Think They're Great Coaches Often Aren't. Retrieved from *Harvard Business Review*: https://hbr.org/2016/06/people-who- think-theyre-great-coaches-often-arent.

Ziglar, Z. (n.d.). Retrieved from Goodreads: https://www.goodreads.com/quotes/80212-a-lot-of-people-have-gone-further-than-they-though.

Edward Stanoch, nuChapter, Poland

Tiina Hoffman, Firstbeat, Finland

Health & Resilience: An Important Aspect of Leadership Development

Abstract: We will first discuss the concepts of health-promoting leadership and ideal performance state and then focus more closely on the role of personal stress management, recovery practices, and physical fitness, as well as effective habit formation, as core components of better physical and mental health. In the end, we will share a few case studies based on physiological data and coaching, to show how managers have been able to improve their health and performance on a very practical level. This kind of data and experience can be applied in the education process to support leaders' self-awareness and self-assessment.

Keywords: Health at Work, Resilience, Stress Management

1. Background & facts

'Health is essential for human performance and sustainable development.' The events of 2020 unexpectedly and brutally highlighted the importance of these words. The COVID-19 pandemic confronted all managers with one of the largest global health, social, and economic crises in the history of modern management. With skyrocketing numbers of infected people, prolonged lockdowns, blocked economies, and overloaded health-care systems, leaders and their organizations were exposed to unprecedented health concerns, uncertainty, anxiety, and high-stress levels. Unfortunately, we entered the pandemic with already growing numbers of lifestyle-related diseases, caused by smoking, unhealthy diet, physical inactivity, poor quality of sleep, and chronic work-related stress. According to the World Health Organization (2021), chronic diseases were directly related to 41 million deaths each year, accounting for 71 % of all deaths globally. With the additional health debt caused by the pandemic, these numbers will keep growing.

Nevertheless, with all its negative outcomes, the pandemic has elevated the significance of workplace well-being, especially in the field of physical and mental health, from a nice-to-have employee benefit to a critical business priority. According to Gallup's research (Harter, 2021), burnout increased significantly for managers in 2021, rising from 28 % in 2020 to the level of 35 %. Moreover, according to another global study (Greenwood & Kroll, 2020) conducted in April 2022, almost 42 % of respondents declared that their mental health had declined since the outbreak began. Unsurprisingly, employees seek and expect more support and assistance from their leaders in health-related issues, including the promotion of a health prevention culture and behaviors. This is an excellent opportunity for leaders to reshape their organizational culture to be more human-centric and become role models in health prevention and healthy lifestyle. With this approach and mindset, mutual benefits can be achieved both for employees and employers.

Health-promoting leadership

Health-promoting leadership can be defined as leadership that works to create a culture for health-promoting workplaces and values, and to inspire and motivate employee participation in such a development (Eriksson, 2011). As the research published in *Forbes* (Kohll, 2018) indicates, organizations whose leaders are role models in health prevention and work-life balance have higher average satisfaction rates with the offered well-being programs (85 %). There is also an increase in participation in pro-health diagnostic programs, which is key to identifying potential health risks in the organization. In addition, research shows that so-called health-promoting leadership (Yao, Li & Wildy, 2021):

- reduces health risks and occupational burnout,
- reduces sickness absence and related productivity losses,
- increases the attractiveness of the employer as a pro-health organization,
- increases the level of commitment, which translates into better business results,
- strengthens the resilience of the entire organization,
- reduces the costs of poor quality and wrong decisions that arise in situations of excessive workload, stress, and lack of adequate recovery.

Health-promoting leadership is not a new concept. At the end of the twentieth century, it received much attention from scholars and business management authors searching for an integrated theory of performance management that goes far beyond the traditional approach, where peak performance is purely related to cognitive capabilities and brainpower. In the search for a more holistic approach to human performance, the world of professional sports offered a great source of inspiration.

Ideal Performance State

Based on the experience from two decades of working with elite athletes (Groppel, Andelman & Loehr, 1999), performance psychologists came up with the concept of 'the Corporate Athlete' primarily dedicated to top executives to help them achieve and sustain their Ideal Performance State (IPS). According to this concept, IPS can be achieved by addressing, in a balanced way, four sources of vital human energy: physical, emotional, mental, and spiritual. These four constitute the performance pyramid (Figure 1), with overall fitness and physical well-being as its foundation. Each of the four areas influences the others, and failure to address any one of them impacts individual performance negatively.

Based on extensive research, the authors of this concept also concluded that effective personal energy management has two key components: 1) proper balance between energy expenditure (stress) and energy renewal (recovery) and 2) lifestyle habits/rituals that help to achieve this balance. When these principles are applied, sustainable growth can be achieved (Stress+Rest = Growth). Still, paradoxically, the corporate world often keeps pushing its employees to the edge of potential burnout, with a significant deficit of recovery that ultimately undermines business performance.

Thus, it has become essential to develop new skills for managing vital energy in parallel with developing a standard set of leadership competencies and skills to drive change on the individual as well as on the organizational level. To lead others, leaders should be role models in achieving their Ideal Performance State by identifying the habits that feed and energize them and those that stress and drain them. In the same way, they should be capable of viewing their employees' well-being holistically.

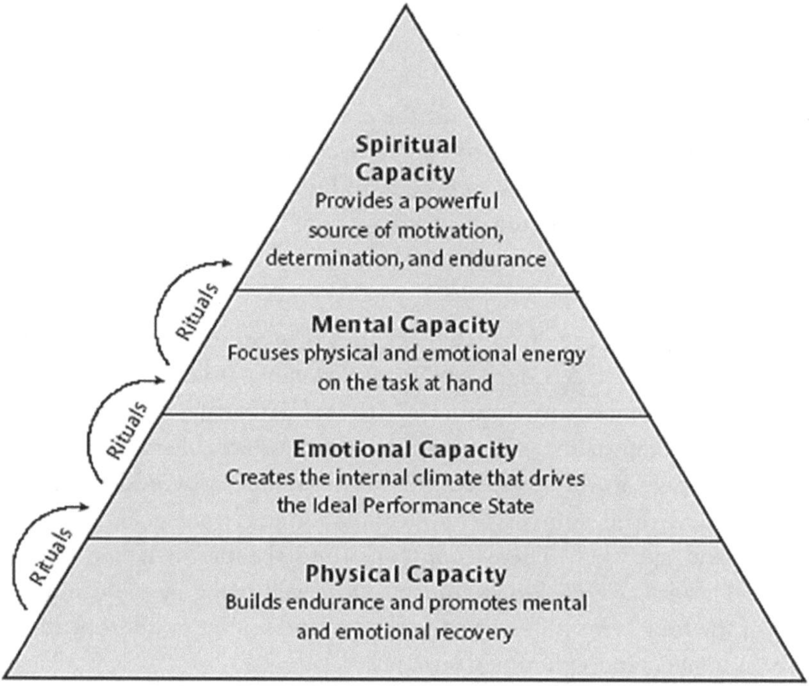

Figure 1. The High-Performance Pyramid (Lohr & Shwartz, 2001)

Leadership behavior has a significant impact on the behavior, well-being, and performance of employees. Apart from acting as a role model, four other related pathways can be identified, with the following potential outcomes:

1. Directly promote (or damage) employee health through healthy (unhealthy) habits/rituals.
2. Promote (or damage) employee health by designing work systems that reduce the pressure on employees and increase their resources.
3. Play a moderating role in the relationship between environmental factors and employee health.
4. Cultivate a healthy climate.

A better understanding of some basic aspects of human physiology and sources of vitality is a key starting point for health-promoting leadership and optimal performance, and next, we will focus on that.

2. Stress management, sleep, and physical fitness at the heart of performance

Excessive stress, lack of sleep, and poor fitness are associated with several physical and mental health problems. In the context of individual and organizational performance and the physical and mental health of managers, these are core topics that any manager looking to stay ahead of the curve cannot ignore. Understanding the basic facts behind these topics, supported by evidence from physiological data, can be helpful in the development of health-promoting leadership.

Understanding stress

Simply defined, stress is a physical response that helps us survive. When we face some kind of physical or mental stress, the body switches to a fight or flight mode (e.g., Cannon, 1915) and the sympathetic branch of the autonomic nervous system takes over: various hormones are released, heart rate and blood pressure increase, and blood flow is directed to where it is most needed. Psychologically, stress can be described as a situation where the demands that we are faced with are greater than the available resources (Lazarus & Folkman, 1984).

Chu and associates (Chu et al., 2022) state that the goal of a stress response is a restoration of homeostasis, but if this does not happen, and the stress response becomes chronic, it can lead to many health problems, such as heart disease, stomach ulcers, sleep problems, psychiatric disorders, and a weakened immune system. Exposure to chronic stress is also associated with burnout, depression, and anxiety (for a review, see Koutsimani, Montgomery, & Georganta, 2019).

Stress-related health issues are widespread. Stress is listed as the second most common health problem addressed by occupational healthcare providers in Europe, and in the EU area, 25 % of employees report that they experience negative work-related stress (European Community

2020). According to the American Institute of Stress (2022), an estimated 1 million workers are absent in the US every day due to excessive stress.

Even if a certain level of stress is acceptable and belongs to life, healthy stress management means that we learn to identify factors that cause stress, recognize harmful stress, and develop practical stress management strategies. This requires a holistic approach and is closely connected to the next part which looks at sleep and physical activity.

We need sleep

Sleep is a cornerstone of good health and one of the most obvious, yet undervalued aspects of human performance. Instead of regarding the ability to get by with little sleep as a badge of honor, individual and corporate attitudes need to switch towards sleeping for success.

Sleep plays a key role in numerous fundamental functions of the body. Therefore, it essential in the maintenance of physical health: our immune system depends on a sufficient quantity and quality of sleep, whereas lack of sleep is linked to a poorer capacity to fight infections and an increased risk of sickness (e.g., Ibarra-Coronado et al., 2015; Besedovski et al., 2012). Sufficient sleep is also important for cognitive functions, such as memory, learning, and decision-making (e.g., Krause et al. 2017).

According to the Joint Consensus Statement of the American Academy of Sleep Medicine and Sleep Research Society (2017), sleeping less than 7 hours per night regularly is associated with many adverse health outcomes, such as obesity, diabetes, hypertension, heart disease, and stroke, depression, an elevated risk of death, impaired immune function, and an increased risk of errors & accidents. Lack of sleep has also been found to be associated with depression (e.g., Franzen & Buysse 2008) and suicide (Bernert & Joiner 2007).

The economic costs of poor sleep are staggering. For example, the estimated annual cost of lost sleep to the UK economy is 30 billion pounds (Public Health England, 2018) and fatigue has been calculated to cost 115–240 million pounds per year in work accidents in the UK (Health and Safety Executive, 2018).

Despite the powerful statistics, sleep is often regarded as a nice-to-have luxury rather than a must-have necessity. It is up to the individual to prioritize enough time for sleep and take steps to ensure high-quality sleep, but companies need to do their part to promote better awareness, for example, by establishing a work culture that does not promote excessively long work hours or late-evening emails. This kind of culture starts at the top: a well-rested leader is more likely to make good decisions in this area.

Physical fitness and health

The positive connections between physical activity and good mental and physical health are supported by extensive research and it is easy to state that leaders looking to optimize their performance need to understand the relevance of fitness.

Aerobic (endurance) exercise improves cardiovascular fitness and promotes healthy functioning of the heart, blood vessels, and lungs. It also improves blood's lipid and glucose profile and helps with weight management. Strength and coordination exercise improves muscular strength, maintains good mobility, promotes musculoskeletal health, and increases bone strength (for a review, see Warburton, Nicol & Brendin, 2006). Studies also show that physical activity has positive effects on mental health (Paluska & Schwenk, 2000), for example by improving mood, relieving stress, and depressive symptoms, and promoting better sleep.

On the contrary, low levels of physical activity are associated with an estimated $117 billion annually in healthcare costs in the US, due to an increased risk of, e.g., heart disease, type 2 diabetes, some cancers, and obesity – U.S. Department of Health and Human Services (2018).

When discussing exercise habits, it is important to highlight that to gain physical and mental health benefits is not necessarily to aim at an athletic level. Indeed, any exercise is better than no exercise, but to optimize the benefits, a universal recommendation is to engage in at least 150 minutes of moderate or 75 minutes of vigorous aerobic exercise per week. That is, for example, a 30-minute walk 5 days a week.

Supercompensation of life

Supercompensation is a basic principle of athletic training, first introduced by Russian physiologist Yakovlev in the 1950s (Viru, 2002) and now

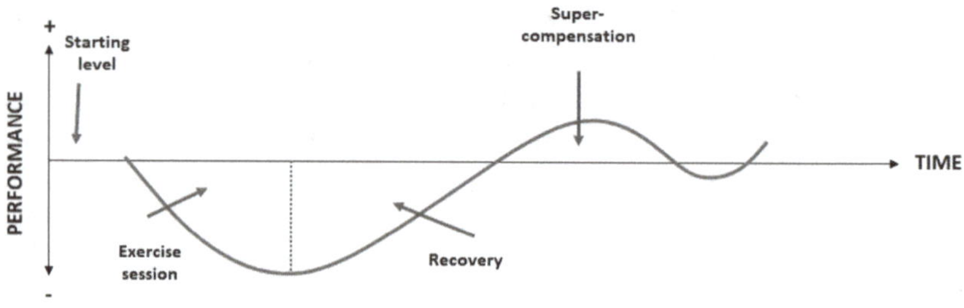

Figure 2. Supercompensation principle

widely understood to mean the balance between the right amount and intensity of training versus sufficient recovery, to improve performance. This balance determines whether athletes can improve their performance. They need to push their limits, but if they train too hard, with insufficient recovery, performance stagnates or worsens.

The same principle can be applied to regular people and leaders, and we refer to this as **supercompensation of life.** It requires a good balance between the different demands of life and is closely tied to stress management, sleep, and fitness. To achieve supercompensation and optimal performance, a leader must be able to balance their workload, stress, and exercise with sufficient recovery. The body resources graph below (Figure 3) illustrates this, and we will further discuss the theory behind this with concrete examples in our case study section.

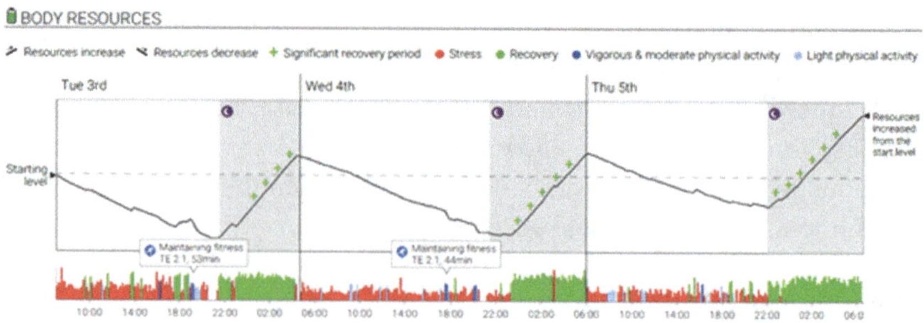

Figure 3. Firstbeat lifestyle assessment covering stress (red), exercise (blue) and recovery (green)

Similarly, the McKinsey report on stress (Asher & Tonis, 2021) suggests that we need to turn stress into an opportunity for growth and find our optimal stress point: the right amount of stress that still allows us to perform at a high level. This is essentially the idea behind supercompensation and the ideal performance state: if the amount of stress is appropriate, we can recover from it and keep performing well. The challenge is that the 'optimal amount of stress' is not permanent or an easily quantifiable, universal figure, but a very personal variable that everyone must figure out for themselves.

Power of habits in changing the leader's lifestyle

Personal habits play a critical role in our lives and impact our daily performance and overall well-being, constituting our lifestyle with positive and negative qualities. Unsurprisingly, it is said that our daily habits determine our future. Thus, understanding how they are formed, and how they can be changed is essential in the leader's self-development process. In the end, habits determine whether we can reach our full potential and achieve the Ideal Performance State, as described above. Following the idea of self-development, we believe that the leadership self-reflection moment should be directed towards one's behaviors, searching for the habits that are strengths and those that waste inner resources and energy. From this perspective, leaders should also analyze their teams and the organization to identify value destroying routines to be corrected or eliminated.

The key learning outcome should be understanding the relationship between lifestyle behaviors and optimal well-being, which can be bidirectional. But there is evidence (Prendergast, Schofield, & Mackay, 2015) to suggest that optimal well-being is enhanced by healthy lifestyle behaviors, especially physical exercise, healthy eating, and quality sleep, which constitute the base of the Ideal Performance Pyramid described earlier (Sherman & Lynch, 2014). These behaviors positively impact our mental and emotional energy and promote the brain's neuroplasticity, enhancing creativity, curiosity, and capacity to learn, critical in any leadership role.

Numerous studies (see for a review Gardner & Rebar, 2019) have been conducted to understand the nature of habit formation, whether good or bad. The primary learning is that habits can emerge unconsciously, without our permission, but can also be deliberately designed and implemented in our daily rituals. A given habit is not a destiny but can be modified or replaced by another habit.

MIT researchers at the Brain & Cognitive Sciences Department conducted in-depth studies on habit formation (MIT News (1999) They concluded that any habit can be formed in a three-step loop: 1) cue – a trigger initiating a particular behavior, 2) routine – an act of performing this behavior (physical, emotional, or mental), 3) reward – a signal to your brain that this behavior is worth repeating. It is based on the general premise that habits emerge because the human brain looks for ways to save the effort and energy required to perform cognitive functions. When the new habit is born, the brain stops participating in the decision-making process and uses its 'auto-pilot' mode. Many of our daily routines are performed unconsciously, and in the background, there are more than 10 000 choices we make each day. We do not think about how to tie the shoelaces, brush our teeth, or ride a bicycle. These are well-formed habits that run automatically when a specific trigger occurs.

Thanks to scientists (Fogg, 2019; Carden & Wood, 2018), we know that the core mechanism for forming habits is the same for good or bad ones. The same principles are applied whether we have a daily routine of a 30-minute walk or scroll our smartphone before sleep. According to the widely recognized and popularized Fogg Behavior Model (Fogg, 2019), a particular behavior can happen when three elements come together at the same time 1) *motivation* to perform this specific activity 2) *ability* – to perform this activity 3) prompt – which acts as a trigger to initiate this specific behavior. In the book 'Tiny Habits,' Fogg articulates the importance of our emotions in building both good and bad habits. Understanding these dynamics and interdependencies is crucial for the conscious practice of modeling one's habits, which can impact the overall lifestyle, health, and well-being.

Thanks to the newest technology advances, behavior modeling can be effectively enabled with dedicated applications and devices that work along with the principles of habit formation. In recent years, wearables (HIMS, 2022) and mobile devices have started to play a pivotal role in changing our lifestyle from merely monitoring specific health conditions (heart rate, temperature, quality of sleep, level of physical activity) to educating and motivating us to change behaviors that are critical for well-being and health. Several online applications are available (PDD, 2020) to help track habits, observe and analyze patterns, monitor progress, and act as a virtual prompt for a given behavior.

Conclusion: 43 % of our daily activities are rooted in our habits that impact our lifestyle and performance, so understanding and practicing habit formation principles should be an essential part of leadership development programs (Palmer, 2020). By providing in-depth knowledge of the various frameworks, leaders will be able to shape their lifestyle, as well as help their teams and organizations to strengthen and sustain positive habits. In this journey, leaders can use and promote various technologies that can help navigate the behavior change process and sustain desired behaviors in the long term.

Case study: Individual lifestyle assessment, coaching, and the impact of micro-corrections

Utilizing data to promote change

Heart rate variability (HRV) is the variation in time between consecutive heartbeats. In general, high HRV is viewed as a marker of good fitness and health, whereas low HRV is associated with negative health outcomes and stress. HRV is regulated by the autonomic nervous system: its sympathetic branch gets the body ready for action, increasing the heart's contraction rate and force and decreasing HRV, whereas the parasympathetic branch allows the body to recover by slowing the heart rate and increasing HRV (e.g., Kim et al. 2018, Singh et al. 2018). The interplay between these branches allows the heart to respond to different situations. HRV varies naturally between days, depending, for example, on the amount of activity and stress, but chronically low HRV can be a sign of excessive stress or imbalance.

To demonstrate the applied value of HRV, we will share some examples from Firstbeat measurements that utilize accurate HRV data, measured with an ECG-based device that detects every heartbeat in daily life. This data is converted, via a sequence of calculations, into a result that illustrates what events cause stress or promote recovery, how good the quality of sleep is and whether the day includes exercise with positive health effects (Firstbeat, 2014). The method originated in Finland and is used in professional corporate wellness programs globally to highlight the importance of lifestyle and early detection of potential problems. The goal is to help people at all levels of an organization make meaningful lifestyle and behavioral changes to support better well-being and performance at work and in their personal life.

In the 24-hour graph below, the red color means stress or activation (sympathetic nervous system dominance) and is considered a normal state that includes positive and negative stress and helps us perform. To stay resilient, we also need recovery, illustrated by the green color (parasympathetic dominance). The main time for recovery is sleep, but ideally, we will also see some recovery during the day. The blue color means physical activity (in this case, an exercise session around 19.00) to show if the day includes enough physical activity to provide positive health effects. Work and sleep periods are marked under the graph.

The report provides a numerical score for stress-recovery balance, sleep, and physical activity, to help the client understand their strengths and development areas. In this example, the stress-recovery balance and sleep scores were moderate because there was very little recovery during the day and recovery only started after several hours of sleep. The exercise session provided a good physical activity score, but because the intensity was high, and performed late at night, it might have contributed to the delayed recovery during sleep. The result is typically discussed together with the client in a 1-2-1 session, to draw accurate conclusions and make meaningful lifestyle and work adjustments.

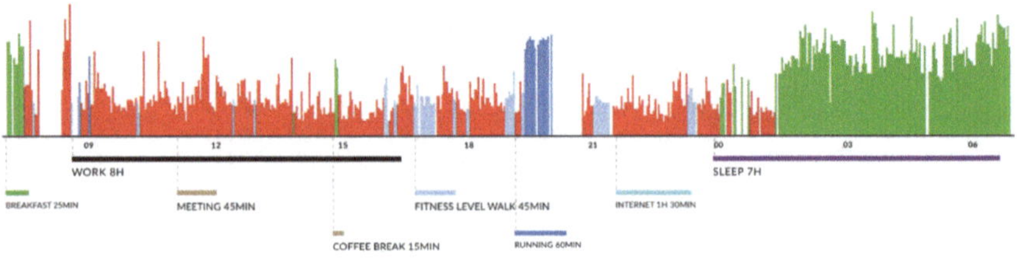

Figure 4. Example of a 24 h measurement demonstrating a moderate result for stress-recovery balance and sleep, and a good result for exercise

Case 1: Busy marketing manager

This marketing manager from Finland underwent the assessment at a very busy time in her life: heavy job demands, increased responsibilities, and 2 children that kept her busy outside of work. She was happy with her job and performing well, but starting to feel stressed, with difficulties disengaging from work. She was not sleeping well and had no time for exercise. The result supported this: all 3 days showed a lot of stress (red), little recovery (green), and very little physical activity (blue). Figure 5 below shows an example from her initial measurement. In the discussion with a performance coach, they acknowledged the challenges and decided on a few action points to improve her well-being, with two main goals:

1) Regular exercise.
2) 1–2 relaxing breaks every day to help manage the level of stress.

A follow-up measurement three months later (Figure 6.) demonstrates the positive effect of changes. Her sleep result was better on all 3 nights, likely because she was structuring her days better to include some exercise and relaxing moments. She felt that in her current situation, she did not have time to go to the gym, so instead, she started walking to and from work on most days. On remote workdays, she took a 15–20-minute walk before and after work. Her workload had not changed, but she had more

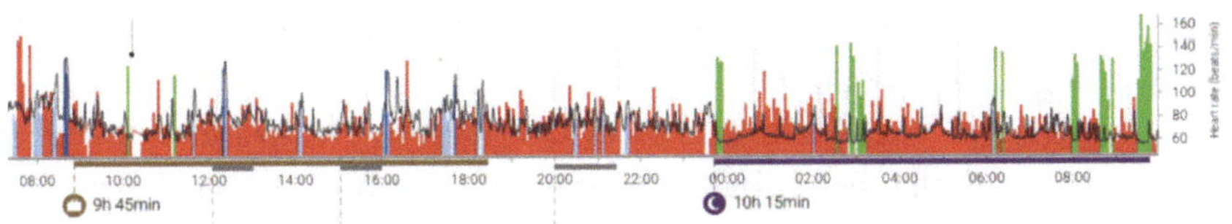

Figure 5. Measurement 1 showed signs of excessive stress and lack of recovery

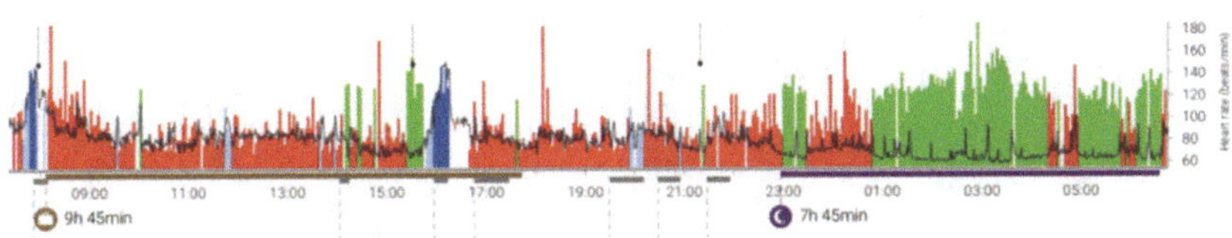

Figure 6. A follow-up measurement showed better sleep, some recovery during the day, and a short walk twice a day to boost her energy level

energy to get the job done, due to the dedicated physical activity and at least one recovery break during the day.

Case 2: Fitness Buff

This 50-year-old upper-level manager from the UK was an athlete in his youth and continued to exercise hard to stay fit. He felt that exercise was a good contrast to his stressful job and he made sure that he fit in a workout even when very busy. Sometimes this meant exercising late at night or continuing his work late at night, after his exercise. He often felt tired but had come to accept it as a normal part of life.

His initial result across the 3 measured days suggested that he might be exercising too hard: the high-pressure job plus the intensive workouts were starting to hurt his recovery during sleep, with an average sleep score of only 45/100, far below optimal. Maintaining a high level of performance requires enough good-quality sleep. In the long run, an imbalance would hurt his sports performance as well as his overall well-being.

On the positive side, he was feeling well and able to get a little bit of recovery even during work (the green bars in the example graph). His good fitness and exercise habits support good performance and stress management, but to keep getting these benefits, he needed better recovery. The discussion with a coach helped him understand the value of easy exercise and the importance of recovery. He learned not to let his exercise regimen cut into his sleep time and started to accept that skipping a workout or doing something easy after a stressful day can sometimes be a smart option, to ensure recovery. Going forward, structuring his training program more sensibly, with a better balance between easy and hard workouts, will allow him to improve his performance.

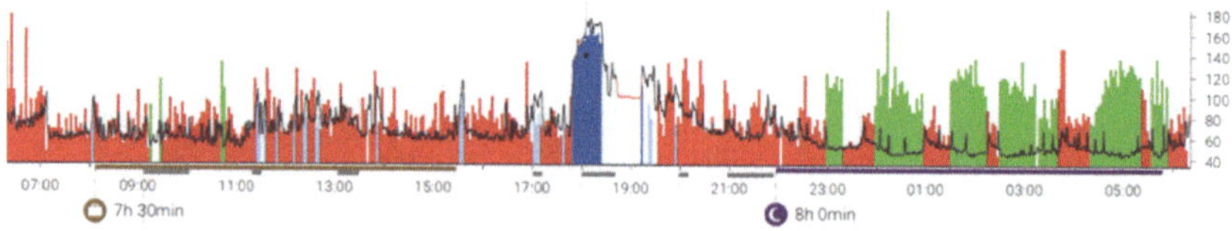

Figure 7. A high-intensity run in the evening (blue bar) is followed by restless sleep, with compromised recovery

Conclusion: Self-awareness is crucial for the self-development of leaders, including managers. Understanding how the human body reacts to different stressors and how an imbalance between stress (or any kind of load) and recovery impacts the ability to stay healthy and perform at a high level should be an important leadership competence. Adding this kind of learning content to the leadership development programs, with dedicated self-diagnostic technology and biofeedback, can help leaders better develop their resilience by proper modeling of their daily habits.

Case study: Impact of team vitality on team performance, productivity, and positivity

Leaders play an important role in enabling team performance and leveraging the human potential of team members. According to Team Coaching International, only 10 % of teams can achieve a high and sustainable level of performance (TCI, 2022). According to numerous studies by Team Coaching International, team productivity is highly correlated with team positivity, which refers to the quality of relationships among team members, level of mutual trust, psychological safety and overall engagement. Both variables of team performance can be influenced by the individual habits of team members as well as team management practices and cooperation principles. Thus, understanding team dynamics, resilience and the level of vital energy is a key competence of effective leaders.

Figure 8. Drivers of High & Sustainable Team Performance

To provide an example, we will share a case study from Poland: ten management team members of a manufacturing company in the phase of major business transformation and restructuring. Due to many projects and parallel initiatives, without sufficient additional resources, the team faced a significant vital energy crisis that impacted its results and overall engagement. The team leader and CEO of the company were concerned about the situation and were looking for support and a dedicated team coaching intervention. He experienced a lot of negative emotions in the team, such as irritation, frustration, blaming, and growing impatience. He also was dealing with extra pressure from the company shareholders, who started to be concerned about the pace of the transformation project. To assess the team's stress level and lifestyle, the same Firstbeat methodology was used as presented in the previous section.

Based on insights from the individual assessments, conducted at the same time for all team members, a team report was generated from the anonymized data. Insufficient or poor-quality-sleep was one of the major challenges in this group, with only 21 % of the measurements showing good recovery during sleep. A majority of the group members slept less than 7 hours, with 24 % sleeping less than 5.5 hours. The average sleep duration was 6h 15 minutes. Moreover, the group was lacking sufficient recovery during the workday, with an average of only 7 minutes of recovery. Leisure time recovery was also fairly low, with an average time of 30 minutes. Studying the individual reports and reviewing the team's weekly practices and calendar led to the conclusion that the team's most important weekly strategy meeting was held at the least optimal time from the team's energy standpoint. Interviews with the team members revealed that the meeting was perceived as highly stressful and unproductive and as a result, the team had trouble gaining consensus on its priorities.

As a result, the team was faced with many additional ad hoc meetings that created extra pressure and defocus. The team members and leaders felt overwhelmed, close to burnout and very concerned about their health status.

Thanks to the diagnostics and the team coaching process, the team decided to make changes to address these issues: 1) the team's strategic meeting was moved from Thursday afternoon to Tuesday morning, with a new agenda and meeting preparation principles 2) after each meeting, short breaks were planned and respected 3) the time between 13.00 – 15.00 was blocked for lunch and administrative work for each team member; team meetings or calls were not allowed during this block 4) no emails or work calls during the weekend.

After the implementation of these corrective measures, overall team performance and positivity improved significantly. Based on a qualitative assessment and an interview with the team leader, rearrangement of the daily and weekly team practices resulted in improved productivity and reduced stress levels, and created the required space to change individual habits, especially those related to physical and emotional energy. Several team members started exercising to improve their overall fitness and reported better sleep habits. The openness and strong support of the team leader were essential to initiate and sustain the behavioral change in this case.

Conclusion: It is the leaders' responsibility to ensure a healthy working environment and culture to leverage the full potential of their team members to achieve sustainable and good performance. Understanding team dynamics in the area of team vitality and individual performance state can be critical to ensure a proper balance between the workload and proper recovery. According to WHO, one in four employees will experience symptoms of burnout during their careers. Therefore, knowledge about practical ways to mitigate the risk of burnout in the workforce should be an obligatory element of leadership development programs.

Final recommendations

'Not everything that matters can be measured.'

Measuring stress and the quality of lifestyle has only become possible during the last decade, whereas in the past, it was a more qualitative discussion and subjective assessment based on questionnaires, such as the Energy Audit or Well-being Score. Thanks to technology development, especially in the field of wearables, leaders today have a tremendous opportunity to get quantitative insights into the key drivers of their vital energy and lifestyle. Real-life cases presented in this chapter demonstrate the benefits that this kind of approach can produce. Monitoring some of the key lifestyle parameters, such as the balance between stress and recovery, quality of sleep, and fitness can become an important part of a leader's agenda and self-reflection practice. Thanks to the growing popularity of such solutions, extensive benchmark databases are available that allow the comparison of one's results to those of one's age group.

As part of self-development, it is recommended to also monitor and review your daily habits and rituals, either using traditional journaling or a dedicated habits application. As part of this self-reflection, it can be useful to map the current activity and stakeholders' bandwidth to identify potential sources of energy waste and extra stressors.

The above-mentioned team-level parameters can also be great indicators of future team performance, engagement, and resilience. Understanding them can help leaders mitigate the risks of potential burnout or other health issues among the team members. It is important to note that group-level data is always anonymous to ensure the privacy of the individuals involved. The individual result is only seen by each individual and the coach involved in the case.

It is said: 'Good health is good business' (Remes & Singhal, 2020). Leaders' awareness and empathy, supported by technological developments can lead to truly human-centric organizations, where health and well-being are not a nice-to-have, but an authentic transformational agenda and attribute of their organizational cultures. This strategy pays off. According to the Virgin Pulse (2022) program, investing in employee well-being and health delivers significant value on investment, with 44 % of employees feeling more productive and engaged. The leader's role is to enable this potential and sustain a healthy and productive working environment for the sustainable development of their organization, employees, and overall ecosystems. From this perspective, ensuring proper leadership education and development support in this domain becomes essential.

References

American Academy of Sleep Medicine (2017). Seven or more hours of sleep per night: A health necessity for adults. https://aasm.org/seven-or-more-hours-of-sleep-per-night-a-health-necessity-for-adults/.

American Institute of Stress (2022). Workplace stress. https://www.stress.org/workplace-stress.

Asher, J. & Tonies, F. (2021, Feb. 18). How to turn everyday stress into 'optima; stress'. *McKinsey Quarterly*. https://www.mckinsey.com/capabilities/people-and-organizational-performance/our-insights/how-to-turn-everyday-stress-into-optimal-stress.

Bernert, R. A., & Joiner, T. E. (2007). Sleep disturbances and suicide risk: a review of the literature. *Neuropsychiatric disease and treatment*, *3*(6), 735.

Besedovsky, L., Lange, T., & Born, J. (2012). Sleep and immune function. *Pflugers Archiv: European Journal of Physiology*, *463*(1), 121–137. DOI: https://doi.org/10.1007/s00424-011-1044-0.

Cannon, W.B. 1915. *Bodily changes in pain, hunger, fear, and rage*. Appleton-Century-Crofts.

Carden, L., & Wood, W. (2018). Habit formation and change. *Current opinion in behavioral sciences*, *20*, 117–122.

Chu, B., Marwaha, K., Sanvictores, T., & Ayers, D. (2021). Physiology, stress reaction. In *StatPearls [Internet]*. StatPearls Publishing. https://www.ncbi.nlm.nih.gov/books/NBK541120/.

Eriksson, A. (2011). *Health-promoting leadership: a study of the concept and critical conditions for implementation and evaluation* (Doctoral dissertation, Nordic School of Public Health).

European Community (2020). Health and Safety at Work in Europe. https://ec.europa.eu/eurostat/web/products-statistical-books/-/ks-31-09-290.

Firstbeat (2014). Stress and Recovery Analysis Method Based on 24-h Heart Rate Variability. Firstbeat Technologies Ltd.; Jyväskylä, Finland.

Fogg, B. J. (2019). *Tiny habits: The small changes that change everything*. Eamon Dolan Books.

Franzen, P. L., & Buysse, D. J. (2022). Sleep disturbances and depression: risk relationships for subsequent depression and therapeutic implications. *Dialogues in clinical neuroscience*. *10*(4), 473–481. DOI: 10.31887/DCNS.2008.10.4/plfranzen.

Gardner, B., & Rebar, A. L. (2019). Habit formation and behavior change. In *Oxford research encyclopedia of psychology*. DOI: https://doi.org/10.1093/acrefore/9780190236557.013.129.

Greenwood, K. Krol, N. (2020). 8 Ways Managers Can Support Employees'. *Harvard Business Review, August. https://hbr.org/2020/08/8-ways-managers-can-support-employees-mental-health*.

Groppel, J. L., Andelman, B., & Loehr, J. (1999). *The corporate athlete: How to achieve maximal performance in business and life*. John Wiley & Sons Incorporated.

Harter, J. (2021), Retrieved from https://www.gallup.com/workplace/357404/manager-burnout-getting-worse.aspx.

Health and Safety Executive (2018). *Human factors: Fatigue:* https://www.hse.gov.uk/humanfactors/topics/fatigue.htm.

HIMSS (2022). The endless possibilities of wearable technology in healthcare. www.himss.org/resources/endless-possibilities-wearable-technology-healthcare.

Ibarra-Coronado, E. G., Pantaleón-Martínez, A. M., Velazquéz-Moctezuma, J., Prospéro-García, O., Méndez-Díaz, M., Pérez-Tapia, M., Pavón, L., & Morales-Montor, J. (2015). The Bidirectional Relationship between Sleep and Immunity against Infections. *Journal of Immunology Research*, 678164. DOI: https://doi.org/10.1155/2015/678164.

Jansen, A., Nguyen, X., Karpitsky, V., Mettenleiter, M. (1995, Oct. 27). Central Command. Neurons of the Sympathetic Nervous System: Basis of the Fight-or-Flight Response. *Science Magazine*. 5236, 270, 644–646.

Kim, H. G., Cheon, E. J., Bai, D. S., Lee, Y. H., & Koo, B. H. (2018). Stress and heart rate variability: a meta-analysis and review of the literature. *Psychiatry investigation*, *15*(3), 235. DOI: 10.30773/pi.2017.08.17.

Kohll, A. (2018). The Evolving Definition Of Work-Life Balance, *Forbes,* March 27. https://www.forbes.com/sites/alankohll/2018/03/27/the-evolving-definition-of-work-life-balance/?sh=44fc2f169ed3.

Koutsimani, P., Montgomery, A., & Georganta, K. (2019). The relationship between burnout, depression, and anxiety: A systematic review and meta-analysis. *Frontiers in psychology*, 284.

Krause, A. J., Simon, E. B., Mander, B. A., Greer, S. M., Saletin, J. M., Goldstein-Piekarski, A. N., & Prendergast, K.B., Schofield, G.M. & Mackay, L.M. (2015). Associations between lifestyle behaviours and optimal wellbeing in a diverse sample of New Zealand adults. *BMC Public Health,* 16, 62. DOI: https://doi.org/10.1186/s12889-016-2755-0.

Lazarus, R., & Folkman, S. (1984). *Stress, Appraisal, and Coping*. Springer.

Loehr, J., & Schwartz, T. (2001). The Making of a Corporate Athlete. *Harvard Business Review*, *79*(1), 120–128.

MIT News (1999, Oct. 20). MIT researcher sheds light on why habits are hard to make and break. https://news.mit.edu/1999/habits.

Palmer, C. (2020). Harnessing the power of habits, *APA Monitor on Psychology*, 51, 8, 78.

Paluska, S. A., & Schwenk, T. L. (2000). Physical activity and mental health. *Sports medicine*, *29*(3), 167–180.

PDD (2020). The growing role of wearables in healthcare. Retived from https://www.pddinnovation.com/the-growing-role-of-wearables-in-healthcare/.

Public Health England (2018, Jan). Is lack of sleep affecting your work? https://publichealthmatters.blog.gov.uk/2018/01/30/is-lack-of-sleep-affecting-your-work/.

Remes, A., Singhal S., (2020, Jul. 9) Good health is good business. Here's why. McKinsey Global Institute. www.mckinsey.com/mgi/overview/in-the-news/good-health-is-good-business.

Sandhal, P. (2022). Breaking code on high performing teams. https://teamcoachinginternational.com/breaking-the-code-on-high-performing-teams/.

Sherman B., Lynch W., (2014). Connecting the dots: examining the link between workforce health and business performance. *The American Journal of Managed Care*, *20*(2), 115–120.

Singh, N., Moneghetti, K. J., Christle, J. W., Hadley, D., Froelicher, V., & Plews, D. (2018). Heart rate variability: an old metric with new meaning in the era of using mhealth technologies for health and exercise training guidance. part two: prognosis and training. *Arrhythmia & Electrophysiology Review*, *7*(4), 247. DOI: 10.15420/aer.2018.30.2.

U.S. Department of Health and Human Services (2018). Physical Activity Guidelines for Americans, 2nd edition. Washington, DC: U.S. Department of Health and Human Services.

U.S. Department of Health and Human Services (2018). Physical Activity Guidelines for Americans, 2nd edition. Washington, DC: U.S. Department of Health and Human Services.

Virgin Pulse (2022). https://international.virginpulse.com.

Viru, A. (2002). Early contributions of Russian stress and exercise physiologists. *Journal of Applied Physiology*, *92*(4), 1378–1382.

Walker, M. P. (2017). The sleep-deprived human brain. *Nature Reviews Neuroscience*, *18*, (7), 404–418. DOI: https://doi.org/10.1038/nrn.2017.55.

Warburton, D. E., Nicol, C. W., & Bredin, S. S. (2006). Health benefits of physical activity: the evidence. *Cmaj*, *174*(6), 801–809.

World Health Organization. (2021). Retrieved from https://www.who.int/health-topics/noncommunicable-diseases.

Yao, L., Li, P., & Wildy, H. (2021). Health-promoting leadership: Concept, measurement, and research framework. *Frontiers in Psychology*, *12*, 602–333.

Sandra Bichl, Career Angels, Europe

Rikard Larsson, Decision Dynamics and Lund University, Sweden

From Linear Career Planning to Diverse Career Development

Abstract: The chapter discusses the evolution of contemporary career planning. A career is conceived here broadly as the life-long development of one's work which pertains to people in managerial and non-managerial positions. Year-long experience supports the differentiation of career advancement in terms of *Career concepts* (images of one's successful development at work) and *Career motives* (which pertain to deeper levels of work drivers). Several practical tips are offered to those who are (or consider being) involved in supporting career planning. The presented real-life case of a female manager encapsulates our assumptions and methodology while working on career development with others.

Keywords: Career concept & Career Motives, Career Planning & Development, Work Motivation

To discuss the evolution of career planning toward more diverse career development, we build upon over 40 years of research and practice of over a million career respondents (e.g., Brousseau et al., 1996; Larsson et al., 2007; Larsson et al., 2016). Traditionally, the concept of the career has been viewed relatively narrowly in both research and practice, such as persons' long-term choices of professions or upward progression along the hierarchical manager ladder in organizations. When a career was viewed as a professional choice, the main career problem became career indecision and the career solution early career counseling (Hall, 1992). On the other hand, when a career was viewed as a managerial upward progression, the main career problem became career plateauing and the related solution career planning (Milliman, 1993). But in the second half of the twentieth century, both research and practice led to new ways of thinking about careers, such as the idea of 'boundaryless careers' (e.g., Inkson, 2006). To better grasp this career diversity, the word career is understood in the broadest sense of the word – not only advancement in a company, but professional activity throughout a person's life like being a freelancer, becoming an entrepreneur, different patterns of changing job areas over time and other ways that people view and experience the development of their working lives (Hupkens et al., 2021).

Two items of data we have collected over the years – to be discussed later in more detail – appear particularly relevant for the discussion on career development:

- 64 % of employees do not have careers they are engaged with.
- Bias against those who are different from us can be harmful to ourselves and others.

In other words, we tend to reinforce or discourage certain career decisions in ourselves or others that we might not even truly identify with in the first place.

What is a '**successful career**'? Ask several persons this question and one will get many different answers. People's perspectives on careers vary in terms of, for example, how long one would ideally stay in the same occupational field, or in which direction one's career should develop (e.g., becoming and remaining a lawyer for the entirety of one's professional life, serial entrepreneurs, professionals turned consultants).

There is a risk of misunderstanding one another if career differences are not acknowledged. This can happen when an organization offers someone a career path that is believed to be rewarding, but a given person might view it as more or less a nightmare.

Traditionally, the word career has been strongly associated with words such as 'go-getter,' 'climber,' higher salary, and status. Those without managerial positions have not been thought of as having a career in this meaning. The word can also be understood as the life-long development of one's work.

Based on the aforementioned research, our definition of career is formulated as follows: 'how a person develops in their work life, which includes that different people can develop their tasks and positions in different directions and for different durations in different positions, fields, and organizations' (e.g., Brousseau et al., 1996; Larsson et al., 2007; Larsson et al., 2016). It is the very work-life development that one finds most engaging, where one may draw benefits from different interests and competencies, discover one's potential, realize one's dreams and perform well to appreciate both oneself and others. From this definition, everyone has a career. We need to find out what career suits us the most.

An essential part of career dynamics that the researchers identified is the difference between 'what one thinks one wants' vs. 'what one actually wants.'

Career research has grown significantly during the last 50 years, including several theories and studies of individual differences in career development, such as Holland's (1997) vocational interests typology with Realistic, Investigative, Artistic, Social, Enterprising, and Conventional. Super (1990) developed a contextual lifespan and life-space approach to career development involving roles and career maturity as key issues. Schein (1996) began developing his Career Anchors approach with 5–8 sets of values, motives, and needs (Autonomy, Security, Technical, Managerial, Entrepreneurial, Service, Challenge, and Lifestyle) at about the same time as Driver (1979) started to develop the Career Concept model (Expert, Linear, Spiral, and Transitory). Driver and Schein were also two of the founders of the Career Division of the Academy of Management in the late 1970s.

Career Concepts & Career Motives

In scientific terms, we look at the difference between 'Career Concepts' and 'Career Motives.'

Career Concepts

Career concepts form the picture of successful development in one's work life. The career concepts are the 'spectacles' with which one views one's own and others' work life and what is a successful career. The concepts are important since these direct most of one's choices in one's work life.

Most of us are not well-informed when it comes to making career decisions. It is not unusual for people to look back at their career and wish they would have gone another way in their work life. There are two usual reasons for this: either they do not know what careers are possible to have or they believe that there are 'good' and 'bad' careers.

Types of Career Concepts

The Decision Dynamics research team has identified four main Career Concepts or views of the ideal career:

1) Expert Concept

The Expert Concept is the most stable and historically dominant view of a successful career as being a lifelong commitment to a profession with which one identifies (one is an engineer, a teacher, or a farmer, etc.). Therefore, success is a process of continually mastering the knowledge and skills of the profession.

Threats: The challenge is to be able to turn one's in-depth knowledge in the right direction. It matters especially when re-organizations and changes in markets and technologies dominate, to what extent these changes are undermining the value and relevance of the made long-term investments in special expertise.

Opportunities: Future possibilities for the Expert career lie in the insight that the strongly growing global body of knowledge will clearly also need many more specializing in more in-depth knowledge, including to complement possible superficiality resulting from today's focus on speed and flexibility.

2) Linear Concept

The Linear Concept is instead focused on rapid movement upward the 'corporate ladder'. A successful career is made by gaining increased levels of responsibility, authority, etc. Success is made as one achieves these higher levels and is measured on an external scale, for example, work status, salary, or power.

Threats: Challenges include downsizing and flattening of managerial hierarchies as well as to leave enough space that it takes to carry through one's own vision while having a good balance between work and spare time. The threat of 'having to sacrifice oneself for the career' would be a barrier to a good balance.

Opportunities: Future possibilities of the Linear career lie in insights such as that there will always be needs for leadership contributions and a high position means having the influence and authority it takes to get results leading to success.

3) Spiral Concept

The Spiral Concept is a less traditional view where one rather discovers one's career, in contrast to the Expert's being and Linear's making their careers, through periodic (5–10 years) lateral changes of occupational fields. These changes tend to involve the development of broader skills and new applications of previous experience.

Threats: Challenges include to find what kind of job changes that one is missing and make those changes in work that it takes to reach a broadening of competence while choosing the combination of experiences that will be attractive to the employer/market. A threat is that possibilities to broaden competence never will come up, or these possibilities will not be acknowledged.

Opportunities: The future opportunity of the Spiral career is in the insight that a broad competence span will give the person a general picture of their work and find personal development in the desired direction.

4) Transitory Concept

The Transitory Concept is the most change-oriented and least conventional view, even to the extent that many consider it as not even being a career. The more different a job change, and the more frequent the changes, the better according to this 'consistent pattern of inconsistency' perspective on careers.

Threats: Historically, the Transitory career concept is the most misunderstood and devalued of the four concepts. A challenge is to not be influenced by others' values about work life, but to have the courage to go one's way, marketing it. The threat is that future employers will think that a disjoint curriculum vitae means that the person cannot be trusted.

Opportunities: A future possibility of the Transitory career lies in the insight that a variety of work experiences will compensate for in-depth knowledge when it is important to identify new situations that require unconventional and not tried methods. Shorter assignments will decrease the dependence on specific competencies of the individual.

Career Motives

Apart from differing in Career Concepts, people also differ in terms of what motivates them at work. While the Career Concepts represent our most idealistic ideas of what a career should be like, the Career Motives involve factors that resonate with us on a deeper level. Finding out what one's motives are, is vital to have the most satisfying work-life possible since they may or may not overlap with one's Career Concepts.

Motives are very individual and vary greatly. Consequently, a 'stable' expert career path is 'motivational heaven' for a person with Expert Motives and 'hell' for a person with Transitory Motives. Managing human resources effectively demands understanding how people's career motives differ.

1) Expert Motives

Many of those agreeing with the Expert career only have a few focused and precise values. This makes the Experts rather easy to satisfy in work life. Their foremost motives are:

- Security. They want security in their work life, that is, stable employment and career.
- Expertise. They want to develop high levels of expertise in a specialized work area and feel as knowledgeable and skilled in their work as possible.
- Safety. Given their long-term orientation, they also prioritize safety issues to avoid unwanted risks in their work environment.

2) Linear Motives

The Linears usually want plenty of things in their work. They have many motives and high expectations which makes them rather demanding when it comes to rewards of their work. Their foremost motives are:

- Achievement. They want results and to be competitive.
- Power. They want power and influence in the organization. They want to maximize their possibility to make important things happen.

- Promotion. The best way to satisfy the above stated motives is to climb the career ladder to positions with more influence and power.
- Prestige. The kind of prestige means higher income and more benefits.

3) Spiral Motives

The Spirals are not interested in knowing a little bit about everything, and yet not knowing anything completely. Instead, they would rather have a base of knowledge within each work area and then change to a related area. Their foremost motives are:

- Personal development. They would like to broaden their skills and knowledge.
- Creativity. The Spiral wants the opportunity of 'breaking new ground' and to be there when something new is to be developed, for example, a new product or service.
- To invent things. While in the process of inventing or creating something new, they acquire new knowledge and skills.

4) Transitory Motives

The Transitories are fond of challenges and new situations. They are very much focused and have precise motives. Their foremost motives are:

- Variety. Variety is the spice of life if it is new and challenging this means attractive.
- Independence. They want their independence and freedom to be able to make their own decisions in their work life.
- Involvement of other people. They are looking for jobs in which they will be in contact with others. They enjoy a lot of interaction, and they like to make new contacts.

Individual Profiles and Bias

Summarizing, the Concepts of persons are what they 'think in their head,' to be the best possible career development, while the Motives signify what the persons 'feel in their heart' that they would most want to have. The two do not necessarily coincide – statistically, only about 40 % of people have alignment between their primary Concepts and Motives.

When looking at individual profiles, we can identify so-called primary and secondary Career Concepts and Motives; in other words, what a person prefers the most. By looking at the combination, we can find illustrative career paths that the person will thrive in:

1. Expert & Linear: Functional Manager
2. Expert & Spiral: General Consultant
3. Expert & Transitory: Freelancer
4. Linear & Spiral: General Manager
5. Linear & Transitory: Independent Business Owner
6. Spiral & Transitory: Entrepreneur/Intrapreneur

Let us look at these in more detail:

1) Functional Manager Path

This is a relatively traditional career path in which individuals develop special expertise in a management function (e.g., finance, marketing). Competence in one's specialty with acceptable management skills is the basis for advancement.

2) General Consultant

There are several possible versions of this career path. The most obvious is to work for a large, established consulting firm, where a person will have the opportunity to get involved in many kinds of projects in a wide range of organizations. People pursuing this path should focus on developing a specialty that forms the basis for their consulting services. Another version of this path is to work in an organization where one can play the role of an 'internal consultant' who provides advice and expert services throughout the organization.

3) Freelancing

This path is a good fit for people who want to develop an area of special expertise, but who also want a lot of variety and freedom. Freelancers or independent consultants usually enjoy a very high level of variety and freedom. Obviously, these subjects pressure on being self-employed. They are free to make their own decisions about the kind of work they do, work methods, and work schedules.

4) General Manager Path

This path involves moving through a series of different functional positions over time, while moving upward in a management hierarchy. The pattern for this path is an upward moving spiral. Over the course of a career, a person pursuing this path will be exposed to many different kinds of positions that provide the opportunity to develop a wide repertoire of skills and knowledge.

5) Independent Business Owner

This path provides Linear/Transitory motives the opportunity to exercise influence, set organizational strategy, play a central role in achieving major business objectives, and work independently without being constrained by close supervision or by bureaucratic rules and policies.

6) Entrepreneur/Intrapreneur

In this path, a person concentrates on getting new businesses off to a successful start and then moves on to new opportunities. When professional entrepreneurs get involved in a new venture, they always have one eye on an eventual 'exit' that will allow them to cash in their interest and move on. Another variant on this theme is working for an innovative organization as an 'intrapreneur.' This path focuses less on making a profitable exit and more on just playing a key role in getting new ideas converted into new products, services, or methods.

One set of key patterns that we have found over the years is that the national culture often influences how ideal persons view different career concepts (Larsson et al., 2007). Experts tend to be more valued in Japan and Germany with their more long-term and uncertainty avoidance orientations (Hofstede, 1991). Linears dominate more in many countries, like the individualistic US and UK as well as France which is high on Hofstede's power distance dimension. On the other hand, Sweden, Denmark, Norway, Finland, and Holland all have high percentages of primary Spiral career concepts, and these countries are also high on Hofstede's femininity dimension. For example, in a Swedish study of 7308 career profiles, 55 % viewed Spiral as their most ideal career concept (Larsson et al., 2016). In this way, we are often socialized into more traditional career values of what our respective society views ought to be the best career path. In contrast, the underlying career motives do not show such clear national career preferences.

Note that these recommendations are based on Career Motives, not Career Concepts as we operate under the assumption that people want to have satisfying and fulfilling professional lives. Having said that, when it comes to moments when decisions need to be made, Career Concepts 'win.' In other words, if somebody with the primary and secondary Career Motives Expert & Spiral and Career Concept Linear & Spiral is offered a promotion, they'll accept it although 'their heart won't be in it' and tasks related to the development of their expert competencies would be much more engaging and rewarding.

Thus, when it comes to our own career decisions, the advice we give, and the bias we develop – Career Concepts always rump Career Motives. Consequently, when looking at career planning, we need to start with awareness – of our preferences and the aforementioned 'career spectacles.' Once we are conscious of the prejudice, we recommend reframing our negatives views into positive attributes.

Reframing Career Views

Experts *could be* seen as a management problem as they are not flexible, overly specialized, rigid, or narrow-minded, instead, they can be valued for adding in-depth knowledge, high quality work, their corporate memory, or being loyal.

Linears *could be* seen as people who decide more than they know or conventional careerists instead they can be valued for taking charge, leading competitive growth, being a performance driver and creating efficient formal structures.

Spirals *could be* seen as lacking focus with a faulty compass instead they can be valued for being a broad bridge to others, for being creative developers, enabling synergistic teamwork and their holistic skill diversity.

Transitory *could be* seen as 'jacks of all trades' with a hopeless CV; instead, they can be valued for being quick and mobile fixers, having customer flexibility, being fast learners, enjoying networking as well as spotting new opportunities.

That bias influences people's internal narrative that they tell themselves which allows them to do and not do certain things professionally. It also takes over the advice we all share with others – which is an important aspect for everyone involved in the careers of others, including:

- professors, lecturers, trainers;
- managers, board members;
- HR professionals;
- career advisors, mentors, coaches.

Over 40 years of our research show that 64 % do not have careers they are engaged with – in other words: Career Concepts and Career Motives are not aligned – which leads to professionals choosing career paths that are not the best fit for them. For instance, functional managers at heart (Career Motives: Expert and Linear) are choosing to become entrepreneurs (Career Concepts: Spiral and Transitory), which leads to:

- frustration, anxiety, burn-out, feeling 'lost';
- low(er) performance;
- engaging in additional activities outside of work (studies, volunteering, hobbies, etc.) to make up for what is missing.

The 4 Stages of 'Intentional' Career Planning

Career Planning is sometimes misunderstood as organizations planning suitable career paths between jobs to solve the succession of job holders. It also assumes that careers should be planned, which is only suitable for some – mainly Linears, while:

- Experts have already made their long-term professional choice.
- Spirals discover their careers over time.
- Transitories definitively do not want to 'pre-plan' their future thereby constraining their freedom.

Additionally, to some extent, most career paths are 'on autopilot' – as people subconsciously allow Career Concepts to take over or automate the decision-making process.

So, when we speak about 'intentional' career planning, we refer to the following moments when the direction is wanted or needed – irrespective of career patterns:

- when feeling unfulfilled/dissatisfied with one's current professional situation;
- when being made redundant or the fear/anticipation of it or similarly the threat of losing a/the source of income;
- after an event that inspires reflection (a conversation, attending a webinar, listening to a podcast, reading an article, observing a situation, etc.);
- being part of a community that shares or indoctrinates the same values and expectations which often happens at Business Schools and MBA programs that reinforces Linear beliefs and career paths;
- based on observations from Career Angels, many professionals arrive naturally at a moment of critically assessing their career path after approximately 12 years of having been professionally active.

In these moments, 'intentional' career planning is advised – with the word 'intentional' seeming redundant but justified given the above context. In these moments, an important aspect is understanding that the job market – like any other market – is governed by supply and demand:

- the supply of candidates;
- the demand for them.

In other words, the candidate is the 'product' that needs to be marketed – adhering to the 4Ps: product, price, place, and promotion. Translating that into a marketing strategy and plan, we arrive at the four stages of 'intentional' career planning.

1) Career Clarity[1]

Career clarity is about being aware of one's own Career Motives and Concepts and translating them into a career goal. Depending on how close it is to the person's competencies and background, the time to achieve that goal can take anywhere between three to 24 months. In some cases, it takes more, if professional training of several years is required.

---

1 Sometimes Stage 1 and 2 are inverted as reflecting upon one's strengths (as well as Career Motives) leads to understanding the most suitable career path.

The difficulty and challenge often lie in correctly identifying and separating the so-called must-have criteria from the nice-to-have ones that describe the future professional situation. Nice-to-haves like gym memberships, free apples, a fancy building/location, or a parking spot often distract unnecessarily from what is really, truly important. It is recommended to go through a so-called 'parameter bidding' process where one enlists the 10–15 most important criteria and their opposites that describe the next role – e.g., ideal income of 100,000 vs. 65,000. Then the criteria are 'bid' against each other: A vs. anti-B, B vs. anti-A, A vs. anti-C, C vs. anti-A, and so on – and then B against C, etc. The results will show 3–5 objective must-have criteria that will help clarify on how to further develop one's career and what to focus on in one's career management or active job search.

2) Understanding one's competencies and differentiators

To understand the viability of one's career goal, one must objectively first assess one's competencies. One study by Tasha Eurich and her associates (2018) of more than 5000 leaders across a variety of roles and industries found that, relative to lower-level leaders, higher-level leaders more significantly over-valued their skills (compared with others' perceptions). This pattern existed for 19 out of the 20 competencies the researchers measured, including emotional self-awareness, accurate self-assessment, empathy, trustworthiness, and leadership performance. Only 10–15 % get it right!

In other words, it is advised to be critical of any tests based on self-assessment or self-reflection in the context of career planning, especially since every Career Pattern demonstrates different tendencies. On the job market, being able to a) know one's competencies and b) understand how one is different (and better) than others, then c) be able to communicate it, is key.

Self-assessment and communication types:

- Experts only feel confident about a skill or area of expertise after they've spent min. 10–15 years in it. They can be seen as self-conscious, introverts. They have difficulties identifying what makes them stand out and speak about themselves in superlatives.

- Linears are on the opposite spectrum of self-assessment, often being overly self-confident and ascribing the financial success of their business units or companies to their leadership skills as opposed to looking at factors like market growth, available budgets, brand recognition, etc.
- Spirals are dedicated to their own and other people's growth making them usually rather accurate in self-assessment exercises. When communicating about themselves, they are more likely to use 'we' instead of 'I.'
- Transitories feel comfortable with understanding topics superficially and are good at marketing themselves accordingly. They interact with ease with others and have no problem taking credit for their work, as they are often a one-man show.

Irrespective of one's type, the following methods can be applied to increase one's competency-related self-awareness:

- the variety of accessible tests on the market (personality, competency, psychometric);
- assessment/development centers;
- feedback (e.g., in the form of conversations or structured 360* assessments).

How the professional position themselves on the job market is also known as Personal Branding, Professional Identity or Executive Identity – depending on the person's career path and seniority.

3) Having the right tools

Career Planning can entail changing or further developing a career path one is already on, for instance: advancing within one's organization, gaining more clients, improving one's career reality, or being recognized in one's field. The most used tools and methods that are worth looking into:

- Job crafting is a work design process for an individual which refers to self-initiated, proactive strategies to change the characteristics of one's job to better align the job with personal needs, goals, and skills. By striving to enhance 'person–job environment fit,' the 'goals of job crafting align with positive psychology's emphasis on taking personal initiative to leverage one's strengths in ways that promote human flourishing' (Dik et al., 2015).

- CV which used to be a list of described past and current professional experiences, but now has morphed into a document that summarizes one's potential added value and can be compared to a 'marketing flyer' of relevant information – from the reader's perspective.
- LinkedIn profile – a summary of a professional's CV that needs to take into consideration two target groups: the algorithm of the platform as well as the 'human' reader.

Naturally, there are more tools to consider – they are any element/channel that is used to communicate with the target group – a recruiter, a future boss, a prospect, and so on.

4) Understanding and navigating the market

Every market is defined by supply and demand – in the case of the job market, it is the supply of available candidates (i.e., expressed in unemployment rates) and the demand for candidates – that is, the available opportunities, out of which only 20–30 % are published (depending on the source of data) and according to data from Hyper Talent (2017) – it is only 10 % for executive roles. The remainder is distributed in the so-called hidden job market through intranets or word of mouth of employees or contacts or is in the hands of recruitment agencies. Based on the data of Career Angels (2021), the job search channels have the following efficiency (average efficiency 2019–2021):

- Networking: 28.66 %
- Direct approach: 35.33 %
- Headhunters: 13.00 %
- Job ads: 23.00 %

The length of the entire process (Stages 1–4) will depend on the following two aspects:

1. How easy/realistic the goal is – in other words: how close the goal overlaps with the current competencies and industry.
2. How systematic & intensive one's activity is.

How to support career planning

Depending on our roles as educators, managers, or HR professionals, we need to be mindful of our influence. We recommend the following tips:

1. Understand your preferences, resulting in potential bias, but also competencies.
2. Be critical of declarations that seem overly self-conscious or self-confident. Invite others to objectively assess their competency profile.
3. Encourage people to seek advice from a trained professional instead of transferring one's own bias to them. What is good for one and what worked for one, will not necessarily be that way for others – even if it might seem so superficially.

BOX

After Linda (not the real name of a primarily Linear manager) was promoted to supervisor, she wanted to learn more about those she managed by looking at their individual career profiles. Noticing the several Experts among them, she commented that while she knew she should trust their expertise, she often ended up feeling as if she had been misled. Consequently, she mistrusted the Experts.

When asked what she expected from her Experts, Linda answered that she wanted them to perform competitively and deliver on time. Asking her then what she thought Experts tend to deliver, Linda replied that they contribute long-term focus with high quality. How did she view these contributions? Linda's initial answer was that they were slow and, therefore, costly, as well as not focused on the customer. She felt disappointed.

By answering these questions, Linda realized that the problem was her own misguided expectations. She was viewing the Experts' contribution from her Linear perspective. She had discounted their talent unintentionally which skewed her perception of their motives, and this had eventually turned into distrust.

References

Brousseau, K. R., Driver, M. J., Eneroth, K., & Larson, R. (1996). Career pandemonium: Realigning organizations and individuals. *Academy of Management Perspectives*, 10(4), 52–66.

Career Angels (2021). *Efficiency of job search channels*. Unpublished report.

Dik, B. J., Duffy, R. D., Allan, B. A., O'Donnell, M. B., Shim, Y., & Steger, M. F. (2015). Purpose and meaning in career development applications. *The Counseling Psychologist*, 43(4), 558–585.

Driver, M. (1979). Career concepts and career management in organizations. In C. Cooper (Ed.) *Behavioral problems in organizations*. Englewood Cliffs, NJ: Prentice-Hall.

Eurich, T. (2018). What self-awareness really is (and how to cultivate it). *Harvard Business Review*, 1–9.

Hall, D. T. (1992). Career indecision research: Conceptual and methodological problems. *Journal of Vocational Behavior*, 41(3), 245–250.

Hyper Talent (2017, April 19). Businesswire. Retrieved March 18, 2022, from www.businesswire.com/news/home/20170419005527/en/Accessing-the-Hidden-Market-for-Executive-Positions-HYPER-Research-Reveals-Over-75-of-Executives-Lack-Visibility-and-Access.

Hofstede, G. (1991). *Cultures and organizations: Software of the mind*. McGraw-Hill.

Holland, J. L. (1997). *Making vocational choices: A theory of vocational personalities and work environments*. Psychological Assessment Resources.

Hupkens, L., Akkermans, J., Solinger, O., & Khapova, S. (2021). The dynamics of subjective career success: A qualitative inquiry. *Sustainability*, 13(14), 7638.

Inkson, K. (2006). Protean and boundaryless careers as metaphors. *Journal of Vocational Behavior*, 69(1), 48–63.

Larsson, R., Brousseau, K. R., Kling, K., & Sweet, P. L. (2007). Building motivational capital through career concept and culture fit: The strategic value of developing motivation and retention. *Career Development International*, *12*(4), 361–381.

Larsson, R., Kling, K., Häggberg, A., & Månsson, G. (2016). *What engages Swedes the most: Do not let our heads fool your heart*. Decision Dynamics Research Report, Lund, Sweden.

Milliman, J. (1993). *Causes, consequences, and moderating factors of career plateauing*. Doctoral dissertation. University of Southern California.

Schein, E. H. (1996). Career anchors revisited: Implications for career development in the 21st century. *Academy of Management Perspectives, 10*(4), 80–88.

Super, D. (1990). A life-span, life-space approach to career development. In D. Brown & L. Brooks (Eds.), *Career choice and development: Applying contemporary approaches to practice* (2nd ed., pp. 197–261). Jossey-Bass.

MANAGEMENT IN DIGITAL TIMES

Edited by Piotr Olaf Żylicz

Vol. 1 Krzysztof Kasianiuk / Bohdan Szklarski / Piotr Olaf Żylicz (eds.): Failed Leadership. 2021.

Vol. 2 Piotr Olaf Żylicz / Vartika Dutta / Rathish Bhatt: Mapping Manager Development. Current and Upcoming Trends. 2023.

www.peterlang.com

Printed by
CPI books GmbH, Leck